BREAKING OPEN THE HEAD

BREAKING
OPEN

DANIEL PINCHBECK

BROADWAY BOOKS
New York

A psychedelic
journey into
the heart of
contemporary
shamanism

THE

HEAD

BROADWAY

A hardcover edition of this book was published in 2002 by Broadway Books.

BREAKING OPEN THE HEAD. Copyright © 2002 by Daniel Pinchbeck. All rights reserved. No part of this book may be reproduced or transmitted in any form or by any means, electronic or mechanical, including photocopying, recording, or by any information storage and retrieval system, without written permission from the publisher. For information, address Broadway Books, a division of Random House, Inc.

PRINTED IN THE UNITED STATES OF AMERICA

BROADWAY BOOKS and its logo, a letter B bisected on the diagonal, are trademarks of Random House, Inc.

Visit our website at www.broadwaybooks.com

First trade paperback edition published 2003

Book design by Lee Fukui
Photo on title page and opener pages courtesy of PhotoDisc, Inc.

Cataloging-in-Publication Data is on file at the Library of Congress.

Sections of *Breaking Open the Head* have appeared in somewhat different form in *Details, Men's Journal, Rolling Stone,* and the *Village Voice.*

ISBN 0-7679-0743-4

10   9   8   7   6

One must explore deep and believe the incredible to find the new particles of truth floating in an ocean of insignificance. —JOSEPH CONRAD

For Laura
And in memory of my father,
Peter Pinchbeck

contents

Part Two
STRANGE GROWTHS

Part Three
LEAVE NO TRACE

Part Four
SHAMANISM AND MODERNISM

Part Eight
INCONCEIVABLE NEW WORLDS

introduction

When I began this book, I wanted to solve a mystery. I wanted to know why certain substances are revered in tribal societies throughout the world but repressed as well as ridiculed in contemporary Western cultures. In the West, these substances are called "psychedelics," a class of drugs that radically alter consciousness and perception. Unlike heroin or cocaine, most psychedelics are neither physically harmful or habit-forming. Yet they are considered so frightening and dangerous that possession of them is punished by long prison sentences. Although they were once thought to "expand consciousness," which sounds at least theoretically desirable, no sane adult can be allowed legal access to them.

The word *psychedelic*—"mind-manifesting"—was coined in the 1950s during our culture's brief enthusiasm for chemical self-discovery. The term itself is a bit vague, as the entire set of these substances tends to escape precise classification. In this book, I have, for the most part, limited my discussion to traditional and well-known visionary catalysts including psilocybin-containing mushrooms, peyote, the Amazonian potion ayahuasca, LSD, iboga, and dimethyltryptamine (DMT). I have also looked into a few recent discoveries. To keep my task manageable, I have not discussed marijuana or ecstasy (better described as an "empathodelic"), or ketamine (an anaesthetic inducing out-of-body experiences).

In the mid-1960s, most of the known psychedelics were outlawed, and the mainstream vogue for consciousness expansion ended soon after. In the next decades, the media repeatedly associated psychedelics with blown minds, wasted potential, and social chaos. The notion persists that to dabble in psychedelics, to trip, is to risk madness.

Preserved in pockets of the undeveloped world, shielded from the rapid ravages of modernization by dense jungles or mountains, it is still possible to encounter intact shamanic cultures. Among these people, plants that induce visions are the center of spiritual life and tradition. They believe that these plants are sentient beings, supernatural emissaries. They ascribe their music and medicine, their cosmology and extensive botanical knowledge to the visions given to them in psychedelic trance. For tribes in Africa, Siberia, North and South America, and many other regions, rejection of the visionary knowledge offered by the botanical world would be a form of insanity.

While researching this book, I visited shamans in West Africa, Mexico, and the Ecuadorean Amazon. In Gabon, a small country on the equator, I went through a Bwiti initiation, eating iboga, a psychedelic rootbark that induces a trance lasting for thirty hours. Some of the Bwiti call this ceremony "breaking open the head." The bark powder temporarily releases the soul from the body, allowing the initiate entry into the African spiritual cosmos, where he is shown the outline of his fate.

Breaking Open the Head follows two tracks. On the one hand, I examine the cultural history of psychedelic compounds in the modern West, looking at the intersection of archaic drugs and modern thinkers leading to the 1960s—a failed mass-cultural voyage of shamanic initiation—and up to the present day. One inspiration is Walter Benjamin, the German Jewish thinker who experimented with hashish and mescaline in the 1920s. Benjamin thought that visionary intoxication, achieved through drugs or other means, could be a "profane illumination," shattering the hypnotic trance of modern life. "The reader, the thinker, the flaneur, are types of illuminati just as much as the opium eater, the dreamer, the ecstatic," Benjamin wrote. "Not to mention that most terrible drug—ourselves—which we take in solitude."

"That most terrible drug," myself, is the subject of the book's other inquiry. Once upon a time, not so long ago, I was a typical Manhattan atheist, suspicious, cynical, disbelieving in metaphysical possibilities. Due to a tweak in my character, my cynicism increasingly tormented me. Without any higher vision, life seemed unbearable and pointless. Compelled by my despair and self-disgust, I decided to poke at the limits of my disbelief. If not the safest or most legal route, certain chemical catalysts seemed the fastest and most direct means of self-testing whether this reality was all that could be known.

Taking myself as a psychedelic case history, I describe my own leaps and crashes through the neurochemical looking glass. *Breaking Open the Head* tells the story of how my own head was broken open, and how I have gingerly tried to put the pieces back together. It is the record of a subjective, incomplete, occasionally harrowing, often alienating, yet exhilarating and fun process of discovery and transformation.

I believe that psychedelic drugs, used carefully, are profound tools for self-exploration. The forbidden substances can be a precision technology for revealing the interstitial processes of thinking, the flickering candle sputters of emotion, the fine-tuned machinery of sense perceptions. The unfolding of the self through an increase in perception, cognition, and feeling is one level of the trip. On low doses, that is all you get, and often it is enough.

The next level begins where consciousness, suddenly able to go beyond its normal boundaries, bursts open on the nonordinary world. It fascinates me that these two levels are so closely related. It is as if the mind were a rocket, gathering force as it speeds along a runway until it finally lifts into space, beyond the tug of gravity, where all the rules are different. Why should a process that begins by sharpening normal perceptions—making colors brighter, enhancing awareness of patterns in nature—lead seamlessly into "abnormal" perceptions, into paintings that breathe, statues that dance, trees that writhe with faces and limbs? Not to mention, as yet, those geometric and hallucinatory vistas of unleashed Otherness, revealed to the closed eyes.

The visionary power of psychedelics remains a mystery, one that was abandoned by the scientific academy when psychedelics were made illegal a generation ago. Equally mysterious: Why should the private exploration of one's inner reality, by chemical or other means, be considered a serious threat to a "free society"?

In *The Long Trip*, a study of visionary drug use through history, Paul Devereux muses: "I sometimes wonder if our culture, acting in the manner of a single organism—in the way a crowd of people or a classroom of students sometimes can—somehow senses a deep threat to its own philosophical foundations residing in the psychedelic experience. This might help account for the otherwise irrational hatred and repression of the use of hallucinogens, and the smirking dismissal of the psychedelic experience as a trivial one by so many of our intellectuals."

It is the nature of repression to be invisible. Something that is repressed can't reveal itself to us, can't appear as a break in our awareness—then we would see its workings, and the repression would be dispelled. In a world of information overload and perpetual distraction, repression manifests as a dismissive giggle, a yawn of boredom, a sin of omission.

"Repression is reflexive," notes the literary critic Frederic Jameson, "that is, it aims not only at removing a particular object from consciousness, but also and above all, at doing away with the trace of that removal as well, at repressing the very memory of the intent to repress." For over thirty years, a tremendous force of cultural repression has been exerted on the subject of psychedelics.

And yet it cannot be said that our culture frowns on the use of consciousness-changing substances. Marijuana is forbidden, but alcohol and nicotine—far more destructive drugs—are consumed in mass quantities. While psychedelics are outlawed, 27 million Americans currently take antidepressants such as Zoloft or Prozac. These days, most people are far more suspicious of plant compounds safely ingested by human beings for tens of thousands of years than they are of selective serotonin reuptake inhibitors (SSRIs) or other powerful, utterly synthetic, mood and mind-altering drugs created in the last decades by a pharmacological industry motivated by profit.

Antidepressants fit our society's underlying biases. Psychedelics, emphatically, do not. Is it possible that we have demonized hallucinogens because we fear the contents of our own minds?

When he tried mescaline for the first time, the chemist Sasha

Shulgin found "the world amazed me, in that I saw it as I had when I was a child. I had forgotten the beauty and the magic and the knowingness of it and me." He realized the tiny amount of white powder he had ingested could not have caused such profound visions. It had only revealed what was inside of him. He understood that "our entire universe is contained in the mind and the spirit. We may choose not to find access to it, we may even deny its existence, but it is indeed there inside us, and there are chemicals that can catalyze its availability."

The nature of consciousness remains a mystery that Western science cannot penetrate. It is not only that our scientists can approach the mind from outside, through descriptions of its functions and logical deductions. There is no means for science, as it is presently constituted, to ask, let alone seek, an answer to the question, Why am I here now? And yet that question forms the basis of an individual's thoughts and perceptions. Of course, I am not saying that psychedelics provide an instant answer to that question, but they offer a different set of lenses through which to look at the problem.

The self-enclosed logic of secular materialism denies any independent existence to the soul, attributing all facets of the human personality to the synaptical wiring of the brain. Psychedelics indicate that this is not the whole story—especially the lightning strike of dimethyltryptamine (DMT), a chemical produced by our own bodies and by many plants. Smoking DMT is like being shot from a cannon into another dimension and returning to this world in less than ten minutes. The DMT revelation strongly suggests that the psyche cannot be reduced to a manifestation of our physical hardware.

Carl Jung wrote: "People will do anything, no matter how absurd, in order to avoid facing their own souls." Is it possible that our society has built up a vast edifice of technology and propaganda in order to avoid that inner confrontation? Enveloped by media and technology, we have come to prefer secondhand images to inner experience—what Jung called "the adventure of the spirit." The self-knowledge achieved through personal discovery and visionary states seems alien, even repellent, compared to the voyeuristic gaze, the virtual entertainments and hypnotic distractions of contemporary culture. Perhaps we are due—even overdue—for a change.

Considering the world's present state of uncertainty, it might seem a strange moment to argue for the validity of controlled shamanic explorations. The entire subject is fraught with prejudices magnified by decades of propaganda. My hope is that people will reserve judgment while reading this book. They are free to consider it as fiction, or as a slightly laborious thought experiment. I do not advocate or suggest that anyone should violate any law, no matter how poorly conceived, antithetical to human nature and dignity, or excessively punitive that law might be. While undertaking this experiment, I have kept in mind a comment by the philosopher Jean-François Lyotard: "Being prepared to receive what thought is not prepared to think is what deserves the name of thinking."

Our society has not been prepared to think seriously about the possibility that plants and even chemicals that transform consciousness might reveal an essential link between the human mind and the natural, and supernatural, world. It may well be the case, as the late Terence McKenna wrote, that "the suppression of the natural human fascination with altered states of consciousness and the present perilous situation of all life on earth are intimately and casually connected." We have pursued frighteningly Faustian knowledge about the physical world without developing deeper awareness of our inner selves. If we don't find some means of correcting this imbalance, we may face the most dire consequences.

Some might consider this book a provocation. It was not meant as one. What took me to Gabon and Ecuador and into the inner recesses of my own psyche was a yearning for meaning and spiritual truth in a world that seemed devoid of both. The study of psychedelic shamanism encompasses a vast number of areas, from botany to chemistry, from cultural history to mysticism. I am an expert in none of them. All I can offer is a record of my own findings—it is, of necessity, incomplete, personal, and highly subjective.

It is, from this vantage point, difficult to conceive that psychedelics might ever receive official sanction, or that the diabolical "War on Drugs" will ever come to an end. But who knows? Above all else, the psychedelic experience continues to reveal, as it did a generation ago, that reality is far more mutable, capacious, and capricious than we generally allow ourselves to imagine.

Part One

MY INITIATION

Whenever there is a reaching down into innermost experience, into the nucleus of the personality, most people are overcome by fear and many run away. . . . The risk of inner experience, the adventure of the spirit, is in any case alien to most human beings. The possibility that such experience might have psychic reality is anathema to them.

—CARL JUNG, *Memories, Dreams, Reflections*

Chapter I

THE KING OF THE BWITI

"The Bwiti believe that before the ceremony, the neophyte is nothing," Daniel Lieberman told me on my first morning in Gabon, as we took a cab from the Libreville airport. "It is only through the initiation that you become something."

"What do you become?" I asked.

"You become a *baanzi*. One who knows the other world, because you have seen it with your own eyes."

"What do the Bwiti think of iboga?" I asked.

Lieberman barely hesitated. "For them, iboga is a super-conscious spiritual entity that guides mankind," he said.

"Okay."

Lieberman, an ethnobotanist from South Africa, wanted to make a business out of taking Westerners through the extreme Bwiti initiation. I had found him on the Internet. On his Website he posted photos from Gabon that seemed unreal—tribal dancers in grass skirts, smiling shamans, and images of iboga itself, a modest, even unassuming-looking plant. The Bwiti's botanical sacrament, *Tabernanthe iboga,* is a bush that grows small, edible orange fruit that are tasteless and sticky. Under optimum conditions, iboga can grow into a tree that rises forty feet high. The hallucinatory compound is concentrated in the plant's rootbark, which is scraped off, dried, and shredded into gray powder. For an outsider coming from the United States, the Bwiti initiation costs over $7,000 with plane ticket, the cost of the ritual, and the botanist's fee. "I have spent time in the rain forests of Africa east and west, Madagascar, and the Amazon working with shamans, *brujos,* witch doctors, healers," Lieberman e-mailed me before the trip. "Iboga I feel to be the one plant that needs to be introduced to the world, and urgently."

In person, the botanist was thin and pallid, wearing Teva sandals and safari clothes. He seemed younger, less professional, more ill at ease than I had expected. He was an entomologist as well as a botanist—later he would show me hundreds of photographs he had taken of insects in the African rain forest. He seemed the type of person who would be happiest alone, trekking through a forest in search of rare beetles and butterflies. He told me his pale complexion and twitches appeared during a near-fatal bout of cerebral malaria. "I caught it during a Bwiti ceremony," he said. "It took me months to recover."

I expected my guide to be robust and adventurous. Instead, at thirty, he turned out to be two years younger than me, and shakier. He also told me that the last time he took iboga, he had been shown the date of his own death, and it wasn't too far away. From the somber way he said this, I knew he believed it was true. I didn't press him for details—later I wished that I had.

Libreville was hot, stagnant, without vitality. The city seemed pressed under glass. Blinding sunlight reflected off the black mirrors of corporate towers, the headquarters of oil companies. Because of its oil deposits, Gabon, a small West African country on the equator, is richer, more secure, than other countries in the region. Iboga is another natural resource, but it will never be exploited for export by the Gabonese. Half the population of Gabon belongs to one Bwiti sect or another. Even the president-for-life, Omar Bongo, whose neutral and uninterested visage gazed down at us from posters around town, was known to be an initiate. The Bwiti seem to tolerate foreign interest in their sacred medicine, but they do not encourage it in any way.

"Why would the Bwiti allow me to join their sect?" I now asked.

"Bwiti is like Buddhism," he said. "Anyone can join if they are willing to be initiated. The word *Bwiti* simply means the experience of the iboga plant, which is the essence of love."

While Lieberman equated Bwiti with Buddhism, to most observers it remains an enigmatic cult. Some sects of Bwiti, such as the Fang, incorporate elements of Christianity, even wearing ostentatious costumes that resemble Mardi Gras versions of the vestments of Catholic bishops and nuns. Other groups, such as the one we were visiting, hold on to tribal beliefs. James Fernandez, an anthropologist who studied the sect at length, ended his book *Bwiti: An Ethnography of the Religious Imagination in Africa* inconclusively: "In the end, any attempt to demonstrate the coherence of the Bwiti cosmos founders upon the paradoxes with which it plays." For Fernandez, the Bwiti religion worked by "indirection and suggestion and other kinds of puzzlements," leaving "many loose ends and inconsistencies." In the text, a typically distanced work of anthropology, there was no indication that Fernandez had tried iboga himself.

I knew there was one other customer for this journey. A woman. I had fantasized, in advance, about hooking up with some brave and beautiful Australian heiress or young Peace Corps volunteer. Instead, to my dismay, I was introduced at the hotel to Elaine, a short, talkative, middle-aged Jewish psychoanalyst with a heavy New York accent.

"I just came from Bhutan where I got a terrible bladder infection," the analyst immediately announced. "You're a New Yorker also? What a surprise! I'm a psychoanalyst in the West Village. Maybe you know my friend who works for the *New York Times*? Or my sister, the novelist?"

I nodded at the familiar names, trying to recover from the shock of unwanted familiarity. I had yearned for some severe and pristine pursuit of the sacred, the exotic "Other" encountered in novels of Joseph Conrad or Paul Bowles. Instead, I would be sharing my tribal adventure with a woman I might have tried to avoid at a Manhattan cocktail party. I admired Elaine's courage and her reasons for taking this trip— she said that some of her patients abused drugs, especially coke, and she wanted to know if she should recommend ibogaine to them. But her presence on my journey seemed like some carefully orchestrated karmic punishment.

We went to meet our shaman, Tsanga Jean Moutamba, who called himself "The King of the Bwiti." What we would later discover about

The King's belligerence and greed and tyrannical theatricality was not evident during this first encounter. At his Libreville house, The King seemed gruff but basically friendly as we set the arrangements for the trip. His purple robe, ample stomach, bushy gray beard, and necklace of lion's teeth gave him the larger-than-life presence of a 1960s avant-garde jazz musician. With shy smiles, members of his huge family came to shake hands—we were told by Lieberman that he had eight wives and fourteen children, plus an untold number of Bwiti initiates who called him "Papa." The tribe packed our bags into a jeep, and The King himself drove us down Gabon's single highway, four hours into the dense jungle, while green foliage unfolded monotonously under a lead gray sky. He played a tape of the twangy, unsettling Bwiti music over and over again on his tape recorder as we drove. The music did not sound tribal; to me it had a sci-fi quality. When we stopped at one of the frequent military checkpoints, the guards would take one look at his lion's tooth necklace and wave us past.

During my time in Gabon, I kept trying to find out the meaning of Moutamba's status as "Le Roi du Gabon Bwiti," as the hand-painted sign outside his tribal village proudly proclaimed. I received different answers, sometimes from the same person. Alain Dukaga, an English-speaking Gabonese with a limp, who acted as our translator, first told me: "Moutamba is like Jesus to us. Most of the people now are like lacking roots. They got tied to the Christian ways and forgot their culture. Moutamba is helping to bring back our culture. We hope soon they will start teaching Bwiti again in the schools." A few days later, when relations soured between us and our shaman, Alain reversed himself. "Moutamba?" he scoffed. "He's not the king of anything. He just call himself that."

It was my first time in Africa, the one continent I had never wanted to visit. When I thought of Africa I thought of vast disasters, cruelty on a biblical scale: famines, tribal wars, inescapable poverty, despotic dictatorships, epidemics of AIDS and ebola. It was a continent where friends of mine went to prove themselves—writing journalism, photographing exotic atrocities, acting out Hemingway-esque safari fantasies, joining the Peace Corps, contracting bizarre diseases. The ebola virus first appeared in the forests of Gabon. Sometimes I mused on the unsettling near-homophony of ebola and iboga.

My trip seemed to be tempting fate. Every detail of it gave me as much resistance as I could handle. I had an assignment to write about the iboga initiation for *Vibe Magazine*, but I only received the money I needed a few days before the trip. After paying off Lieberman and everyone else, my bank account was reduced to a few hundred dollars. The visa I needed to enter the country—a full-page purple passport stamp of a mother and baby—was held up, for no obvious reason, at the Gabonese consulate in Washington. It finally arrived at my apartment via FedEx a few hours before my departure, interrupting my fit of hysterics. When I reached Charles de Gaulle Airport in Paris, I learned that Air France had canceled their once-a-week flight to Libreville, which was supposed to leave that night. Air France gave me 1,500 francs in consolation and stashed me in an airport hotel for two nights, before the next departure to Libreville, on Air Gabon. At the hotel, I ate with a few elegantly dressed Gabonese people who were also stranded. They mocked the wine and the service in rapid-fire French. I told one of the men I was planning to visit the Bwiti. He gave me a strange look. *"Les Bwiti, ils sont dangereux,"* he said solemnly, quickly turning away. I had no way of getting in touch with Lieberman to explain the delay; I could only hope he would still be waiting for me when I arrived.

In retrospect, and even at the time, it almost seemed as if the difficulties were a kind of test, an ordeal prepared for me before I could even reach the ordeal of the initiation. Although I was anxious, it did not occur to me to turn back.

I was driven to try iboga by a yearning that went far deeper than the desire to get a good story. I saw the assignment as a mystical lottery ticket. I was committed to this once-in-a-lifetime long shot to visit the Bwiti, to access their spirit world. Or any spirit world.

Chapter 2

MAD TO BE SAVED

My initiation into the Bwiti came at a time when I was losing interest in myself. I felt like an actor who had lost the motivation for his part. Or I was like the character of "Daniel Pinchbeck," trapped in a half-finished novel that an incompetent author was in the sluggish, surly process of abandoning.

I fell into a spiritual crisis.

I fell, and I could not get up.

Wandering the streets of the East Village, I spent so much time contemplating the meaninglessness of existence that I sometimes felt like a ghost. *Perhaps I am already dead,* I thought to myself. The world seemed to be wrapped in a cocoon I could not tear open, and I was suffocating in it. I did not want what other people wanted, but I didn't know how to find what I needed. I wanted truth—my own truth, whatever bleak fragment of whatever hellish totality it might turn out to be.

There are reasons why I, particularly, got sucked into this spiritual void. When I look back over my life, I can see the open jaws of the abyss awaiting me. Through my mother, Joyce Johnson, a writer of novels and memoirs, I was linked to the often maligned and sometimes revered writers of the Beat Generation, frantic in their pursuit of mystical experience across the globe (when Jack Kerouac was on a TV talk show in the late 1950s, he was asked what he was looking for. Drunk and defiant, he replied, honestly, "I am waiting for God to show me His Face." At the time, my poor mother, all of twenty-two years old, was anxiously waiting for him backstage). My mother sent mixed signals about her Beat past. On the one hand the high school yearbook quote she dedicated to me was from *On the Road*: "mad to live, mad to love, mad to be saved. . . ." Yet the life she seemed to want me to lead was that of a sheltered middle-class intellectual. She had seen too many friends destroyed by bohemian excesses, ruined by alcohol or speed.

A second reason lies in my preposterous last name, which sometimes feels like wearing a clown's red nose. The word can be found in any good dictionary: "pinchbeck" is a type of false gold. This shiny alloy of zinc and copper, still used in costume jewelry, was invented by Christopher Pinchbeck, an eighteenth-century English alchemist who was also a maker of intricate mechanical clocks for British aristocrats. Later, the definition of "pinchbeck" expanded to mean anything false or spurious—for instance, according to the example in one old dictionary, "The 19th Century was a pinchbeck age of literature." James Joyce included the word in *Ulysses*. Recently, William Safire championed its revival.

This spurious moniker has kept me remote, to some extent, from the hard facts of existence. Behind the pinchbeck facade, life always seems slightly illusory, an alchemical and improbable process. Perhaps I also inherited my ancestor's urge to seek out wonder, as well as my father's yearning for transcendence, expressed in his enormous and brooding abstract paintings. In the quest described in this book, I suspect I am working through some business left over from my heritage, as if mystical yearnings run, like rogue genes, in family trees.

My reference points for a spiritual crisis were books and authors—*Nausea, Notes from Undergound, The Stranger*; Kafka, Beckett, Rilke—the eloquent despair of twentieth-century literature. As I wandered the streets in a desolate funk, I would ask myself the impossible, the embarrassing, the ultimate childish question of Why?—Why this city? Why this life? Why anything? Of course I knew that "why" was a question you were supposed to stop asking around the age of ten, but I couldn't free myself from it.

I mocked myself by recalling a sequence from *Hannah and Her*

Sisters where the character portrayed by Woody Allen first learns he has a brain tumor, then finds out he doesn't have one after all, yet still realizes—no matter how improbable it seemed before, when he was, like most of us, in cheerful denial—he will die someday. Suddenly obsessed with finding a meaning to life, he joins several religions including Hare Krisna and Catholicism—for the skit's high point, he goes to the supermarket to buy a loaf of white Wonder Bread as a sign of his new Christian faith. In the end, he resolves his crisis at a Marx Brothers double feature, realizing that laughter is, if not an answer, at least the only solace he can imagine.

I was in a worse place than Woody Allen. I needed some solace beyond laughter.

My options looked pretty bad.

We live in a world of media overload and data smog, where everything distracts us from everything else. Yet underlying this noisy assault, our culture offers us nothing transcendent. No deeper meaning, no abiding hope. In my crisis, every facet of the contemporary world seemed part of a diabolical mechanism carefully designed to keep people from wondering about the real purpose of their endless frantic activity.

When people find themselves sinking into a spiritual crisis, many turn to the established religions of Christianity or Judaism—or Buddhism, or some New Age consolation—to haul themselves from the depths. This was not an option for me.

My parents were antireligion. My mother was Jewish by birth but a committed nonbeliever. Even my grandmother and her older sisters, who had been born in Poland, avoided the subject of religion. Our small family Passover was a dinner without ritual or prayer. My father, forced into being an altar boy, hated Catholicism and shuddered when he recalled the priests who oppressed him as a child. Anyway, I had no interest in received wisdom or traditional faith. I wanted inspiration of my own, inner knowledge.

Ralph Waldo Emerson is one of those writers we study in high school and then forget. When I encountered his essays as an adult, I realized he was speaking to me: "Why should not we also enjoy an original relation to the universe?" Emerson asked. "Why should not we have a poetry and philosophy of insight and not of tradition, and a religion by revelation to us, and not the history of theirs?"

That was what I demanded, "an original relation to the universe." Nothing abstract, secondhand, or second-rate. No history of somebody else's transcendence. Why should not I also enjoy it? Why did it seem such an impossible goal?

My parents were part of the Beat and Abstract Expressionist upsurge of the fifties and sixties. A generation later, I watched the wrecking ball of economic determinism destroy the remnants of their liberal, idiosyncratic culture—the quaint, slow-motion world of antiquated cafes, old revival houses, independent bookstores. Through the 1990s, New York transformed from a city where culture and commerce lived together symbiotically into a commercial center where artists clung to the margins. There was certainly no longer anything like a redemptive "high culture" to provide a brake on the capitalist juggernaut.

I felt as if I were becoming a ghost, a disembodied survivor from some distant epoch. I realized that if this monotonous materialist culture was "the end of history," as some writers proclaimed—without spiritual reality, without access to any other level of consciousness or meaning—then life for me was almost intolerable.

At a low point, I recalled illicit illuminations received from certain dried bits of chewy fungus and tiny paper squares I had last eaten in college. Most of all, I remembered my encounters with psilocybin mushrooms. What I recalled was the sensory glow—the expansion of colors, sounds, smells. It had been a revelation—how the veils of abstraction suddenly seemed to fall away from my mind. At the time, mushrooms cut through my painful feelings of postadolescent alienation, although they sometimes magnified my deepest anxieties.

While tripping, I felt how I was embedded in the social and biological processes that were spun like the intricate filaments of a spider's web all around me. The world returned to the status of an original mystery, but nothing was more bizarre than my own consciousness, my place in the structure of all I could see and sense and know.

I started experimenting with mushrooms and LSD again. At first, finding these drugs was a surprisingly difficult task in New York. Heroin and cocaine were easily available on any number of street corners, but psychedelics required serious effort and research. Once supplied, I took them at home, in parks, and before visiting grungy East Village bars. On mushrooms, a friend and I perceived Max Fish, a bar on Ludlow Street, to be a medieval pub, full of wounded knights and crippled plague victims, scoundrels, and wastrels. I took a strong dose of LSD with another friend in my apartment on Avenue B in the East Village. We watched, amazed, as music generated rainbow shimmers and our words turned into stained-glass pictures before our eyes. The acid temporarily wiped out my identity. I knew I had chosen to perform some type of experiment on myself, but I couldn't recall my own name. This was interesting rather than threatening—in another circumstance it might have been terrifying. As the walls trembled like running watercolors, I asked my friend, "Did I, at some point earlier this evening, take a drug that altered my mind?"

A year later, I tried the Amazonian jungle drug ayahuasca—the legendary substance, also known as *yagé*, that William Burroughs pursued through South America in the early 1950s, seeking a visionary cure for his heroin addiction. Cups of the drug were doled out at a $200 ceremony in a downtown apartment, organized by a couple from California. Before drinking, we were given Adult Depends diapers to wear, and plastic buckets for vomiting. The sour potion produced a few startling insights and images—emerald-green vines wavering in front of a waterfall—and hours of nausea. One woman groaned and retched for hours as the New Age shamans shook rattles and feathers around her. It sounded like she was vomiting out her very being. Her sickness kept me from my own inner journey.

The ayahuasca trip, while intriguing, left me deeply unsatisfied. My ability to have visions seemed extremely meager. A hardhead, I lacked the capacity to "hallucinate." Even my dreams were meager gray voids. I wondered if my intense desire to reach the visionary state stemmed from some intrinsic physical flaw.

Most of my friends dismissed my new enthusiasm. Psychedelic drugs were weird and childish, something you did in high school or college and got over. You tried them a bunch of times, had some freaky trips, then moved on to the adult lubricators of social interaction— booze, coke, Valium, pot, heroin. Heroin, above all, was the downtown hipster intoxicant of choice. Over a decade, I knew at least half a dozen people—bright, artistic, confused—who died from overdoses. Compared to these hipster intoxicants, mushrooms and LSD were seen as silly, somehow regressive, or weak. In my crowd, even Ecstasy was not popular—only alcohol in massive amounts, then heroin and coke, and sometimes the volatile mixture of the three. While I took those substances in social circumstances, I never felt the slightest compulsion about them. I never touched them when I was alone.

I first heard about iboga at Black Out Books, an anarchist bookstore on Avenue B. The clerk showed me a book on the Ibogaine Project, a twenty-year effort to bring attention to a rare African hallucinogen purported to have a miraculous effect on heroin and cocaine addiction. Ibogaine, I learned, was an underground legend for its anti-addictive powers. This property was discovered in the early 1960s by Howard Lotsoff. Lotsoff was a young addict when he read about the African bark somewhere, obtained the powder through a mail-order catalog, and took it for extra kicks. Instead of an added high, he was sent on a stern and somber tour of his entire past. Finding the trip unpleasant, he tried to shake out of it by taking a walk. Crossing a street at one point, he looked back and saw seven copies of himself, freeze-framed, crossing the street behind him. At the end of the trip, he found he had lost interest in heroin, as well as any desire for it—an inadvertent and not even desired side effect. Lotsoff went on with his life but never forgot this episode. Decades later, he patented the iboga molecule under the name of ibogaine, specifically for use in treating drug addiction. After fifteen years of effort, Lotsoff had failed to get his treatment legalized.

If this were all true, then the mythic dimensions of the ibogaine story were fascinating: A plant from equatorial Africa (the archaic birthplace of humanity) that cured addiction (the modern scourge of African Americans in the inner cities of the United States) by sending addicts on a long psychedelic trip (a voyage into an archaic spiritual dimension whose existence is dismissed by modern "rationality").

I personally did not believe in the existence of a "spirit world."

Still, I wanted to try it for myself.

Chapter 3

YOU WANT TO CHEAT ME?

We drove to The King's village, forty kilometers of dirt road and red dust–covered jungle away from Lambaréné, the riverside town where Albert Schweitzer had his hospital. Moutamba's homestead was a compound of modest buildings in a jungle clearing. Children, hens, and roosters wandered freely around dirt paths and chaotic patches of garden. One roofless structure decorated with palm fronds was the Pygmy House, honoring the region's native inhabitants for discovering *le bois sacré,* "the sacred wood," another name for iboga.

According to legend, the Pygmies used iboga for centuries before they gave the secret of the plant to the neighboring Bantu tribes who kept attacking them, forcing them deeper into the jungle. The Pygmies showed their enemies how to use iboga so they would discover their place in the spirit world. The Pygmies knew that once the Bantus made that discovery, they would lose interest in waging wars. If that was the plan, it worked: Gabon remains the only peaceful country in a region of inescapable hostility, tribal conflicts, mindless genocides. The cult of Bwiti may be the reason for its pacifism.

The Pygmies still live in small bands in Gabon's most inaccessible jungles. Theoretically, it is possible to have a Pygmy initiation. I will have to save that adventure for another trip. Or more likely a future life.

The stone walls of the temple were painted with crude portraits of Moutamba's ancestors. A wooden statue of the original Bwiti couple stood at the entryway. In the nineteenth century, Gabonese wood-carvers were renowned for their skill, but their artisanship degenerated after the French colonial occupation and the oil boom, and this statue was of poor quality. I gave the sculpture a careful look. The figures were crude and uncuddly, squared off and dark. A small iboga plant sprouted up between their legs. Before arriving in Gabon, I read accounts of Westerners taking iboga—there were quite a few reports posted on the Internet. The Bwiti version of Adam and Eve, the cult's archaic father and mother, often appeared in iboga visions, even showing themselves to people who knew nothing about Bwiti before taking it. I hoped they would appear to me.

We stayed at the village the night before the ceremony. The analyst, the botanist, The King, and I slept in the temple on mattresses under mosquito nets, along with various members of the tribe. People came and went throughout the night. Lizards skittered across the tin ceiling. A small child arrived and nestled close to me. When we awoke, The King gave us what the Bwiti call *la liste*, the traditional roster of things neophytes buy for the ritual. *La liste* included a mirror, a tin bucket, a red parrot's feather, yards of fabric, candles and copal incense, a machete, a woven mat, and supplies for the next day's feast for the tribe—a live *coq du village*, and a large quantity of sweet liquors such as rum and cassis. The analyst, the guide, and I spent the morning driving around the market stalls of Lambaréné with three of The King's sons, whose unsmiling severity as they assisted us made me conscious of the serious nature of the ceremony. Everywhere we went in the virtually all-black township, people peered into our car with curiosity, and the tight-lipped Bwiti clan seemed proud to parade *les blancs* around like exotic trophies.

On the way back to the village, the jeep kicked up clouds of the red dust that covered the palms and banana plants along the dirt road. Sitting next to a jet-black young man with a long knife at his belt, the analyst was chattering nervously, talking nonstop. The botanist admitted he didn't have a girlfriend. The analyst told him how to improve his love life. She said he should move to New York and take out some personal ads.

"Lately my friend Mark has met so many wonderful men through the *New York Review of Books*," she shouted over the wind.

The Bwiti stared silently into the jungle.

. . .

WHEN WE RETURNED, The King called us to the temple. "It was good you stayed here last night." He smiled broadly, flashing white teeth. "Last night, I dreamt that *le journaliste*"—he pointed at me—"will have many wonderful visions. Now it is time. You must give us the rest of the money."

This was a surprise. We had already handed over the agreed-upon $600 for the ceremony, at least double the fee paid by the average Gabonese. We reminded him of this, but The King started shouting.

"You want to cheat me?" He demanded another $600 from each of us. Our guide tried to bargain with him, but Lieberman seemed to have little authority among the Bwiti. The argument went on for hours. Moutamba raged at us, shouted his demand over and over again. He would go away for a while, then return to scream some more. The young men of the tribe stared at us coldly, as if they were shocked we would challenge The King's authority.

Later I learned that shamans tend to be tricky when it comes to matters of payment: It is tough to set a price tag on transcendence. During an interval when The King stopped yelling at us, he approached me through Alain, the translator. I was told that, in the future, they didn't want to work with the botanist anymore. "You yourself should bring more Americans to him for initiation." I said I would see what I could do.

Lieberman kept assuring us the Bwiti were pacifist, but the situation seemed out of control. He certainly did not have control over it. Lieberman's extensive Website gave the impression he had led numerous people through the Bwiti ceremony. When I actually questioned him about it, I learned he had brought only one other customer to The King, a Dutch computer programmer. The Dutchman lost his nerve before the initiation, swallowed a fistful of tranquilizers, and did not eat any iboga. Lieberman had also told us that Moutamba had initiated many outsiders. The King presented us a large ledger for foreigners to sign before the ceremony. There were only two other names in the book's yellowing pages.

We did not feel safe; later on the analyst told me she had never been so terrified in her life. We were completely in their power. While The King ranted that we had cheated them out of money, all of our belongings, our bags and passports and wallets, were stashed in one of their unlocked houses. During one meeting with The King and his retinue, a hunting rifle lay on the table in front of them. As The King screamed at us, one of his sons carefully cleaned it, then loaded it up.

"I'm not sure I like the power dynamics I see here," the analyst whispered to me.

While the analyst had earlier seemed a karmic curse, I now considered her a good-luck charm. It was easy for me to imagine myself and the botanist burned at the stake by angry Bwiti who felt we were ruining their ritual—we were two pale-faced sad sacks desperate to know the tribal mysteries—but it was impossible that they would hurt the analyst. With her "Free Tibet" T-shirt, Patagonia pants, bug-eyed glasses, and incessant chatter, she had a curious quality of indestructibility.

Finally it was decided that the initiation would proceed even though we had cheated them. At the end of the ritual, however, The King would not give us the special oil that bestows a deeper understanding of our visions through the year. "He himself will not walk with you into the forest and explain to you the myth of the Bwiti, the origin of the plants," Alain translated. Now Moutamba's tribe seemed to regard us with contempt. Bwiti no longer seemed quite the "essence of love" Lieberman had described.

.   .   .

IT WAS ALMOST DUSK. I was told to sit alone in front of the temple. As night fell, the men of the Bwiti came to me. They were an impressive sight. They had changed from their everyday jeans and T-shirts into tribal dress. Limbs and torsos bare, they wore animal pelts and loincloths, with armbands and necklaces made from shells and feathers. Their jet-black skin was painted with white stripes and dots.

We walked in single file, away from the simple wooden houses of the village, taking a path through the jungle to the banks of a small stream. Among the Bwiti, I felt absurdly self-conscious: I knew I was not a person to them so much as an archetype. To the Bwiti, I was a white ghost, a pale interloper from the colonial world seeking to return to the spiritual source. I wanted to laugh—the initiation seemed like an act of insane hubris on my part.

Some of the men held torches. Others played drums and rattles and horns in a weirdly humorous march. The young men of the tribe had the sleek and muscular bodies of hunters. White-painted patterns glowed like neon on their bodies in the flickering flames.

Moutamba, wrapped in a leopard skin, ordered me to undress completely and step into the middle of the stream. As I shivered in the icy water, the young man assigned to be my "Bwiti father" poured a soapy liquid over me—a protective spirit-medicine. He smeared a rough red paste across my face and torso. The Bwiti sang while I put on the initiate's outfit—straps of tanned animal skins and shells looping across my chest and upper arms, a short red tunic. A red feather was twirled in my hair.

It was time to begin eating the iboga.

Chapter 4

TOUCHERS TEACH TOO

The King raised up the plantain with two hands.
My Bwiti father carried this sacrament to me gingerly while the others
watched. I looked at the fruit held to my lips; it had been split open and
filled with the gray flecks of iboga powder. The Bwiti men on the hillside sang and drummed a dirgelike melody. By casting off my clothes
and putting on the red robe of the initiate, I had symbolically died.
After eating the dry powder, I would be reborn.

For years after, whenever I recalled the flavor of iboga, I shuddered
with disgust. The powder tasted like sawdust laced with battery acid—
it was entirely revolting, the most bitter substance I ever put into my
mouth. Worse yet, the plantain was dry and hard and each bite required extensive chewing. My tongue became dry and swollen, my
throat gagged as it tried to reject the vile stuff.

After I finished the plantain, I was fed a few more spoonfuls of the
drug mixed with honey. The shaman nodded encouragingly. I fought
to keep the stuff down.

"*Le journaliste a mangé beaucoup, beaucoup,*" he said.

We returned to the village. My legs had turned rubbery and I felt
queasy. In the main courtyard, a few of the men sat around me, playing
drums. One of them strummed the *m'congo,* a one-stringed mouth

harp resembling a bow, which has the eerie tonality of a mocking voice. I had been told that the *m'congo* channels the voices of the Bwiti ancestors. They put a bundle of leaves in my right hand and a whisk of dry thistles in my left and told me to keep shaking both in time to the music. This mechanical gesture would help to steady me throughout the visions. The Bwiti were strict about this rule; whenever I stopped shaking the rattles throughout the night, a tribesman would rush up to me and force me to continue.

They fed me more iboga and brought me, shuddering, into the torch-lit temple. I was unbalanced, confused. They sat me alone at the center, in front of my mirror, which was surrounded by fern leaves and carved figurines. The King and the tribal elders sat to my left, and the rest of the tribe was on benches to my right, perhaps thirty people in all.

The analyst was telling her visions, which seemed to be pouring into her. She lay along a wall of the temple surrounded by Bwiti women who murmured supportively as she recounted what she saw.

"There's Buddha," Elaine said, pointing at the ceiling. She turned around. "And I see my dead grandma over there." She waved at the wall. "Hello, Grandma."

Around me, the atmosphere was tense. The King had decreed I would have "wonderful visions." I began to realize that not satisfying him was not an option.

A long time passed, and nothing happened.

In the mirror, I saw my face change shape. I seemed to age, lines and wrinkles spread across my skin. Then I appeared younger, my features smoothing out, impacting into the scrunched face of a baby. These effects fluctuated, lasting a few instants. Then I was staring at myself again, a bewildered pale face in tortoiseshell glasses and tribal outfit.

"I don't see anything," I said to the impatient tribesmen watching me.

Finally, out of the corner of my eye, I had my first vision: A large wooden statue, a dark and faceless golemlike figure formed out of rough logs, walked across the room and sat on the bench. Crossing its legs, it leaned forward, as if to watch me with interest. The vision happened quickly. It seemed utterly real. A moment later, a tiny screen opened in the mirror's scratched, pockmarked surface. On that screen I looked into the window of my Manhattan apartment. Through the hanging plants, I saw into my living room, which was empty. Then I watched crowds crossing a Broadway intersection, holding umbrellas in the rain. The images were ghost impressions in shades of gray, like images from an old movie; they were clear, totally distinct, but only for a moment. When I tried to study them, they wavered and disappeared.

"If you see a window you must try to go through it," The King instructed me through the translator, "and if you meet somebody there you must try to talk to them. Perhaps they have a message for you, some information."

The Bwiti kept insisting I should relate my visions out loud. I was not ready for that. I had expected whatever I saw to be my own concern. But the Bwiti didn't sympathize with my Western ideas of privacy. "Everything you see must be shared," The King urged. "You might have a message for the tribe, some information." In my stoned state I was tongue-tied, and I sensed the Bwitis' rigid disapproval of my silence.

Other images passed quickly before my eyes—a *memento mori* arrangement of candles, burning skulls, and goblin faces; the figures of women in black dresses stretching out long white arms toward me from the edges of my vision—but when I tried to speak of them, they disappeared.

The King began to shout again. "When is he going to see the fabulous castles? The cities of the spirits?" he asked, exasperated. He stormed out of the room.

"I think they're going to keep feeding you iboga until you start talking," Lieberman whispered.

Meanwhile, I was fighting against pulses that gathered into waves of nausea. I wanted to reach the deepest visionary state. I was also scared. If iboga was indeed a "super-conscious spiritual entity," I wasn't sure whether this entity liked or hated me. Perhaps it wanted to kill me. I was an outsider, a stranger to its meanings. They brought me outside, where I stood under the cool stars. I remembered King Moutamba saying, earlier, *"Le journaliste a mangé beaucoup, beaucoup."* Had I eaten too much?

I was drenched in sweat. My head seemed like a balloon, blown up

several times its normal size. I wondered if I was going to die. I retched
and vomited green slime into my pail.

When I was no longer sick, the Bwiti took me back inside the temple. They brought me to a mat on the hard-packed earth and instructed
me to lie down. The King returned to his seat. The Bwiti tribesmen
started drumming and singing. The awesome sound filled the temple,
pounding against the walls of my skull. I felt an incredible sense of failure as I scorned my own foolishness: Who was I to try to enter the
African spirit world?

From time to time the drums and the singing stopped, and The
King would make a speech to his tribe, slipping between Bantu and
French. I didn't know either language, but I felt I could understand
every nuance of every word he spoke. He was deriding me, making
fun of my anatomy, my visionary failures, my weakness—several times
I had asked for a blanket to cover myself, and a pillow for my head, but
the Bwiti rejected these requests.

"The foreigners, they say they want the true Bwiti initiation," The
King seemed to say with a sneer. "Well, this is what they are getting.
Now they complain: 'I want a blanket, I want a pillow,' they say. The
true Bwiti doesn't want any comfort."

Finally The King took a break from mocking me. The impossibly
beautiful music—polyrhythms, call-and-response songs—started up
again.

Closing my eyes, I saw brightly colored patterns. Spiraling plantlike forms and dancing geometries swirled with the music. I fell into a
trance, floating with the Bwiti songs. I drifted into a new phase of the
trip.

Piece by piece, the pattern of my past began to flare up in my
mind. For the next several hours, I forgot about the tribesmen watching me. I was witnessing a "memory theater," a scrupulous replaying
of all the forces that sculpted me into the person I was. I reviewed the
elements of my early life—my parents' separation, my father's absence
from my childhood, the imprint of my mother's loneliness and depres-
sion, my own solitude and love of reading, the many months I spent in
a hospital bed at the age of eleven with a bacterial infection in my
spine. I went back to the secret, baroque sources of childhood nightmare and fantasy—the primal fear of the monsters under the bed, the

cave of darkness inside the closet. I saw the desperate, desolate parts of my life and the flashes of power and invention that were also mine. Separate from myself, yet enclosed within myself, I followed the traces of the being that I was, that was given to me, as it unfolded over time.

Laid out for me was the entire, intricate process of my self-development. The process was complex yet ultimately organic. The extension of the self was, I realized, a natural process, akin to the blossoming of a plant. While a plant extends toward the sun throughout its life, human beings evolve internally. We rise up and flourish, or become stunted, involuted, as we react to the forces that press against us. Our growth takes place in the invisible realm of our mental space, and the unreachable sun we rise toward is knowledge—of the self and the universe.

Henry James once described human consciousness as "a helpless jelly poured into a mold." Iboga compelled me to perceive the exact shape of that mold; at the same time, it allowed me to escape that sense of helplessness. I felt a mingling of wonder, sorrow, and freedom. By letting me perceive the shape of my past self, iboga also seemed to be freeing me from the burden of that past. The action of the drug actually was—as I had heard it described but wouldn't believe—the equivalent of ten years of psychoanalysis compacted into one interminable night.

For a brief time I mulled on my drinking habits. I knew I wasn't an alcoholic, but since high school I had relied on booze as a tool for socializing. For the first time I fully realized the negative impact that alcohol had on my relationships, my work, on me in general. Alcohol fired up my id, sent me staggering across endless parties and barroom floors in an aggressive, sometimes successful, pursuit of sex. But drinking was holding me back—it was like a weight I was dragging around. It was keeping me from my own self-development. I saw myself as a drunken idiot at parties, cycled through many nights where I drank to blot myself out. There was a dark tinge of shame and self-disgust entwined in my overuse of alcohol. I realized I didn't need to do it anymore.

Through iboga, I recognized my existing self as the product of all the physical and psychological forces that had acted upon me. Yet there seemed to be something beyond all of it, something that was "mine," an energy projected from outside of my biographical destiny. That energy was the self—and the self's tremendous capacity for transformation.

The trip turned to a cinematic cyclone, whirling images and scenes at high speed. A series of unknown houses appeared, ghostly gray suburban landscapes I had never seen before. I drifted down into them as they faded away.

Impressions of old girlfriends dispersed like fog, their bodies dancing away from me into the ether. I saw the sign for a restaurant, Teacher's Too, a childhood haunt. In its heyday, Teacher's Too (across the street from the original Teacher's) was a maroon-colored meeting place for publishing types, professors, the lost liberal intelligentsia of the Upper West Side.

Teacher's Too was the place where I met my first serious girlfriend, after I dropped out of college. I arrived early for a lunch date, and started to chat with the restaurant's cute hostess. She was sipping a Bloody Mary at the bar, wearing a plastic hat for St. Patrick's Day. She was giggly, vivacious—it was as if an electrical current flowed around her. Julie told me she was also a college dropout. Suddenly I remembered her: We had met once at a party during high school when she was dating a friend of mine. After that chance meeting, we started seeing each other, and stayed together for three years.

The letters of the restaurant sign peeled off one by one in small squares, as though they were pieces from a board game. The squares spun around in my mental space with a clicking sound. It was like a cheap special effect from an old movie. The letters reassembled, rebus-like, to spell out a phrase that was either "Touchers Teach Too" or "Touchers Teach Two."

This ambiguous message, this telegraphic koan, seemed to contain a code about my future relationships. There was a sense of reconciliation and hope in the phrase, but what did it mean? It seemed to suggest the possibility of having children—two to be exact—an option I had rarely considered, certainly not at the time of my trip to Gabon, when I had no money, no girlfriend, and no prospects for either.

The drumming and singing became deafening in the low-ceilinged temple. In my altered state the songs were awesome in their beauty. There was a strain of self-aware humor in the melodies. Intricate rhythms unfolded organically as if the music, channeled by the Bwiti, was emanating from the plant's essence. I realized the depth of the tribe's bond with this plant that showed them things. I felt how complete their culture was in itself. So complete that no outsider could disturb it. The music expressed the botanical symbiosis, essence of the Bwiti's pride and power.

Late that night the Bwiti made us rise and dance with them. The men tried to teach me the basic steps—hard for me to follow in my state of stoned self-consciousness and my sensitivity to The King's disapproval. Then we sat down to watch as each man in the tribe danced around the temple, whirling a torch, scattering shadows across the walls like living forms. They executed their steps with expert grace and gravity.

"After you take iboga you will know what Bwiti is," The King had told me the day before the ritual. I was still trying to understand. Perhaps iboga opened a symbiotic link between plant and human, a doorway for interspecies communication. But if that were so, who or what was communicating from the other side? I was left with an impression of contact with some other intelligence or entity existing in a realm outside of our own. I wondered if what my guide said was true, that in Bwiti, like Buddhism, there is no ultimate deity, just an endless play of forms, vast hierophanies of spirits, spinning like pinwheels across the Eternal Void.

I knew, intellectually, that tribal groups attribute spirit and sentience to plants. Claude Lévi-Strauss wrote about this in *The Savage Mind,* giving some examples of a universal phenomenon: "When a medicine man of eastern Canada gathers roots or leaves, he is careful to propitiate the soul of each plant by placing a tiny offering at its base." My iboga experience tested the limits of my own beliefs: How could eating a bitter bark take me on such a profound and carefully structured journey through my past, into my future? Could a plant have a "soul" or an intelligence? I had never taken this idea seriously before.

At dawn, the Bwiti led us outside to watch the sunrise. Pink light filtered over the palm fronds and fruit trees, across the dusty disorder of the village. They sang, and we sang with them.

The analyst and I staggered woozily as the ritual ended, but The

King immediately started shouting at us again. "Now you have been initiated, you give me presents of money!" he screamed. "I demand more money for the visions I have shown you!" We decided to escape his shouts and check into a hotel in Lambaréné. This required another long and tense negotiation.

"*J'ai eu des visions de ruine terrible,*" The King shouted.

Because *le journaliste* had not seen or told all of his visions, he explained, we would be in mortal danger if we did not stay another night. As the botanist insisted we were leaving anyway, The King tried to make a fast bargain. Introducing the analyst to the father of a nine-year-old girl, he suggested that, instead of paying more, she take the man's daughter and raise her in America. This was crude but pragmatic psychology on the part of The King: While tripping, the analyst told the Bwiti she regretted not having a child, but she didn't expect an instant chance to rectify the situation.

We convinced one of The King's sons to drive us to the Ogobue Palace, a placid hotel overlooking the river. In my hotel room, I found the iboga trip was still going on. I was wide awake and without hunger, although I had not slept or eaten in over thirty hours. Lying in bed, an eerie strain of Bwiti music returned to my ears. I watched a parade of fleeting phantasms that drifted across cracks in the white wall. Solemn men in funny hats and antique coats marched away, melting into the plaster, trailed by fading rhythms. I realized these were the "ancestor shades," ghost-impressions of my forefathers, a vision that the iboga trance often produced, according to accounts I had read.

I descend from Europeans—Polish Jews and Irish Catholics—and know little about my ancestors, my history. As the figures paraded across the wall, I wished I could linger among them, see them more clearly.

So faint—so quick—they melted away.

Chapter 5

I AM THE ONE YOU SEEK

I did not undergo the most extreme form of Bwiti initiation. The award for most extreme initiation goes, hands down, to the bad-ass Bwiti of the Mitsogho, who live in the southern reaches of Gabon. Before the ceremony, the hardcore Mitsogho shave off the initiate's hair. They pierce his tongue with a long needle. Then, after he has eaten iboga, his skull is hit with a hammer three times in order "to break open the head," helping him enter the spirit world. In reports of visions from the Mitsogho ritual, the *baanzi*, the initiate, meets the original Bwiti man and woman, then visits the "Village of the Dead":

> Suddenly, the "Village of the Dead" is covered with increasingly intense sparks, a "ball of light" takes shape and becomes distinct (Kombe, the sun). This ball of light questions the visitor as to the reasons for his journey. "Do you know who I am? I am the Chief of the World, I am the essential point!"

The brutal Mitsogho initiation lasts for days, during which they induce the *baanzi* to eat such a huge amount of iboga that he lapses into complete unconsciousness. For years after the ritual, fragments of his visions will come back to him in dreams and intimations.

By comparison, the Bwiti of the Fang is a gentle branch of the cult, offering a syncretic mixture of Christian and native beliefs. A standard vision from the Fang ceremony substitutes Christian symbols for native mythology, but is otherwise similar:

> During his journey, he sees many saints, Noah, priests in their cassock. Christ, dressed in gold garments, questions the stranger as to the reason for his visit. And the neophyte answers: "I am seeking, I want to see the Lord Jesus Christ." "I am the one you seek," Christ replies.

These descriptions come from Robert Goutarel, a French chemist who studied iboga in depth. Goutarel defined the meaning of the botanical revelation for Bwiti initiates: "Iboga brings about the visual, tactile, and auditory certainty of the irrefutable existence of the beyond." The plant-spirit directly reveals that the human soul is a "spiritually immutable substance." Through initiation, the *baanzi* discovers that man exists on two planes of existence at once—the material plane and the spiritual one. "Physical death loses all meaning because it is nothing but a new life, another existence," Goutarel writes. "It is iboga that conditions the several existences."

Goutarel also thought the iboga visions differed in character from those induced by LSD. LSD hallucinations "belong to a high and angelic domain of esthetic sensations." The ibogaine domain, on the other hand, "is that of the subterranean world of Freud, of animal impulse and of regression." Similarly, Claudio Naranjo, a Chilean psychiatrist who used ibogaine in therapy, compared the iboga visions to those produced by harmaline and harmine, the psychoactive compounds in ayahuasca. He found, with ibogaine, "the quality of the fantasy is generally more personal and concerns the subject himself, his parents and significant others."

. . .

IBOGA—like heroin, marijuana, ecstasy, and LSD—is a Schedule One drug in the United States, outlawed in most Western countries. "Schedule One" means that it is considered to have potential for abuse but no medical value. Iboga was given this status in the late 1960s, when anxiety about recreational use of psychedelics reached a fever pitch and governments reacted with hysteria. "The 1967–68 resolutions of the World Health Assembly classified ibogaine among the drugs capable of producing dependency or impairing human health," Goutarel wrote. "The fact is, however, that even though ibogaine is considered as a hallucinogen (oneirophrenic), it produces no drug dependency and it has proved to suppress dependency to opiates, amphetamines, cocaine, LSD, and even alcohol and tobacco." Ibogaine made a brief appearance in the sixties underground drug trade, then vanished. He writes, "Ibogaine suddenly disappeared from the market and it seems that the drug dealers rapidly became aware of the fact that its use would deprive them of part of their clientele."

Dr. Deborah Mash from the University of Miami is the only government-sanctioned researcher currently studying ibogaine as a treatment for addiction. Mash has set up a clinic for this purpose on the island of St. Kitt's. In a September 2000 paper for the *Annals of the New York Academy of Sciences,* Mash and her collaborators compiled the effects of a single ibogaine dose, followed by posttreatment therapy, on twenty-seven addicts. They concluded the following:

> After treatment with ibogaine, opiate-dependent subjects were less likely to anticipate positive outcomes from heroin (or other opiate) use, less likely to believe that heroin (or opiate) use would relieve withdrawal/dysphoria, and more likely to believe in their control for abstaining or stopping their drug use. Ibogaine treatment also decreased participants' desire and intention to use heroin.

Scientists currently know something about how iboga affects the brain, but not much. The ibogaine molecule is an extremely complex alkaloid (the intimidating chemical name is 3-methyl-5-ethylpyridine). Like most of the known psychedelic drugs, it has a structure similar to the neurotransmitter serotonin, which is believed to perform many functions and helps to regulate sensory information—whether sense data trickles, flows, pours, or floods into the brain. Psilocybin, mescaline, and LSD are also alkaloids that resemble serotonin. The superpotent hallucinogen DMT (NN-dimethyltryptamine) is a very close cousin to serotonin—a similar molecular structure with the difference of two methyl groups. Selective serotonin reuptake inhibitors (SSRIs), such as the antidepressants Prozac and Zoloft, limit mood swings by modulating the release of serotonin.

Because they are so closely related to serotonin, psychedelics bond temporarily to many of the same receptor sites as serotonin and similar neurotransmitters—and that is the principle cause of their activity. I now think of the brain (as distinct from the mind) as a kind of radio. With "normative" levels of serotonin, the brain is tuned to the "consensual reality"—something like the local pop or talk radio station. By substituting psilocybin, ibogaine, dimethyltryptamine, or some other psychedelic compound for serotonin and other neurotransmitters, you change the station and suddenly you begin to pick up the sensorial equivalent of avant-garde jazz, Tibetan chants, or another channel resonating with new and astonishing information. Yet your mind, the perceiving core of the self, remains more or less unaffected. In that sense, psychedelics, unlike alcohol or heroin, are not even intoxicating.

Goutarel wrote, "Ibogaine inhibits the oxidation of serotonin and catalyzes that of catecholamines by a MAO (monoamine oxidase), ceruplasmin." Monoamine oxidase is an enzyme in the stomach that renders many potentially mind-influencing compounds inactive before they reach the brain. Ibogaine, like the Amazonian psychedelic ayahuasca, contains a natural MAO inhibitor. The ayahuasca potion, however, is a mixture of two plants with different properties. All by itself, the iboga plant is an extraordinary chemical factory.

Currently, no scientific theory explains why plants like iboga go to the trouble of creating psychoactive alkaloids. The compounds seem to convey no evolutionary benefit to the botanicals, and they require a great deal of effort and time to produce.

"Why do plants make alkaloids?" the psychedelic chemist Sasha Shulgin asked at a lecture I attended in Mexico. "It's basically unknown. Maybe to keep ants away? Some people say alkaloids are garbage dumps for nitrogen, but why produce a compound that takes two years to synthesize?" No science can explain the drawn-out phases of a large-dose ibogaine trip, the twenty-hour passage from vision to insight, experienced almost universally.

The ibogaine molecule is especially complex—more than most psychedelics. It is so intricate that it cannot be synthesized in a laboratory. Besides being "a potent serotegenic" compound, meaning it works at serotonin-receptor sites, ibogaine also seems to interact with dopamine, another neurotransmitter, which regulates the body's experience of pleasure and is associated with the cravings of addiction.

In 1994, the *New York Times Magazine* published a feature on ibogaine that was full of interesting information but was an unfortunate disaster for ibogaine's future as a mainstream treatment for drug addiction. The article followed an experimental ibogaine treatment program in Holland. During the writer's visit to Holland, the program was discontinued due to the death of a young woman addict. The addict probably continued to take heroin right before she started her ibogaine treatment. It is not a clearly understood mechanism, but ibogaine seems to dramatically increase the potency of all drugs in the bloodstream. For addicts seeking to use ibogaine, a one-day period of detox is necessary first, to avoid a toxic reaction.

But how could ibogaine help break addiction? The *Times* noted: "Heroin and cocaine ordinarily trigger dopamine's release in the brain's 'reward center,' producing feelings of euphoria. Ibogaine appears to disrupt this mechanism, blocking some releases while stimulating others." This might temporarily impede the effects of drugs, but, the article went on to ask, "how can ibogaine affect behavior long after it disappears from the bloodstream?"

One theory is that ibogaine restores a balance between the brain's two hemispheres. Dr. Carl Anderson of McLean Hospital, Virginia, believes that people prone to addiction suffer from an imbalance between the left and right hemispheres. The conventional model is that our "rational" processes—language, logic, scientific thought—spring from the left hemisphere, while the right hemisphere controls the "irrational" processes—emotions, intuitions, dreams, etcetera.

Anderson suggests, "Interhemispheric struggles, primarily a result of child abuse, may be the fundamental psychological root of drug addiction." This is probably an exaggeration. In any case, disparities between the left and right brain disrupt REM sleep, which, as Anderson notes, is "essential for emotional regulation, learning, and memory consolidation." Iboga, or ibogaine, accesses REM cycling in a powerful way, and because of this, most people need less sleep for weeks or even months after one strong, and long, dose.

Drug abuse is, for Anderson, "strongly associated with asymetric hemispheric function." If ibogaine causes "bihemispheric reintegration," it might return to psychically damaged people the healing power of their sleep and dreams. The ibogaine trip would be "a healing journey through the fractal hyperspace of emotionally indexed childhood memories." This is an elegant, but highly speculative, theory about an area that remains largely unresearched.

Chapter 6

I SEE YOUR GRANDMOTHER

We did not see The King again. After a night's rest, Lieberman and I went on a search through Lambaréné for other Bwiti shamans. The botanist wanted to buy iboga seeds and powder to take back with him to South Africa. I hoped to learn more about the Bwiti. Off the main streets, you could walk for hours on jungle footpaths between small settlements. The town's back alleys formed mazes of little houses and shacks in the woods, and each separate maze was its own community where people worked and hung out. Each neighborhood seemed to have its own Bwiti temple. Built out of wooden boards and palm fronds, they were modest, unpretentious structures compared to The King's concrete sanctuary.

In one of these local shrines we found Papa Simone, a young, bearded shaman with a wise face and a pensive, gentle manner. I described my visions, scant though they seemed, to Papa Simone, and he interpreted them thoughtfully. The wooden statue, he said, was the spirit of *le bois sacré* itself, "which comes out and engages you in conversation." The pictures of my apartment and the city streets were a telepathic check-in, showing me that everything was calm—*"tranquille"*—at home. The beckoning female figures, he said, indicated what paths to take. I was sorry I hadn't known better how to follow them.

Outside Simone's temple we met a thin young girl in the *baanzi*'s red outfit, sitting on a tree stump. She had just gone through her Bwiti initiation, Papa Simone told us. Iboga had revealed some dangers facing her, so she was staying at the temple for a few days of healing rituals. She shared with Papa Simone a quality of calm intelligence. I asked her why she went through the iboga initiation.

"I wanted to know what was going on," she said. I loved her dignity and the simplicity of her answer. What she wanted was exactly what I wanted, distilled to its essence.

Lieberman asked Papa Simone to organize another all-night ceremony for us with his Bwiti village, a closing ritual to give us the oil that The King had withheld. During that night of dancing, drumming, and singing, I saw what Lieberman had described as "the essence of love" in the community around Papa Simone. There were secret parts to this ritual, involving the sacrifice of a rooster in a fire, and sacred ceremonies of bonding, done among the company of men. One after another, the Bwiti men let out long, whooping cries in their language, and helped me to imitate them. At the end of the night, each of the Bwiti embraced the analyst, then me, and danced us around the temple fire like we were huge rag dolls, swinging us as violently and quickly as possible. The embraces told us, more directly than words could, that despite our alien language and culture and pale skin, we were accepted among them.

For the ceremony they wanted us to eat iboga again. They seemed curious to find out what *les blancs* could see. After the previous night's indulgence, I tried, shuddering, but I couldn't swallow more than a spoonful of the bark (it was green and fresh rather than dried and white, but terrible, terrible). This was not enough to cause visions. Papa Simone's tribe included a large, laughing man wearing a red loincloth, his sleek black body daubed with white paint. As one of the tribal elders, he ate iboga throughout the ceremony. He kept pointing at the bowl of shavings, and then at his own eyes, then at me, trying to convince me to eat more so I would see things.

Toward morning, this man, the whites of his eyes gleaming in the firelight, announced he was having a vision. He said he saw a spirit hovering over me where I sat by the yellow flames of the bonfire. With matter-of-fact certainty, he specified that this spirit was my grandmother on my mother's side.

"You were very close to your grandmother, your mother's mother," he told me. "She loved you very much, but now she is dead, and she doesn't want to let you go. Her spirit is hanging over you. She is stopping you from seeing visions, from visiting the other world."

. . .

THE TRIBESMAN'S VISION shocked me. This shock continued to reverberate through my life. I was surprised that he specified my mother's mother. She was the only grandparent I knew—the others died before I was born. She had lived to be eighty-eight, dying only a year before my trip to Gabon. I had told the Bwiti nothing about my life. If this man was guessing, if he was exaggerating or lying about what he was seeing, he had only a one-in-four chance of getting it right.

I did have a close relationship with my grandmother, in a way. She took care of me as a child when my mother went out of town. As I got older, however, I found her a gloomy, life-denying presence. She seemed utterly fixed, trapped inside herself. After her two gloomy sisters died, nobody or nothing was good enough for her, therefore she had no friends, no life. Until her death, her best furniture remained slipcovered in plastic, waiting for an important and unknown visitor who never arrived. There was something insane yet unnervingly powerful in the way she denied herself all pleasure, all possibility. Denial and endurance—those were the only values that mattered to her as she slowly sank into senescence.

My grandmother's life was a sad story of immigrant America. Her parents came from Poland; her father could not find a decent job in New York, and in 1908 he killed himself, abandoning his family. My great-grandmother, my grandmother, and my two aunts could not forgive him. They burned his papers, destroyed all traces of him. They never spoke of him again. The trauma of his suicide and the vengeful act of annihilation that followed shaped my grandmother's psyche into a forceful mechanism of repression.

Of course, as a rational product of the modern world, I didn't think elements of the psychic life could continue after death. Intuitively, however, within the right-brain world of my intuitions and dreams, the tribesman's insight resonated.

If there was a "spirit world," it was easy for me to think of my grandmother as a possessive, negating phantom anxiously hanging over me, keeping me away from revelations.

Months after the Bwiti ceremony, I had an extremely vivid nightmare about my grandmother, waking up after dawn to write it in my notebook. In the dream, my grandmother called me. She was in my house, cleaning and looking through all of my closets, drawers, and my desk for what she called "the business" or "the papers." I could see her in my apartment, an ancient figure, befuddled and unhinged, rifling through my possessions. I was furious at her, screaming over the phone with almost inhuman fervor, ordering her to leave my stuff alone, to go away and rest, watch television, not to look for the papers anymore. She backed off. Her voice was so real, quavering.

In the days afterward, I felt cleansed—it was as if my spirit, gaining strength, had evicted her from the premises. I felt as if some dark veil had been lifted from me. Of course, most Westerners would interpret this dream as metaphor or subconscious symbol. To me, the more I thought about it, the more the dream seemed, intuitively, real—a victory over a residue of her psyche by my unconscious self.

Carl Jung's *Memories, Dreams, Reflections* is an autobiographical meditation on the inner world revealed to the analyst throughout his life by dreams, telepathic incidents, and transcendent hints. In the last chapters Jung does what most scientists would find unthinkable. He speculates on the possibility of the psyche's persistence after death: "There are many human beings who throughout their lives and at the moment of death lag behind their own potentialities. . . . Hence their demand to attain in death that share of awareness which they failed to win in life." According to Jung, these spirits or shades try "to penetrate into life in order to share in the knowledge of men."

Was my grandmother such a spirit?

Could Jung—and the Bwiti—be right?

Does the psyche survive, in some form, after death?

And what was iboga's role in all this?

.   .   .

A FEW DAYS after the second Bwiti ceremony, I returned to New York City. At home, I found that I needed several hours less sleep a night. It was as if I were constantly caffeinated, and this energized state lasted for several weeks. With so much extra time, I kept mulling over the facets of the initiation—the greedy shaman, the shaky botanist, the revelatory plant.

Iboga did not show me much of the African spiritual cosmos, but it revealed my own inner world. For a few hours I was granted a powerful lens through which I could see my life—that complex assemblage of habits, moods, past events, and relationships—like a constellation viewed through a telescope.

I still wanted to know what touchers could teach.

Part Two

STRANGE GROWTHS

Chapter 7

TREACHEROUS
EXCRESCENCES

Once a favorite destination for hippies and bohemian wanderers, Huautla de Jiménez has been out of fashion for so long that the town does not even rate a mention in the latest *Lonely Planet* guides. Huautla was brought to the attention of the modern world when an article appeared in *Life* magazine on June 10, 1957: "Seeking the Magic Mushroom: A New York banker goes to Mexico's mountains to participate in the age-old rituals of Indians who chew strange growths that produce visions."

The author of the article, R. Gordon Wasson, was a vice president of J. P. Morgan; he and his Russian wife, Valentina, were also amateur mycologists. With their impressive erudition, Slavic inspiration, and mandarin style, the Wassons were the great Nabokovian figures of twentieth-century psychedelia—substituting mushrooms for butterflies. They discovered their vocation accidentally, when Wasson could not match his wife's enthusiasm for a group of edible toadstools she picked in the woods outside their home in the Catskills Mountains of New York. She insisted on eating the fungi she had found; he feared she was committing suicide.

"Like all good Anglo-Saxons," Wasson wrote, "I knew nothing about the fungal world and felt that the less I knew about those putrid, treacherous excrescences the better." For his wife, on the other hand, "they were things of grace, infinitely inviting to the perceptive mind."

The Wassons wanted to understand why they had such opposed reactions, and this quizzical challenge mushroomed into a lifetime quest. They discovered that the split between mycophiles and mycophobes was a deep divide among European cultures. Researching linguistic clues and folklore, they found an "aura of the supernatural in which all the fungi seem to be bathed." The hidden traces of mythical mushrooms seemed to unfold throughout European history, leading the Wassons to a wild speculation: "All of our evidence taken together led us many years ago to hazard a bold surmise: was it not probable that, long ago, long before the beginnings of written history, our ancestors had worshipped a divine mushroom?" The Wassons came to suspect that the "divine mushroom" was at the preliterate origin of all human religion.

But why would anybody worship a mushroom? The answer to that question brought them to the remote reaches of Mexico, following faint rumors of a still-extant mushroom cult among the Mazatec Indians. After a series of false starts, they purchased some specimens of *Psilocybe mexicana* and brought them to the skilled *curandera* Maria Sabina. "She was middle-aged, and short like all Mixetecos, with a spirituality in her expression that struck at once. She had presence. We showed our mushrooms to the woman and the daughter. They cried out in rapture over the firmness, the fresh beauty of our young specimens. Through an interpreter we asked if they would serve us that night. They said yes."

They ate the mushrooms in total darkness, with the shamaness and her daughter singing beside them. During his first sessions Wasson saw extremely detailed landscapes and figures—"a mythological beast drawing a regal chariot"—as well as abstract patterns and colorful geometries. He was astounded by the precision of the visions, which were not dreamlike at all; if anything, they seemed more real to him, more objective and accurate, than the world beheld through normal sight.

"I felt that I was now seeing plain, whereas ordinary vision gives us an imperfect view; I was seeing the archetypes, the Platonic ideas, that underlie the imperfect images of everyday life. The thought crossed my mind: could the divine mushrooms be the secret that lay behind the ancient Mysteries? Could the miraculous mobility that I was now enjoying be the explanation for the flying witches that played so important a part in the folklore and fairy tales of northern Europe?" Wasson felt removed from any possibility of contact with the visions shown to him. He became "a disembodied eye, invisible, incorporeal, seeing but not seen."

The bemushroomed state was nothing like intoxication in the ordinary sense of the term. Despite the visionary and sensory overload, Wasson noted that his rational intellect remained intact throughout the journey: "The mind is attached as by an elastic cord to the vagrant senses."

In one of their first séances with the Mazatecs, the Wassons witnessed a demonstration of accurate clairvoyance. After eating thirteen pairs of mushrooms, the shaman Aurelia Carreras told them that a relative would become critically ill within a year, that their son was in trouble and might soon join the army—all of which, to the Wassons' shock, they later verified. They intentionally omitted this episode from their early accounts. "I had always had a horror of those who preached a kind of pseudoreligion of telepathy, who for me were unreliable people, and if our discoveries in Mexico, including our initial velada [ceremony], were to be drawn to their attention we were in danger of being adopted by such undesirables," Wasson wrote decades later, still pondering on the mystery of it: "The entheogen, at least when taken by a wise shaman . . . conveys information, but how?"

After his discovery of psilocybin, Wasson continued his scholarly work on mushrooms around the world. He found hints of psychedelic or entheogenic ("god-releasing") mushrooms in Genesis, in the Eleusinian Mysteries, and in the Hindu sacred text, *The Rig Veda*. Despite his revelations among the Mazatecs, he became convinced that the essential entheogen of the ancient world was Soma—*Amanita muscaria,* which contains the psychoactive agent muscarine rather than psilocybin. He also suspected that an entheogenic plant may have catalyzed our ancestors' psychic evolution:

A prodigious expansion in Man's memory must have been the gift that differentiated mankind from his predecessors, and I surmise that this expansion in memory led to a simultaneous growth in the gift of language, these two powers generating in man that self-consciousness which is the third of the triune traits that alone make man unique. . . . I am asking myself whether Soma could have possessed the power to spark what I have called these triune traits.

It is hard to imagine what middle-class readers of *Life* must have thought as they read about mystical revelations produced in an eloquent WASP banker by eating a handful of foul-tasting mushrooms with a bunch of primitive Indians. Wasson's article was one of a series of cultural shocks that would culminate, ten years later, in the short-circuited fireworks of the Psychedelic Era, although Wasson, ironically, came to deplore the public fascination with the "sacred children," as Sabina called the mushrooms. When Timothy Leary visited him in the early 1960s, Leary was perplexed by the banker's negative attitude.

"Wasson was opposed to any current use of the mushrooms," Leary recalled. "Although these fungi had produced all of the great philosophic visions of antiquity, he proclaimed they had no relevance to the modern world." In the aftermath of Wasson's article, Huautla became a tourist destination for the counterculture and Sabina became the world-famous figurehead for indigenous shamanism—even the Beatles visited her.

. . .

A YEAR AFTER my trip to Gabon, I went to Huautla with Laura, my girlfriend. Undeterred by my rough treatment at the hands of The King, I had continued reading about shamanism and was eager to meet more shamans. We drove for two days, through ever-changing landscapes, beneath stony ridges of giant cacti with clumps of spindles like fingers pointing accusingly at the sun.

At one point—a sudden flash of roadside horror—we passed the carcass of a horse, blind eye staring out at me, as a flock of vultures devoured its flesh. From dry desert land we entered the deep forested valleys and high mountain peaks of the Mazatec region. For six hours we followed a narrow road—the only road to Huautla—winding around high cliffs with numerous blind spots and no guard rail, passing little shrines for those who had plummeted off the edge. Large rocks seemed to tumble off the mountain with alarming frequency. Laura, who was driving, navigated around these boulders and the unrepaired craters they had left. The remote area had a quality of stillness that reminded me of Gabon. Because the Mazatec country is difficult to access, the Indians have preserved their own language and culture—an estimated half of the forty thousand Mazatecs living in the mountainous land beyond Huautla don't speak Spanish.

It is still possible to buy white dresses and blouses embroidered with mushrooms in Huautla's sleepy local shops, as well as posters of Sabina. But the sizzle is gone from the hippie tourist industry. As far as we could tell, we were almost the only Westerners around. The town itself, like our hotel, was rough, functional, and ugly. The hotel was plain, concrete-walled, with a septic smell. From our balcony, we watched a parade of Mazatec women marching in a Saint's Day festival through the crowded market square. They wore colorful outfits, chanted, and carried sheaves of green leaves in their hands.

We went in search of the house of Maria Sabina; I had read that it was preserved as a shrine. We had only vague directions, but as we were riding up the hill, an Indian boy stopped us to ask if we could give him a lift. In the car, he told us that his father was the son of Maria Sabina, also a shaman in the family tradition. Sabina's house was in the middle of a family compound, on a hilltop ridge overlooking the town on one side and a deep, wide valley on the other. The boy showed us a photograph of his father in a book on Mazatec shamans. He asked if we wanted a ceremony. I said yes, if it was possible. The price was around $70.

The ceremony was performed that night. The participants were myself and Carlos, a young Mexican of Spanish descent from Mexico City who looked like a club kid but was a student of alternative healing—Laura bowed out of taking the mushrooms. Luckily for me, Carlos spoke English. He said he had visited the shaman before. He was staying there for a few nights, in Maria Sabina's simple white clapboard house, which looked like a prefab unit from the 1960s.

We waited for Filogonio, the shaman, on the low wooden benches of the temple, which was a large wooden shack. The altar included candles, flowers, stones, and a mix of icons of saints and the Virgin Mary. A carved wooden Christ on the cross had a distinctly Indian look.

Eventually, Filogonia arrived wearing a gray, hooded sweatshirt and smoking a cigarette. He was a small but robust-looking man with tough, dark skin and an incredible face—wise, tormented, gnomic. The mushrooms were passed out. Ten little green bulbs floated in a steaming broth. Laura was shocked by their fluorescent color and extraterrestrial look. I chewed and drank them down; the taste was inoffensive.

"What do you do when you take the mushrooms in your country?" Filogonia asked me, through Carlos. I told him we often walked around and looked at nature.

The shaman chanted for a time in Mazatec, an archaic and Asiatic-sounding language. He came around with the copal we had been directed to buy, a sweet and pungent incense, and bathed us in its smoke. He blew his tobacco-scented breath into our faces. The ceremony borrowed elements from the Catholic mass. For whatever reason, that night the mushrooms had little effect on me—my senses awakened to the world around me, but there was no trace of the deep visionary realms described by Wasson, who had watched "pellucid water flowing through an endless expanse of reeds down to a measureless sea . . . a woman in primitive costume, standing and staring across the water, enigmatic, beautiful."

Carlos, on the other hand, began to weep openly. He begged God for mercy. He called the shaman "Padre," addressing him like a priest, and asked for his blessing. His voice shaking, he confessed recent sins and begged forgiveness.

Filogonio shrugged and smiled shyly. He took us outside and walked us around the family's property. Affected by the mushrooms, I realized this ridge was a sacred, or at least a privileged, ancestral spot. I wondered how many centuries the Sabina family had lived here before Wasson discovered them. The little lights of the town glimmered below us. The stars spiraled across the sky overhead. A mule watched us peacefully. The shaman occasionally made little movements with his hands, like the robot gestures of breakdancers. This was the first time I had seen the "shamanic passes" described by Michael Harner and Carlos Castaneda. At moments he looked weary, heartbroken, close to tears, but his expression would change, and he would laugh.

It was, for me, another unvisionary trip. I cursed my hard head. Although I visited no other realms—no trace of the bejeweled starship factories or strobing Buddha lands I had seen several times on large doses of dried mushrooms in New York—my senses opened to the physical world, and as Laura drove us back to the hotel, I felt the sadness of Huautla. The town had been cheaply and brutally hewed out of mountain rock with little thought for the people forced to inhabit it. It was a grim extraction point for whatever capital could be sucked from this Third World backwater. The smell of cheap gasoline hung in the air. I was glad that the region's inaccessibility had preserved the Mazatec culture. We drove back to the city of Oaxaca the next day.

From Huautla, the mushrooms entered world consciousness. Eventually, Maria Sabina believed that the foreigners ruined the power of the mushrooms. Like most indigenous groups, the Mazatecs only consulted the sacred plants when they needed healing or guidance. The new enthusiasts consumed them indiscriminately. After Wasson, Sabina performed many ceremonies for Westerners seeking spiritual insight or looking for kicks. "From the moment the foreigners came to find God, the sacred children lost their purity," she said in her autobiography. "They lost their force, one has spoiled them. From now on, they will no longer have an effect. There is nothing one can do about it."

And yet, half a century later, the popularity of Sabina's "sacred children" continues, quietly, to spread across the modern world. Despite the illegal status of the mushrooms in the West, increasing numbers of enthusiasts grow their own in basement jars. Recently I have heard credible reports of psilocybin enthusiasts, neopagan nature cultists, who travel across the world spreading the spores around forests and public parks, where they enter the local ecosystem. Species of the mushrooms now grow plentifully in Oregon and Washington State and other areas where they were not known before. A half century after the Wassons' initiation, the dissemination of knowledge has not ended. I began my own psychedelic education as one of its many beneficiaries.

Chapter 8

PROFANE ILLUMINATIONS

I first tried mushrooms at Wesleyan University, a private college in Connecticut. An unhappy nineteen-year-old, I kept tying myself into deeper psychological and intellectual knots. I was taking a seminar on the work of Jacques Lacan, who turned Freud's ideas into seductive gibberish. Our teacher was a chic presence, a twenty-eight-year-old Scottish woman who wore antique gowns and resembled Bette Davis, chain-smoked during class, and drank herself to death a few years later. Lacan wrote about lost objects of desire that could never be recaptured and "the crisis of the real." He described how the sexual act never took place. His contorted concepts seemed painfully persuasive to me at the time.

There was a strong psychedelic undercurrent at Wesleyan, but it wasn't my style. A group of prep school kids in tie-dyed T-shirts spent their weekends pursuing the Grateful Dead up and down the East Coast. I had grown up around the New Wave scene in New York, and the Grateful Dead's twangling blues seemed unbearably outdated and suburban to me. One wintry day my friend Alex—she was several years older than me, an art student—brought me to her house and gave me some mushrooms. The mushrooms were dried shards of stems and caps with an acrid taste. We ate them and walked around the campus, staring at icicles that descended like glittering daggers from roof ledges and tree branches. I felt fizzy, light. My senses seemed to be tuning up, taking in stray bits of reality that I would have ignored otherwise. I bought a soda at a deli and giggled as I pulled a clump of dollar bills from my pocket. What was this nasty stuff? Suddenly I could not fathom the social process that made these wrinkled bits of dirty paper so important. It seemed ridiculous and arbitrary.

From the perspective of the mushrooms, the world revealed different priorities. Trees and plants glowed with patience and intelligence, as if expressing a deeper wisdom. The university buildings were either Modernist prisons or pompous attempts at architectural meaning; the collonaded facade of Olin Library, for instance, was trying far too hard. Cars and junk-food packaging and everything else that was factory-made and shiny seemed like aggressive overkill. The "consensus reality" of the university, of late-twentieth-century America in general, seemed dubiously presumptuous and insubstantial.

Later I made the mistake of writing about psychedelics at Wesleyan. I lived in West College, the bohemian and hippie dorm. Each year, WestCo held two festivals, Uncle Duke Day and Zonker Harris Day, that had a fun-house atmosphere. These events were designed for tripping. The halls organized little events—Day-Glo face painting or ambient concerts—that would appeal to stoned kids with bright eyes wandering through the halls and underground tunnels. For *The Argus*, the student newspaper, I described the goings-on and theorized Uncle Duke Day as an example of "repressive tolerance," a phrase coined by philosopher Herbert Marcuse in the 1960s. Under a regime of "repressive tolerance," individuals are allowed freedom that has been stripped of all political meaning. My editor forgot that the paper went to hundreds of parent subscribers, and some of them were irate. They were not interested in "repressive tolerance." They preferred simple repression, and demanded that the events be outlawed.

. . .

I STARTED READING Walter Benjamin around that time. Benjamin is the kind of thinker for whom I have a perhaps fatal weakness. He could not stop himself from trying to think through everything at once—fashion, Marxism, psychoanalysis, Walt Disney, history, and the mimetic nature of language, to name only a few. This type of thinking is my own habitual curse. At Wesleyan, in the midst of a crisis of alienation, I kept trying to understand my life at the university as if I were some kind of extraterrestrial social scientist observing the culture around me. This effort made me feel trapped outside of myself, a witness rather than a participant even in my own private drama. Neither Benjamin nor psychedelic drugs helped to end my desperation at that point.

More than a decade later, I had the chance to study Benjamin in a graduate course at Columbia University. Each week, twenty of us met in the office of the anthropologist Michael Taussig. Under tingling gray fluorescents, we hunched over copies of Benjamin's unfinished magnum opus, *The Arcades Project*, twelve hundred pages of quotes, aphorisms, and fragments.

Benjamin's writing flashes between poles of revolution and revelation. A scholar of threshold experiences, states of intoxication, and failed philosophies, he is brilliant on the subject of drugs: "The most passionate examination of the hashish trance will not teach us half as much about thinking (which is eminently narcotic), as the profane illumination of thinking about the hashish trance," he wrote. "The reader, the thinker, the flaneur, are types of illuminati just as much as the opium eater, the dreamer, the ecstatic. . . . Not to mention that most terrible drug—ourselves—which we take in solitude."

He saw thinking as a form of intoxication. He recognized that drug-exploration, the pursuit of visionary experience, could be an extension of a rational and intellectual quest: "The dialectics of intoxication are indeed curious," he wrote. "Is not perhaps all ecstasy in one world humiliating sobriety in that complementary to it?"

Writing in the 1920s and 1930s, Benjamin smoked hash, tried mescaline, and enjoyed his own trips: "I thought with intense pride of sitting here in Marseilles in a hashish trance; of who else might be sharing my intoxication this evening, how few." Thinking under the influence of hashish was like unrolling a ball of thread through a maze: "We go forward; but in so doing we not only discover the twists and turns of the cave, but also enjoy the pleasure of this discovery against the background of the other, rhythmical bliss of unwinding the thread."

On hashish, he saw the elaborate furnishings of the nineteenth-century bourgeois interior concentrating "to satanic contentment, satanic knowing, satanic calm . . . To live in these interiors was to have woven a dense fabric about oneself, to have secluded oneself within a spider's web, in whose coils world events hang loosely suspended like so many insect bodies sucked dry. From the cavern, one does not like to stir." The narcotic trance revealed an occult and sinister undercurrent to the bourgeois love of comfort and exotic decor.

For the society as well as the individual, Benjamin realized "the importance of intoxication for perception, of fiction for thinking." The new consumer culture of the nineteenth century induced a widespread trance in the public, as capitalism breathed supernatural power into its products. The World Exhibits, the Belle Epoque's celebrations of global commerce, "open up a phantasmagoria that people enter to be amused. The entertainment industry facilitates this by elevating people to the status of commodities. They submit to being manipulated while enjoying their alienation from themselves and others." The euphoria induced by these spectacles was like a drug that robbed the masses of their will, that taught them how to enjoy being transformed into objects of exchange.

Intoxicated, entranced by the new world of commodities, the West lost its contact with the communal "ecstatic trance," those archaic Dionysian festivals and annual Mysteries celebrating the transformation of primordial chaos into order. The loss of rituals that compelled "ecstatic contact with the cosmos" posed a threat to humanity: "It is the dangerous error of modern men to regard this experience as unimportant and avoidable . . . it is not; its hour strikes again and again, and then neither nations nor generations can escape it." Humanity needed such periodic rites of regeneration to avoid hypnotic episodes of feverish destruction, which served the same purpose at a much greater cost. For Benjamin, this was the real significance of the First World War, "an attempt at a new and unprecedented commingling with the cosmic powers." He worried that mankind's alienation from itself was deepening "to such a degree that it can experience its own destruction as an aesthetic pleasure of the first order."

Benjamin's fusion of sociological, psychoanalytical, and mystical levels of insight reminded me of the integrated vision of myself that I took back from the iboga trip. He saw that no revolution could succeed unless it transformed the inner realm of thought—the meaning of perception, the relationship of the senses to the physical world—as well as economic relations. He was always on the lookout for the secret core of primitive ritual and magical belief hidden within the seemingly "rational" processes of modernity.

He called his great uncompleted work *The Arcades Project* "an experiment in the technique of awakening." On the personal level, awakening is, of course, something we do every morning without a thought. We suddenly emerge into ourselves, arriving in our beds from the evanescent dream dimensions. Occasionally we remember vivid narratives and scenes from our unconscious meanderings. At other times we can reconstruct the stories only with an effort, searching inside our minds for clues to patterns that quickly fizzle out and disappear if we don't pursue them, if we don't make the effort to retrace our steps through the labyrinth. Most often, we don't remember anything at all, and we are happier for it.

Benjamin describes awakening as a historical and generational process as well as an individual one. History is the effort made by each age to bring the "not-yet conscious knowledge of what has been" into awareness. Waking is a "dialectical moment" suspended between the dreamworld of the past and the transformative energy locked within the present. For Benjamin, history advances in sudden flashes and leaps. It is a series of awakenings into deeper and more profound levels of awareness, or falterings into deeper states of hypnosis and trance.

This "dialectic of awakening" has no end point. Just as the individual slips between sleep and waking, reaching different intensities of awareness during the day, generations and epochs also fluctuate between levels of consciousness and unconsciousness. Advertisements, popular entertainment, public architecture are natural expressions of the unconscious desires of the "dreaming collective."

Unseduced by the ideology of modernist progress, he described capitalism as "a natural phenomenon with which a new dream-filled sleep came over Europe, and, through it, a reactivation of mythic forces." Those reactivated mythic forces ended up destroying him: He committed suicide in 1940 while trying to flee the Nazis.

He died before he could begin a projected book on drugs. It would have perfectly fit his intention to "cultivate fields where, until now, only madness has reigned." Paradoxically, Benjamin's work suggests that only intoxication—ecstasy that is also "humiliating sobriety," an apt description of tripping—can awaken the individual by snapping him or her out of the monotonous trance of modern life.

Chapter 9

fUN WITH fUNGI

The creation of the modern Western consciousness required a violent repression of our archaic heritage. That heritage includes the ability to explore sacred and magical realms through spontaneously occurring trance states, through rituals of initiation, or through the visionary compounds found in certain plants. For many thousands of years, direct knowledge of the sacred was a natural and universal part of human existence, as it remains today in tribal cultures. With the rise of the modern state and the Church, interaction with mystical realities was alienated from the masses and explicitly demonized. Communion with the sacred was reserved for the priests. During the Inquisition, cavorting with the spirits of nature or contacting the souls of the dead became heresies. The punishment for these crimes was severe.

The dialectical process that created the possessive mind-set of the capitalist and the "rational" outlook of the technocrat required destruction of the premodern vestiges of communal and animistic beliefs, whether these beliefs were found in isolated pockets of Europe or in the indigenous populations of the New World. This destruction was part of the process that Karl Marx described as the alienation of all of our physical and intellectual senses into one sense: the sense of having.

Of course, "the sense of having" is not really a sense—it is an illusion of fulfillment that seems to extend outside of the self.

Modernism caused a profound shift in the way we use our senses. In his book *Myth and Meaning*, Lévi-Strauss admitted his initial shock when he discovered that Indian tribesmen were able to see the planet Venus in daylight, with the naked eye—"something that to me would be utterly impossible and incredible." But he learned from astronomers that it was feasible, and he found ancient accounts of Western navigators with the same ability. "Today we use less and we use more of our mental capacity than we did in the past," he realized. We have sacrificed perceptual capabilities for other mental abilities—to concentrate on a computer screen while sitting in a cubicle for many hours at a stretch (something those Indians would find "utterly impossible and incredible"), or to shut off multiple levels of awareness as we drive a car in heavy traffic. In other words, we are brought up within a system that teaches us to postpone, defer, and eliminate most incoming sense data in favor of a future reward. We live in a feedback loop of perpetual postponement. For the most part, we are not even aware of what we have lost.

Personally, I was not aware of what I was losing until I took mushrooms. During those early trips I realized I was trapped in a state of deferred expectation and compulsive self-distancing. I had a neurotic intellectual's habit of constantly trying to observe myself from some imaginary point of objectivity outside of myself, and this impossible effort sapped my energy and kept me from connecting to the present. Mushrooms did not cure me of this—for a long time only alcohol could obliterate the division, and it took me some years to resolve the problem—but the bits of dried fungi made me aware, for the first time, of exactly what I was doing wrong.

The modern consciousness is awake to materialism, to the incorporeal "sense of having," to the mechanistic worldview and the scientific method of empirical observation. Its antithesis is the archaic mind, alive to the world of the senses, in close contact with the sacred as it is revealed through the natural world, through dreams and visions. For this kind of consciousness, as Henry Miller once put it, "The goal of life is not to possess power but to radiate it."

There is a cultural split between focus on the brain, the material hardware in which consciousness operates, and study of the mind, the incorporeal nexus of all we experience. Western science obsessively studies the "objective" workings of the brain, its pathways of neurons and dense forests of synapses, without comprehending the nature of consciousness. Archaic shamanism is a technology for exploring the "subjective" truth of the mind through vision, dream, myth, and interaction with nature. According to current psychiatry, mental disorders have physical causes that can be treated, to a certain extent, with appropriate medication. From the shamanic perspective, not only mental but even physical disorders have nonphysical—spiritual—causes that must be addressed if a cure is going to be effective.

The visionary plants are the guiding spirits of archaic cultures. They are sacred because they awaken the mind to other levels of awareness. They are gateways to a spiritual, or multidimensional, universe. In the modern world, the substances derived from these plants continue to be demonized, ridiculed, and above all suppressed. In the early 1960s, when a reviewer reduced Aldous Huxley's fascination with psychedelics to "fun with fungi," Huxley replied in scathing terms: "Which is better, to have Fun with Fungi or to have Idiocy with Ideology, to have Wars because of Words, to have Tomorrow's Misdeeds out of Yesterday's Miscreeds?"

This cultural split remains a deep divide. As I write this, psychedelic drugs have been dismissed, yet again, as "toys of the hippie generation" in the Science section of the *New York Times*. It seems that no mainstream newspaper or magazine can publish an article about hallucinogens without stopping to ridicule them in some way. Psychedelics, chemical catalysts that open up inner worlds, remain banished and misunderstood because they occupy the point of direct contradiction and possible synthesis between brain-based materialism and spirit-oriented shamanism.

The exploration and unbiased study of these mind-expanding molecules—an interrupted legacy of scientific and psychological research begun in the 1950s and shut down with hysterical force during the late 1960s—is one way to unify these opposite approaches to the nature of reality.

Perhaps it is the only way.

Chapter 10

NIGHT TRAVELERS

For Benjamin, the rise of capitalism was not simply an awakening of our technological and rational powers. It was also a "new dream-filled sleep," a surrender to dangerous "mythic forces." Reason, rationality, and scientific empiricism concealed their darker opposites but did not dispel them. In fact, the mechanistic ideology of modernism, by substituting the commodity trance for the "ecstatic trance" known to the ancients, put humanity in an extremely dangerous and vulnerable position. Writers of the past centuries explored this fissure between reason and the irrational by concentrating on the ambiguous nature of awakening, the seductive power of dreams, the magical power of trance states.

No writer explored these transitory and in-between forms of mental life with more wit and daring than William Shakespeare. In Shakespeare's work, conscious life is revealed, over and over again, as a type of trance. For the duration of his plays, we seem to recognize or remember that reality tends to reveal itself in a series of marvelous episodes and peculiar coincidences.

At the beginning of the modern era, Shakespeare helped define the modern consciousness—or perhaps it is more accurate to say that the mercurial ambiguities and linguistic openness of his work indicate a path that the modern consciousness did not take. He wrote his plays as Europe was shaking off the animistic and magical beliefs of the past. Some of his most memorable moments seem like a public staging of this transition—for example, Prospero breaking his staff and giving up his powers at the end of *The Tempest*. "Drama is born in the renunciation of magic," wrote the critic Northrop Frye, "and in *The Tempest* and elsewhere it remembers its inheritance."

As Shakespeare was writing, witches were burning in Inquisitional fires. In *Ecstasies: Deciphering the Witches' Sabbath,* the historian Carlo Ginzburg studied court documents from the Inquisition, a paper trail of persecutions crossing the map of Europe. Ginzburg's subversive strategy was to use the reports of the accusers to recover the actual belief systems and the visionary techniques of the accused. He examined testimonies such as the following, from a Scottish witch trial:

> In 1597 Andrew Man told the judges at Aberdeen that he had paid homage to the Queen of the Elves and to the devil, who had appeared to him in the guise of a stag, emerging from the snow on a summer's day during the harvest. His name was Christsonday (the Sunday of God). Andrew Man had kissed its behind. . . . The Elves had set the tables with food, played music and danced. They were shadows, but with the appearance and clothes of human beings. Their queen was very beautiful, and Andrew Man had coupled with her carnally.

Andrew Man's night of enchantment calls to mind *A Midsummer Night's Dream.* For the scenes of Bottom and the fairies, Shakespeare perhaps borrowed such a trial report, a lifting from eyewitness testimony similar to the use of accounts of UFO abduction stories in Steven Spielberg's *Close Encounters of the Third Kind.*

Shakespeare allowed his audience of merchants and nobles to cathartically relive the animist and fantastic beliefs their society was in the process of shedding. Waking from his affair with the Fairy Queen, Bottom says, "The eye of man hath not heard, the ear of man hath not seen, man's hand is not able to taste, his tongue to conceive, nor his heart to report, what my dream was." For the few hours of the Shakespearean spectacle, his audience reawakened to the archaic power of

BREAKING OPEN THE HEAD

magical thought—a theatrical mimesis that helped them to recognize and suppress their own antiquated beliefs with deeper conviction. The plays helped to mark the separation between the old fictions and the new realities. As the modern era gathered force, artistic depictions of fantasy rather than inner experiences of altered states became the only way most people preserved a tenuous link to magical realms. That remains the situation today.

In Shakespearean drama, magic is staging its retreat—a retreat from the world of doing into the world of saying. His language, with its constant play of similes and metaphors, expresses the alchemical process of transformation. As Theseus declares in *A Midsummer Night's Dream:*

> *The poet's eye, in a fine frenzy rolling,*
> *Doth glance from heaven to earth, from earth to heaven;*
> *And as imagination bodies forth*
> *The forms of things unknown, the poet's pen*
> *Turns them to shapes, and gives to airy nothing*
> *A local habitation and a name.*

Shakespeare's language of metamorphosis drew inspiration from Greek myths about gods and humans morphing into animals and plants, of heroes sneaking into the Underworld and the realm of the gods for various poetic or shamanic purposes. Through language, the poet takes over the role of shaman or mage, shaping the "forms of things unknown," giving to "airy nothing / A local habitation and a name."

The theme of awakening was closely linked to the theme of identity. His characters return to ordinary consciousness from dreams, from magical drugs that warp their senses, from delusions that take a nightmarish hold on them. But awakening, breaking the enchantment, is a paradoxical moment: In the act of becoming conscious—Romeo and Juliet in the tomb, Lady Macbeth startled from sleepwalking, Bottom waking in the forest—Shakespeare's protagonists do not escape their delusions. They slip from one level of trance, one form of self-forgetting, into another.

According to the critic Northrop Frye, the systematic revelations at the end of Shakespeare's plays result from "the talisman of recognition that awakens the mind to reality." The talisman can be a ghost, a statue, the sudden appearance of a long-lost friend, a memory. The "talisman of recognition" restores justice to the world, although the outcome never entirely loses its ambivalence. This awakening leads to a happy outcome in his comedies; in the tragedies it brings inevitable doom.

Shakespeare's plays explore the boundary between dream and waking. Even when they are awake, his characters often behave as though mesmerized. It is easy to forget that, while we are awake, we are constantly submerged in different levels of awareness—semiconscious states in which we daydream, space out, or watch advertisements; concentrate without attention; are "distracted by distraction."

The awakening of modern empiricism negated the Shakespearean faculty of "marvelous intuition," the archaic awareness of the "insubstantial pageant" populated by peculiarly anthropomorphic spirits, fairies, dryads, nymphs, and so on. Puck or Pan and their ambivalent followers, were displaced, in the modern era, by the unambiguous Satan. Cut off from the archaic belief in nature-as-spirit, from the multivalent spirits of nature, the modern mind increasingly fixated on its own solitary status. Nothing else, not animals, not spirits, not even the "noble savages" that explorers encountered in their wanderings, seemed to possess logic or sentience besides itself.

.   .   .

WHAT WERE THE principles of the lost magical world that Shakespeare conjures up, then dispels, in *A Midsummer Night's Dream, The Tempest,* and other plays? In *Ecstasies,* Ginzburg makes a lengthy attempt to peel away the "gradual, centuries-long diabolization of a stratum of beliefs that has only reached us in a fragmentary manner, through texts produced by canonists, inquisitors and judges." He finds, hidden in accounts of the witch trials, records of the thought-system that the Church persecuted to the brink of extinction. An amoral consorting with numerous spirits—good, bad, and indifferent—was twisted into a diabolical frolic with Satan's minions. When the accused, like Andrew Man, threw Christian terms such as "devils" into their testimony, it was, according to Ginzburg, a "profound and unconscious reaction, which spread a Christian veil over a more ancient stratum of beliefs." Ginzburg found examples of these archaic beliefs all across Europe. It was an oral tradition, often a feminine one rather than one preserved in patriarchal texts.

In *The Long Trip,* an overview of the use of visionary plants from prehistory on, Paul Devereux finds that the "Witches" condemned by the Church were actually "the practicioners of an ancient tradition— 'night travelers.' In Northern Europe they were called *qveldriga,* 'night rider,' or *myrkiada,* 'rider in the dark.' " As part of this tradition, a woman known to be a prophetess, dressed in the ritual attire of a goddess—depending on location this could be Freya, Diana, or Hela— "would travel to farmsteads and hamlets with a group of girls to give divinatory trance sessions." Like the weird sisters in *Macbeth,* they were the inheritors of an archaic European shamanism. Like shamans around the world, the seeress and her followers used plant potions to achieve ecstatic states: "The night traveler's flight into the wilderness was, of course, a trance 'journey' into the deep reaches of the unconscious mind, a 'spirit flight' caused, usually, by hallucinogens in the flying ointments."

Across the premodern world, country people maintained an active relationship with the spirits and elemental beings hidden in nature. From secret kingdoms just beyond the margins of the perceptible, the "good neighbors" were known to cast their influence over human relations, the fate of kingdoms, the weather, and all natural events. In many of his plays, Shakespeare drew upon this vestigial awareness of magical realms.

With the arrival of modernity, this arena of folk knowledge, along with all modes of nonordinary perception, was banished from the mainstream of Western literary and intellectual life, exiled to the realms of fairy tale and moth-eaten myth. Modern culture, devoted to mercantilism, industrialism, and scientific progress, enforced a sharp distinction between sleep and waking, idleness and productivity, childhood and adulthood, human consciousness and the nonsentient world of nature. The existence of numerous orders of conscious beings—beings that could show themselves upon occasion, but most often appeared in certain ecstatic states or in dreams—was adamantly denied by both Church and State.

After rooting out its witches and shamans and destroying its visionary traditions, the modern world relied on artists and poets to create pallid simulations of what had been lost. From Shakespeare to Spielberg, William Blake to Joseph Beuys, these artistic evocations substituted for the transformative power of an actual encounter with a supernatural "other," or the personal experience of an altered state. What had been banished from memory and suppressed from awareness could now be enjoyed as cathartic spectacle, or ridiculed from the patronizing perspective of the "rational" critical mind. In the modern world, the artist took over the role of the shaman. To enforce one particular mode of consciousness, modern humanity forfeited all direct contact with its nonhuman shadows.

Chapter II

SHAMANISM AND
THE WORLD TREE

Shamanism is a technology for exploring nonordinary states of consciousness in order to accomplish specific purposes: healing, divination, and communication with the spirit realm. The characteristics of shamanism were defined by the religious historian Mircea Eliade: "special relations with 'spirits,' ecstatic capacities permitting of magical flight, ascent to the sky, descent to the underworld, mastery over fire, etc." Shamanism can also involve magical transformation of humans into animals, prophetic dreams, and interaction with the souls of the dead.

The belief system of shamanism posits, besides the dimensions of space and time that are tangible to us, other dimensions, accessible through heightened consciousness or trance. These other dimensions, which pass through every human being, are often represented by the Axis Mundi, or World Tree, with roots reaching down into the lower domains of ghosts and spirits, and branches stretching up toward the gods. "The underworld, the center of the earth, and the 'gate' of the sky are situated on the same axis, and in past times it was by this axis that passage from one cosmic region to another was effected," Eliade notes.

The phenomenon of shamanism is unfathomably old and amazingly widespread. While some historians believe the nomads of the Siberian steppes were the original shamanic culture—and their nomadism took them across the Bering Straits into the Americas as well as through Asia—that does not help to explain the existence of fully developed shamanic practices among African Pygmies and Australian aboriginals. Shamanism is a fully developed enterprise among Australian tribes who separated from other human populations as much as forty thousand years ago. Outside of the modern Western cultures, shamanism seems to be something close to a universal human phenomenon. Its opposite in archaic traditions are the cults of "spirit possession" still found across Africa. In these traditions, a God or spirit comes down and occupies the body of an entranced participant. In shamanic trances, the shaman holds on to his psychic integrity. He goes out into the spirit realms and returns to his hammock or hut in full consciousness.

Eliade illuminates cross-cultural similarities in shamanic belief systems across the world. From Australia to Brazil to Siberia, he documents myths of ancient "cosmic serpents" that brought life to earth, of an original battle in which the men overthrew a primordial and feminine chaos to begin time, of the healing power of rock crystals and the magic breath of the shaman.

Shamanic initiation often takes the form of a sickness—the cure is the discovery of the vocation. Eliade wrote about a famous Yakut shaman who had been ill as a young man. If he did not shamanize, his illness would return. Shamans often become sick when they are young. During their illness, they may see visions of spirits or meet the ghosts of their ancestors. Shamanism can also be inherited through a family line. A dramatic way to become a shaman is to be struck by lightning and survive. "The Greeks believed a person struck by lightning was in possession of magical powers, and in tribal cultures throughout the world lightning shamans are venerated and feared as mighty shamans," notes Holger Kalweit, a German scholar who recounts several case histories of lightning shamans who manifested superhuman powers given to them by the "Thunder Beings."

Traditionally, the evolution from ordinary human state to shaman is marked by a series of visions and dreams of the novice being killed, dismembered, eaten, regurgitated, and put back together by the spirits.

His or her bones are replaced with quartz crystals, precious metals, or similar magical substances. For instance, in Borneo, according to Eliade, the spirits of past shamans come to the initiate, they "cut his head open, take out his brains, wash and restore them . . . insert gold dust into his eyes to give him keenness and strength of sight powerful enough to see the soul wherever it may have wandered; they plant barbed hooks on the tips of his fingers to enable him to seize the soul and hold it fast; and lastly they pierce his heart with an arrow to make him tender-hearted, and full of sympathy with the sick and suffering." In most cultures the majority of shamans are men; however, when women become shamans they are often especially powerful. In some tribes, shamans have an ambiguous gender-identity, dressing like women, or remaining celibate.

Eliade sums up the vast anthropological literature on shamanic initiations as "the death and mystical resurrection of the candidate by means of a descent to the underworld and an ascent to the sky." The candidate, while he is undergoing shamanic initiation, receives a "massive influx" of the sacred. That temporary unleashing of supernatural forces that the initiate must learn to control can be dangerous to those close to him. According to the historian William Irwin Thompson, the shaman is a "transformer who takes in powerful energies, steps them down, and turns them into a weaker alternating current that can be used in all the homes of the ordinary folk." By mediating between the suprahuman and elemental realms, the shaman allows civilization to take place.

The traditional shaman is healer, gardener, storyteller, forecaster, and initiator into the spirit realms. One of his tasks is to bring the souls of the dead to their place in the underworld. The shaman's wisdom, his relationship with the spirit realm, his capacity for ecstatic experience, makes him "the great specialist in the human soul; he alone 'sees' it, for he knows its 'form' and its destiny," Eliade writes.

Shamanic operations utilize a substance that is produced within the shaman's body and materialized in various ways, as a fluid, rock crystal, or magical dart. According to the anthropologist Alfred Metraux: "The shaman's power also has been described by some authorities as a substance which the magician carried in his body. The gestures of shamans during their magic operations suggested that they were handling some invisible stuff which they removed from the patient's body or transmitted to persons or even things to enhance their excellence. The Apapocuva-Guarani shamans, for instance, were given a substance by the spirits which, in turn, they could communicate to other people to increase their vitality."

Some writers, such as Terence McKenna, have equated this substance with the primal substance, between matter and consciousness, sought by the alchemists. In *The Hermetic Tradition,* a book on the European tradition of alchemy, Julius Evola writes, "the hermeticist performs certain operations by which he actualizes and brings to perfection a symbolic 'Matter.'" In the symbolic language of alchemy, this precious stuff is the "gold" that the alchemists seek to fabricate. It is a byproduct of the interior process of self-transformation.

The local technologies of archaic shamanism are sophisticated, effective, and highly pragmatic. What later became the cliché witch's broomstick was originally a tool for spreading lotions made of extracts from belladonna, henbane, and hemlock, dangerous plants containing poisonous and intoxicating tropane alkaloids. According to anthropologist Michael Harner, the broomstick served as "an applicator for the atropine-containing plant to the sensitive vaginal membranes as well as providing the suggestion of riding on a steed, a typical illusion of the witches' ride to the Sabbath."

Ginzburg suspects that Andrew Man's night of frolic with the "good neighbors" was primed by an ingestion of intoxicating plants. According to Ginzburg, this technique was known to some scholars of the time: "In the sixteenth century scientists like Cardano or Della Porta formulated a different opinion: animal metamorphoses, flights, apparitions of the devil were the effects of malnutrition or the use of hallucinogenic substances contained in vegetable concoctions or ointments." Although Ginzburg doesn't try such an atropine-containing lotion or potion himself, he confidently declares that no potion or plant or shamanic technique could be responsible, in itself, for such a visionary narrative. "Against all biological determinism one must emphasize that the key to this codified repetition can only be cultural."

Ginzburg does not define exactly what he means by "cultural" here, but his declaration that no potion, by itself, could have induced Andrew Man's visions belongs to a tradition of scholarly condescension toward the shamanic use of psychoactive plants. This tradition includes Eliade's insistence, in his classic work *Shamanism: Archaic Techniques of Ecstasy* (1951) that ingestion of visionary flora, whether smoked, eaten, drunk, or snuffed (a.k.a. "drugs"), represents a decadent phase of shamanism:

> Narcotics are only a vulgar substitute for "pure" trance. We have already had occasion to note this fact among several Siberian peoples; the use of intoxicants (alcohol, tobacco, etc.) is a recent innovation and points to a decadence in shamanic technique. Narcotic intoxication is called on to provide an imitation of a state that the shaman is no longer capable of attaining otherwise.

Eliade's statement is not just misleading, it seems to be a reversal of the actual facts.

The use of plants to induce trance states is an ancient and worldwide practice. It is not the only way of seeking visions—dancing, fasting, meditation, self-mortification are other ways—but it seems to be the surefire method. Discoveries in archaeology and anthropology clarified this after Eliade published his book—a few years later, Gordon and Valentina Wasson found the mushroom cult among the Mazatecs. But Eliade's statement revealed his prejudice against "narcotic intoxication," as well as puritanical resistance to any fast track for reaching mystical states.

Ginzburg's *Ecstasies,* written forty years after Eliade's tome, is actually a long-winded attempt to overcome those prejudices, to bring the suppressed facts into historical discourse. "The unfathomable experience that humanity has symbolically expressed for millennia through myths, fables, rituals and ecstasies, remains one of the hidden centres of our culture, of the way we exist in the world." Ginzburg argues that the "unfathomable experience," the revelation of "the forms of things unseen," is often a result of trance states produced through psychoactive plants.

He investigates antiquated terms such as "drunken rye" or "mad wheat" for strains of rye infected by *Claviceps purpurea,* a mushroom, also known as ergot fungus. The terms suggest a lost awareness of ergot's use as a shamanic intoxicant. Ergot was used by midwives to induce labor, and it is also the source from which lysergic acid diethylamide, LSD, was synthesized. He also studies mythic allusions to *Amanita muscaria*, the red-capped mushroom used by Siberian shamans, and finds a relationship between widespread myths involving lameness, from Cinderella's slipper to Oedipus's limp, and these mushrooms, often identified as "the single-footed." In his conclusion, Ginzburg realizes he has been examining not a single narrative "but the matrix of all possible narratives." He equates the historian's task with the shaman's flights: "The attempt to attain knowledge of the past is also a journey into the world of the dead."

In many parts of the world, the influence that shamans had over their tribe was inscribed in the land itself. The earthworks and effigy mounds left by North American tribes across the continent, the vast Nazca lines in Peru, the Ley lines and stone circles of Europe, and the similar straight roads that run across vast stretches of Central and South America are residues of shamanic alignment with the earth's subtle energies. Many of them show animal, bird, and human-bird forms that powerful shamans would take in their trance states. The straight roads may represent paths that shamans used to fly into the "other worlds." Throughout Europe, the Church capitalized on this archaic topography; many cathedrals and chapels were placed along long-forgotten Ley lines. Paul Devereux writes that the straight-line roads "symbolize spirit travel, journeying into the otherworld of spirits, of the ancestors, which . . . can be seen in shamanic terms as simply another level or dimension of the physical landscape."

Bruce Chatwin's *The Song Lines* describes the shamanic geography of Australian aboriginals. All tribal members have their own clan song and personal song, which are directly linked to local geography—a rock, a hillside, a pond might have its own cosmological resonance embodied in a story committed to memory for uncountable generations. Traditionally, these songs even acted as a form of currency. In order to pass through another clan's area, a tribesman had to barter for the appropriate hymn.

The aboriginals believe that their mythological Ancestors sang the land and all of its creatures into existence. A tribesman's religious life "had a single aim: to keep the land the way it was and should be,"

Chatwin writes. "The man who went 'Walkabout' was making a ritual journey. He trod in the footsteps of the Ancestor. He sang the Ancestor's stanzas without changing a word or note—and so re-created the Creation." Like a vast loom, the entire Australian continent is crisscrossed by songs that are, at the same time, interwoven myths of creation, the harmonic residue of geological events, and elements of the earth's surface.

For the aboriginals, the natural and supernatural aspects of reality are inseparable. Humanity has a sacred task in the world, and exists to perform a sacred function. This task is connected to the ability, or gift, that separates them from all other living things: The gift of language.

In "The Mushrooms of Language," an essay on Mazatec shamanism, the writer Henry Munn notes that linguistic inspiration is the most profound effect of eating the mushrooms. "Those who eat them are men of language, illuminated with the spirit, who call themselves the ones who speak, those who say." The ability to heal is directly related to ecstatic and inspired speech, "a primordial activity of signification," imparted by the mushrooms. "The Indian shamans are not contemplative; they are workers who actively express themselves by speaking, creators engaged in an endeavour of ontological, existential disclosure." The shamans are enunciators of revelatory reality.

Walter Benjamin's thoughts about the nature of language echo the indigenous viewpoint: "The existence of language . . . is not only coexistent with all the areas of human mental expression in which language is always in one sense or another inherent, but with absolutely everything," he wrote. "There is no event or thing in either animate or inanimate nature that does not in some way partake of language, for it is in the nature of all to communicate their mental meanings." Signifying is, in itself, a sacred act—"in naming the mental being of man communicates itself to God."

In Benjamin's conception, the existence of language, the possibility of expression, is immanent in every object that exists. For the aboriginal, the ancient act of naming, of storytelling, literally invents, initiates, the world. The shaman's use of language, his chants and songs, is formative, primordially creative, as well as protective and healing. As Terence McKenna put it, for the shaman, "the universe is made of language." Myth weaves the world into being.

In all shamanic cultures, landscapes are psychic and spiritual extensions as well as physical ones. Traditional shamanism has always been deeply rooted in place. A Shuar shaman from the Ecuadorean Amazon told me that he believed his powers of healing came to him from the mountains where he lived. The mountains conveyed some of their elemental energy and magnetic force to him, and through the medium of the ayahuasca vine as well as tobacco, one of the most sacred shamanic plants across South America, he could channel this force to his patients.

It is difficult for those of us, like myself, who grew up rootless in modern cities or suburbs to fully comprehend this sense of the sacredness, the supernatural power, of a land that has been inhabited by the same people over innumerable generations. When we read an article about the Uwa Indians—a tribe in Colombia threatening to commit mass suicide if the oil companies drill on their land—we may feel profound sympathy. But we can hardly imagine having an identification with a part of the earth, the shape of the land and the particular plants that grow there, which is so strong that we would rather die than abandon it.

The modern person drawn to the shamanic archetype—the vision of sacred earth, revelatory word, and multidimensional cosmos—finds himself horrified by contemporary society and the accelerating processes of global destruction it has unleashed. Yet he is cut off from the archaic traditions he might like to embrace. Our tradition seems to deny us access to spiritual vision, and we have lost the Indians' innate relation with the natural world as sacred being.

And yet, if shamanism is a universal human phenomenon, we possess the innate ability to regain everything we have lost.

Part Three

LEAVE NO TRACE

Chapter 12

A CYBERNETIC
PULSE ENGINE

The drive to Black Rock City from San Francisco leads through Nevada flatlands, past the jittering neon sadness of Reno. My friend Adam and I made the obligatory stop at the last twenty-four-hour supermarket and casino, dropping a quarter in the final slot machine, a tiny offering to the gray shroud of flat desert ahead. At the shopping mart, we greeted the other obvious Burners, tattooed or face-pierced or with hair dyed in patterns, their trucks overflowing with PVC pipe and junkyard scraps, taxidermied animals, Christmas lights, battered couches, massage tables, costumes, and turntables. We met Two Feather, a muscular ponytailed Indian riding a giant, shining cherry-red chopper. With his blond travel-weary Austrian girlfriend wedged behind him, he was like a pure emanation of America. While his dust-covered yet still sultry partner watched, Two Feather tied plastic containers of Poland Spring water to the chopper. He gave out his Website address and raised a fist before dustclouding into the distance.

"Sex!" he called out as farewell.

From the last shopping mall, the drive through the night turns increasingly surreal. There is nothing to see but shadowy sagebrush and the occasional suicidal jackrabbit with cartoon ears and flashing eyes suddenly leaping into the headlights. Confronting such oblivion, what living thing wouldn't be tempted to self-destruct? Every year, perhaps imitating the jackrabbits, a few Burners crash their vehicles on this last lap of the hipster pilgrimage.

The Black Rock desert is unique among wastelands. A prehistoric lake bed, it is the planetary equivalent of Absolute Zero. This flat plane, ringed by mountains, is entirely devoid of plant or bird or insect life. Nothing moves except the ever-changing Cecil B. DeMille spectacle of cloud formations and, at night, the moon and its unfurled banner of stars shimmering over the wide-angle sky. The claylike surface of the playa is lunar and unreal, traced with craggy lines and zigzag patterns. In dry weather the playa bounces underfoot like AstroTurf. The local Indians made Black Rock the center of their creation myth. These days, its end-of-the-world ambience is often the backdrop for SUV ads.

"Nothing lives out here unless you force it to," said a Burning Man veteran. The spongy salinity of that alien, inhuman earth changes the metabolism, rewires it in some way. Sleep becomes entirely optional. The desert also does interesting things to your hair; "playa hair" is the condition where the top of your unwashed head turns into a gray, sporelike growth.

I camped with Adam, an editor at *Wired* magazine in San Francisco, and his friends—architects, designers, Bay Area Ravers. Back in SF, Adam had filled me in on the erotic tangles and psychodynamic subtexts among the group—the central figures were a married couple in their late twenties, each with another lover conveniently located in a nearby tent. Likable, taut, photogenic, my campmates emanated an E-lated vibe of hyped-up communion.

We arrived late at night. The next morning we unpacked the rented U-Haul and spent many hours turning a green parachute into a mushroom-shaped shade structure supported by cables that just barely survived the wind's weeklong assault. The city—at its zenith reaching a population of 25,000, making it the third largest urban center in Nevada—was quickly raising itself out of the earth around us. New domes and tents, new turrets and towers appeared each hour.

Across the road from us was the Erowid dome. Erowid is one of the most comprehensive Websites on psychedelics. It features trip reports, resource lists, photographs of plants, diagrams of psychoactive molecules, legal precedents, and much more. I borrowed a hammer as a pretext to meet Earth and Fire Erowid, the husband-and-wife team who run the site. I ended up sweating out the 110-degree afternoon heat sitting in the Erowid center as people came through, to peruse the books and articles assembled in the Erowid library, and share stories of their own adventures.

The trip reports posted on Erowid and other websites make for fascinating reading. Here, you find numerous reports of encounters with "preying mantis entities" and "machine elves" on DMT, mystical meltdowns on LSD and cough syrup, and brave explorations of new chemical and botanical discoveries. Probably through all of history but certainly from the Middle Ages on, drug experimentation has been a secret subculture, essentially oral and underground, a body of knowledge evolving through fable, exaggeration, and rumor. The Internet, the synaptically self-assembling global brain of humanity, has provided system and structure to this formerly esoteric realm. The masses of trip reports allow for verification and cross-checking, and have probably prevented many disasters. Some of the entries are sequential studies of a single substance—the notes of high-level technicians, returning again and again to test-drive some little-known shamanic inebriant. Like committed alchemists, these seekers probe the essence of a particular chemical catalyst or plant spirit.

Other reports, many cautionary tales, describe the fervor of experimenters who mix multiple mind-alterers, looking for a rocket-ride to the far antipodes of the psyche. The trip reports are a road map of spectacular neoshamanic successes, hair-raising failures and fritz-outs, and bizarre sightseeing along the way. "Your mileage may vary" is a common cautionary note.

Even without any chemical additives, Burning Man is deliriously mind-expanding. Black Rock City is the psychedelic vision made visceral. The festival is an homage to the way tryptamines expand awareness, open playgrounds of undreamt potential, reveal the erotic core of all interactions. The event is a highly evolved, brilliantly organized follow-up to the Be-Ins and Happenings of the 1960s. The communal system and "Leave No Trace" ecological rule of the event descend from the conscientious politics of The Diggers, a radical group that ran a Free Store in Haight-Ashbury in the late 1960s. At Burning Man, all the subcultures I had dismissed as trite or uninteresting—Goth, Raver, New Age, hippie, pagan, punk, and pierced, decades of sullen subcultural wreckage—seemed to be melding and recombining like elements in a laboratory experiment, fusing into new, protean life forms.

"What is Burning Man? Burning Man is a cybernetic pulse engine fueled by information," Danger Ranger, a gray-bearded founding father of the festival, told me later that week, as we monitored the windswept chaos from his pickup. "Burning Man is like a program that runs. It comes together, it compresses, then it explodes."

When the sun faded, I rode my bicycle around Black Rock City. Each year, Burning Man consists of a semi-circle of rings, divided into streets with thematic names. That year—2000—the theme was the body. The first street, facing the playa, was Head, followed by Brain, Throat, Heart, Gut, Sex Drive, Anal Avenue, Knee Lane, and Feet. From the center of the city, a main lamp-lit avenue led out to the glowing fifty-two-foot-tall Man himself, ringed by sequenced lights. Along this main drag, the Burn equivalent of the Champs Elysées, I rode past a giant head with three faces: a metal face weeping burning tears, a face made from driftwood, and a clay face weeping water. There was a giant clay phallus and yoni with lit-up clit, and a three-story-high interactive asshole—you climbed the stairs and pushed your way through glowing rectal tissue to slide down a steep chute out the other side.

At night, the festival transmutes into a luminous spectacle. There are generator-powered video projectors on billowing domes, films, man-made lightning bolts, flamethrowers, and multihued lasers arching across the star-saturated desert sky. Personal adornment runs the gamut from glowsticks and fairy wings to extraordinary electroluminescent outfits of flashing wires molded into beasts, demons, serpents, aliens, or angels. One of the best outfits I saw revealed the wearer's internal anatomy in glowing wire, sending trails of light shooting out from the heart along the veins, while other sequenced flashes illuminated the filaments of nerves, erogenous zones, and chakra points.

Besides masses of walkers and people on their glowing or furry bicycles, lovingly decorated art cars and wiggy transport trains promenade across the desert. The art cars in 2000 include the Chromozoom, with a spinning DNA coil; a pirate ship featuring a raucous crowd of drunken sailors; a variety of moving couches and living rooms and toilet seats; a furry neon-colored cat bus, and a mobile lobster. Most fabulous was a long Dragon Train that breathed fire with a full-bar inside one of its always-crowded compartments.

During my first visit, I hardly slept or ate, biking frenetically back and forth over the playa, stopping at whatever caught my attention. One night it was the Flaming Lotus Collective, a team of cool hippie chicks who had built a kiln-shaped launchpad that shot crimson pillars of biblical flame one hundred feet into the air as onlookers backed away from the heat. After each blast, the women cried "Yay!" They jumped up to give each other warm hugs of support. The Flaming Lotus was a harmonious mixture of force, fire, and feminity—the kind of spectacle found at Burning Man, and nowhere else.

. . .

ONE NIGHT, word went around that a famous British DJ was spinning at Illuminaughty, one of the enormous rave camps of glowing purple lights and digital video screens, along the far edge of the playa. Having misplaced my bicycle, I set out for the camp on foot, a several-mile trek, and quickly lost all of my friends. Rain was falling hard, turning the desert dust to thick mud. As I walked alone, the luminous night panorama of Black Rock City revealed a creepy carnival shadow, an undertone of desperation.

At moments, Burning Man reminded me of Norman Mailer's *Armies of the Night*, an ambivalent take on the counterculture during the 1967 Pentagon march. "The dress ball was going into battle," he wrote. "Now the witches were here, and rites of exorcism, and black terrors of the night . . . the hippies had gone from Tibet to Christ to the Middle Ages, now they were Revolutionary Alchemists." Like most literati, the hard-drinking Mailer hated psychedelics: "The nightmare was in the echo of those trips which had fractured their sense of past and present. . . . The history of the past was being exploded right into the present: perhaps there were now lacunae in the firmament of the past, holes where once had been the psychic reality of an era which was gone."

Since Mailer's book, memory loss—mass-cultural amnesia,

rampant Alzheimer's, disconnection from history—has become our dominant cultural paradigm. Burning Man, on the other hand, celebrates "the history of the past" as it is exploded into the present—as kitsch spectacle, mythic image, or, in Benjamin's phrase, "profane illumination." It is possible to witness a fully costumed Aztec sacrifice atop a cardboard ziggurat, undergo a mock Egyptian burial using rites from the *Egyptian Book of the Dead*, participate in a Shivaite fire ritual— all in an hour. The entire event spoofs some 1970s retro sci-fi fantasy of postapocalyptic tribalism, and the big man's climactic burning summons up ancient druidic sacrificial rites from the collective memory banks. The constant riffing on the past amplifies the festival's hallucinatory ambience. Like the effect of certain chemicals, Burning Man changes one's sense of time, revealing the mythic underpinnings, the whispers of eternity, underneath the most ordinary moment. Perhaps this is what Danger Ranger meant when he told me, "I found out there is a way your consciousness can go beyond what we call Now, and I rode the shockwave of inverse time."

. . .

ON THE PLAYA I met a young California kid, light-blond-haired with a baby face, who was escaping the Dragon Train in a hurry. "It's my eighteenth birthday," he told me. "I was in the dragon and this freaky chick with her tits exposed gave me a big sloppy kiss. Then this naked freak named Mustard Seed said, 'I want to tie you to a whipping post, you cute little boy.' I said I'm leaving. I didn't want to be tied to a whipping post. I've seen more psycho shit here than I've seen before in my life."

Rain was splattering as I reached the Thunderdome, a popular haven for fans of the Mad Max flicks, its exuberant mock-violence the opposite of Black Rock City's peace-and-love vibe. Inside the Thunderdome, two opponents on bungee cords were beating the shit out of each other with foam-wrapped clubs, spurred on by the banshee shrieks and bat trills of a huge slavering crowd hanging from the dome's metal cross-sections. An opera singer came out between bouts, accompanied by fire spinners, and her Wagnerian trills sent flutters down my spine.

Past Thunderdome was Emerald City, a Rave-oriented theme camp featuring a formidable laser. This multimillion-dollar party trick had been brought, along with its large cooling tank, by two genius mad scientists. The laser was brand new, designed and built in the months before the event; it shot solid geometric patterns out into the stratosphere, projected fractal patterns and Sacred Geometries on the dancing masses. A balloon held on to its beam refracted rainbows across the dark playa. This magical laser seemed to violate all physical laws—from a distance it appeared to send a bar of solid white light toward the stars, where it stopped in midair.

In front of the speaker towers of Illuminaughty, hundreds were dancing beneath a video projection of churning fractal patterns. But the famous DJ's tinny beats left me cold—Rave's treacly graphics and amphetamine rhythms of repetition are just not my thing. It was past two A.M. Sick of the icy rain, I retreated to the Nipple Lounge, a breast-shaped chill-out tent at the edge of Illuminaughty. Inside was paradise: couches, pillows, rugs, billowing fabrics, hectic dialogues, warm bodies. A glittery teenage Edie look-alike from the Moontribe went around hugging everyone she met. She talked about the squadron of military jets flying across Black Rock with unsettling frequency.

"They are so scared of us," she said. "They know that we have the power."

More likely the pilots just wanted to catch a glimpse of the spectacle. I was beginning to feel a strong sense of déjà vu—not for something I had lived but something I had read and heard about. The next day, I asked John Perry Barlow, a former Grateful Dead lyricist and Silicon Valley polemicist, the inevitable question: Was this anything like the sixties?

"This is so much better than the sixties. So much less self-indulgent and desperate, so much more restrained," Barlow answered. "What you have here is a large group of people trying to practice unconditional love for strangers, and, for the most part, succeeding."

I found Barlow in his rented RV—one of many RVs ringed around Spiral Oasis, a theme camp that was described to me as "among the most successful, richest people you could possibly meet at Burning Man." Although their site was far less luxurious than the nearby Church of Mez—orchestrated by high-level project managers from

Microsoft, Mez featured a sixty-foot DJ tower and an eighteen-wheel truck converted into a costume shop and kitchen presided over by the five-star chef from Seattle's Four Seasons—the denizens of Spiral were enthusiastic propagandists for the festival.

"This is the center of everything that's going on right now, all of the progress. You are seeing the best form of it here," I was told by Ken Goldberg, a robotics expert who had just published a book with MIT, as he did me the favor of shampooing my dust-clotted hair beneath a sun shower.

"It is amazing to see virgins arrive at Black Rock," added Mark Pesce, the inventor of VRML, a virtual reality programming language. "After five or ten minutes, they say, 'Oh my God, I've been looking for this all my life.' This is the epicenter of a free culture." Pesce had founded a group called the "Church of the Motherfuckers," based on an obscure smokable powder that seems to create, in a few minutes, the effect of exploding out into the cosmos. "My God it is amazing," said Pesce. His fellow psychonauts could only describe it as "thermonuclear contact with the Divine."

The centerpiece of Spiral Oasis was a popular trampoline and an open-air sunshower. Its public project was a hypermodern fetish bar called Alien Sex Club (featuring a tank where rubberized alien exhibitionists could display their moves; a wall with tentacles allowing for brusque feel-ups of the unknowns standing on the other side). Along with its Silicon Valley brain trust, Spiral's inhabitants included Hollywood producers and actors, Swedish supermodels, corporate lawyers, a chef, and a hairdresser—130 people in all. Goldberg's wife, Tiffany Shlain, had created the "Webbies" Awards, an annual showcase for the digiterati during their brief golden age. Also present was Tiffany's father, Leonard Shlain, wearing a soft Rembrandt hat. He was the author of *The Alphabet and the Goddess*, a work of New Age prehistorical revisionism with the thesis that patriarchy was inscribed in written language and the new postliterate electronic culture would bring back the Golden Age of matriarchal goddess worship—it sounded a bit shaky to me. I told him I was from New York.

"Ah, New York—a city without foreplay," he said. "When you arrive there, there is no lubrication, no hesitation. They just give it to you straight."

At Spiral, the music was ambient, the mood was mellow, clothing was optional, and it was easy to fall into a discussion stretching from the epistemological conundrums raised by robot consciousness, to the dolphin scientist John Lilly's theories about metaprogramming the human biocomputer, and the anthropological evidence for an ancient tribe of High Plains Indians who smoked DMT all day long.

Chapter 13

DOCTOR MEGAVOLT

Burning Man is more decadent than Warhol's Factory, more glamorous than Berlin in the 1920s, more ludicrous than the most lavish Busby Berkeley musical, more of a love-fest than Pepperland, more anarchic than Groucho Marx's Freedonia, more implausible than any mirage.

The festival rewires your sense of what is possible now.

But perhaps the most intoxicating aspect of Burning Man, as Walter Benjamin might have put it, is thinking about Burning Man. Also dreaming about it—many visitors dream through the year of returning to the playa. In dreams of my own, Burning Man takes place in an abandoned factory building in Queens, now overrun with glittering hipsters; or it has "sold out" and become a sad carnival in a seaside town; or it is the last euphoric gathering of humanity in a radioactive wasteland; or I am waiting, alone, for dawn to rise over the desert's lunar surface. Almost every night for months after my visits, the festival turns up in some form in my interior theater.

A few Burners never return to the mainstream. In New York, I met J., formerly the advertising director of a major business magazine. After he went to Burning Man, he aborted his career and morphed into a mad-eyed avatar of outdoor parties and trance music, living on the bohemian margin of New York—a thin margin these days. He christened himself "Machine Elf," dressing as a sci-fi warlock with horns and cape at all-night outlaw parties he orchestrated under the city's bridges.

Burning Man started in 1986, when Larry Harvey, a barely employed landscape architect and overaged bike messenger, built an eight-foot-tall wooden effigy of a man after a painful break-up, then torched it on Baker Beach in San Francisco. It felt so good that he returned the next year with more of his friends to do it again. As it grew, the event was listed in the newsletter of the Cacophony Society, a loosely knit Bay Area group of "culture jammers," pranksters who distort the messages of the corporate media. The Cacophony Society had developed out of the collapse of an earlier and more insular group, The Suicide Club, a prepunk, posthippie underground network formed in the 1970s.

Harvey intended the Man as a free-floating symbol: an image of transience or spiritual regeneration, a signaling beacon for a new posthumanism, or a reigniting point for the spent energies of a suppressed and depressed counterculture at the end of the Reagan eighties. In 1990, the burn was too big for the beach and they relocated to the barren wastes of the Nevada desert.

"As soon as we stepped onto this desert, I knew this had tremendous potential for growth," Harvey says. "The playa was like an enormous blank canvas."

Harvey is the founder and a beloved figure in Burning Man's self-perpetuating mythology. A gruff chainsmoker in a cowboy hat, he runs the event with a full-time year-round staff of twelve. They pay the Bureau of Land Management about $500,000 to use the site each year. Ticket sales, starting at $125 early in the year and rising to more than $200 for latecomers, as well as donations, cover their costs. Harvey's current plot is replicating Burning Mans across the globe, and his staff is actively networking their expertise to localized, small-scale versions of the festival.

"That first year in the desert, we didn't know anything," recalled Danger Ranger, the gray-bearded founder of the Black Rock Rangers, which is now a corps of two hundred volunteers trained to mediate and problem-solve. "It was so hot we crawled under our cars like lizards."

The rapid growth of the festival and its flawless self-organizing structure are direct products of the Internet. Among the attendants at Burning Man can be found a tremendous brain trust of scientists and technicians, Silicon Valley engineers and CEOs. While artists can access the event's brain trust of technicians to help them achieve their projects—"We have resources of technical knowledge that many corporations lack," said one sculptor—scientists and engineers use the Burn as their creative outlet. Briefly escaping corporate jobs or university labs, they find release in flaunting their tools before a live and jubilant audience. "Black Rock City shows it is possible to create a society based on play," said Russel Wilcox, a laser engineer for Lawrence Livermore Laboratories who donates work to the event—in 2000, he created a green crisscrossing laser display forming a Burning Man insignia, visible from outer space. "Just doing something where play is at the heart of every interaction is implicitly political."

Walking around or hanging out in the cafe, I would make great new friends and just as suddenly lose them forever. At night, at the theme camps, social constellations would suddenly form for a few hours and then disperse into randomness. Like strangers on the Internet, Burners play with their personas, picking up and discarding new identities, new friends, new ideas, at hyperspeed. "During the day, I'm Aladdin riding a magic carpet; at night, I'm a manta ray," said a creative director from Adobe Photoshop, wrapped in Arabian tunic. "I'm a pretty amazing closet exhibitionist. This event feeds my desire for people to say, 'You're wonderful, you're great.' "

In 1995, two people died—one, apparently a suicide; the second, run over in his tent by a car gone off course. In the aftermath, the organizers had to make a choice. Did they want their event to remain a lawless rodeo for freaks, or did they want to change in order to grow? Taking the path of evolution, they banned firearms, took unauthorized cars off the playa, raised ticket prices, and imposed order on chaos. The years of the dot-com bubble brought thousands of new participants, flush with IPO cash. But the bursting of the bubble did not lower attendance. If anything, the 2001 Burn seemed more raucous, more extravagant and exploratory, than the year before.

One of the sculptors told me, "Burning Man was the last great art movement of the twentieth century, and the first great art movement of the twenty-first century." Although art is integral to the event, the individuality of the artist vanishes in the sweeping scale of the festival. Burning Man enacts the German artist Joseph Beuys's concept of "social sculpture"—a communal aesthetic that goes beyond private egotism. Unlike the self-consciously prickly works of the insider art world in New York, the projects displayed at Burning Man are explicitly user-friendly, Pop inspired, community-oriented, experiential. They are not intended for museums. They are meant to be touched and then torched.

A postmodern Pop Art phantasm, Burning Man constantly mocks and undercuts its own pretentions. It is an endlessly involuting imitation of itself. "Everything out here is a myth. You invent your own reality," one of the artists told me. "That's part of the grand experience: We make these grand myths to go with it." The festival is also a self-conscious parody of esoteric initiation, the ritualized ushering into the Mysteries last seen in the Western world at Eleusis.

On Saturday, the festival's crescendo, my friend Jon got lost in the wandering masses. He ended up at the Chapel of Plastic, a beautiful, translucent structure out on the playa that resembles stained glass. He found himself in a mass wedding ceremony. A sex columnist was marrying everyone to themselves. Jon was uncertain whether he wanted to make that kind of commitment, but he took the vow. Later he was watching the preparations for burning down the Man—a fifty-two-foot-tall sculpture that is filled with explosives and ignited. He became increasingly certain that he was the Man—when they burned it down, they would be destroying him as well. He looked at the faces around him and saw sinister motives. "Suddenly I realized that Burning Man was forcing all of these unsuspecting people to join a diabolical cult of devil worship," he said. The day after the burn, he seemed calm and well-satisfied. The flames had consumed his paranoia. If he still saw the event as a Satanic cult, he was proud to have joined.

One of the festival's icons is Doctor MegaVolt, a pair of rattle-shaped Tesla coils, resembling *Bride of Frankenstein* movie props, two-story-tall generators mounted on a raised, mobile platform, with a space between them. Charged with fifty thousand volts of energy, MegaVolt shoots violet-edged lightning bolts in all directions, crackling into the black night in instantly branching and suddenly fading zigzags like electrical orgasms. When a man or woman in a metal suit stands between the Tesla coils, something called the Faraday Principle in physics takes hold, protecting them from frying as they reach out to conduct lightning bolts through their fingers, smash them against their helmet, play with fifty thousand visible volts like a child might dream of doing, to the intense delight of a huge crowd of the naked and the glowing and the fully costumed, screaming "MegaVolt! MegaVolt!" over and over at the top of their lungs, until the last drop of juice is spent.

Later I spoke to Austin Richards, the Berkeley physicist who created MegaVolt. "It is a synthesis of art and science," he told me. "It creates an event that is extremely interactive between man and machine. It allows us, the people in the suits, to commune directly with electricity. The sensation of lightning arcs hitting your body is very cerebral."

MegaVolt embodies the essence of Burning Man. If the event can be reduced to one single concept, it is "transformation": transformation of consciousness, transformation of artistic creativity into ecstatic communion, of sculptures into flames and ash, of the invisible force of electricity into a death-defying game, of all kinds of energy into each other.

Above all, transformation of the self. In the aftermath of the festival, many people start new relationships or end old ones, switch continents or careers, remake their lives in dramatic ways. "After last year, when my boyfriend and I got back to Calgary, we said, 'What are we doing with our lives?' " I was told by a young Canadian giving away her poems in the center cafe. "We quit our jobs and went to Central America for four months." Unfortunately, the modern world doesn't always reward its seekers: "We're back in Calgary now, trying to pay off our debts," she admitted. "It's sort of sad. Reality stepped in front of us like a brick wall." She said she was working as a secretary.

This transformational energy is expressed by the iconic hobby of the festival: fire-spinning, in which a Burner (often clad in Goth leather) spins torches on chains around his or her body, silent except for the rush of air swishing around the pinwheeling flames. For the duration of the flames, the spinner becomes their own solitary atom—a neutron with four flaming electrons swirling around in a solemn balancing act that did not interest me at all until I started to find it mesmerizing and beautiful.

Citizens of Black Rock City are a wide range of types: smug Silicon Valley superstars who fly into the event on private planes, artists of all stripes, tech workers, sex workers, social activists, secretive occultists, bland thrill-seekers, sinister voyeurs. There is a selection of those who have entirely separated from the dominant culture—freaks, if you will. This last group includes women who know they are witches, who are in touch with secret currents of the night, such as Jenny Greenteeth, her name swiped from a fairy tale, who described how, while tripping on an obscure substance, a yin-yang symbol once shot across her room into her Third Eye, sending her into meditative samadhi. There are men with the shamanic disposition, seeking the tools to heal the desouled, such as the two naked guys who sat on the floor of the cafe giving Tarot card readings; or "Teddybear Man," wandering the festival in a thick coat of stitched-together stuffed animals, dispensing hugs and wise words. After the burn, Teddybear Man was going to help the Chumash Indians build a sweat lodge—putting off reentry into the "real world" for as long as he possibly could.

.   .   .

BY SATURDAY MORNING, the entire desert was a mud pile that formed a squishing seven-layer cake under my sneakers at every step. At the center cafe, the band on stage resembled a latter-day simulation of the sixties hippie group The Fugs. They wore Indian robes and kaftans, long beards and hippie beads. Their song consisted of one monotonous chant repeated over and over, as the crowd of several hundred rapturously joined in:

> "Fucking piece of shit!
> Fucking piece of shit!
> Fucking piece of shit!"

That afternoon, the Department of Public Works went on its annual Labor Day march across the playa. Modeling themselves on apocalypse culture of the 1970s and early 1980s—Road Warrier, Devo, the Sex Pistols, the Plasmatics—the DPW is Black Rock's dedicated cadre of free labor. Their slogan is "If you don't matter, we don't care." Harvey calls them "speed freaks with power tools." They build the infrastructure and tear it down in the weeks afterward. Now they were gyrating—raw, cooked, crocked, cracked—atop their trucks and fork-lifts and caterpillars and smashed cars, screaming insults, spitting long funnels of beer, swooshing long tails of fire from flamethrowers at the appreciative crowd. One black-bearded Rasputin-like guy in a small Bobcat crashed repeatedly against the battered trucks, revving against them like a vicious little dog trying to get off on some bigger ones.

"Go back to your cubicle! Go back to your computer! Get out of our reality!" the DPW chanted.

The crowd nodded appreciatively but did not budge.

Chapter 14

GREAT ROBOT EMPIRES

During my first visit to Burning Man, I spent my last night sitting in front of the Heart of the Man. The Heart was a large furnace, welded together from sheets of metal, shaped like the human heart, with stacks of logs next to it for fuel. When it was stoked full and the bellows was pumped, the Heart actually beat a deep red. Yellow sparks shot out of its ventricles. The Heart spread a circle of inviting warmth around it in the cold desert night, and I sank down and stayed there, among other quiet Burners, meditating and half-dozing, until morning.

When I returned to New York a few days later, I checked my e-mail and discovered that Dan Lieberman, the botanist who took me to Gabon, was dead. He had died in a freak car accident on a flat South African highway; he was asleep in the backseat when the accident happened. It was his thirty-third birthday.

I recalled how Lieberman said he had been shown, during his iboga trip, that he wasn't going to live very long. He was very chastened by this. I had taken it lightly. It seemed impossible to me, at that point, that a drug, no matter how visionary, could predict one's fate with any accuracy.

There was an e-mail address for Dan's parents. I wrote a

condolence letter to them, praising his courage and conviction. I assumed that would be my closest brush with death for the day.

Later that afternoon I received some worried calls from friends of my father's. Nobody had heard from my dad for over a week. I had left messages for him at home, but assumed he was staying out in the country—he had recently purchased a tiny cabin in upstate New York. But his friends said he was no longer upstate. With an increasingly heavy foreboding, I went to his SoHo loft with the police that night. While I waited downstairs with Laura and two of my father's painter friends, the police broke in and found my father's body in the bathroom. From the medical examiner, I learned he had died of heart failure some days ago—perhaps my last night at Burning Man, as I sat in front of the Heart. He was sixty-eight years old.

My father had been suffering from a heart condition for several years. But he had not divulged to anybody how serious his condition was—I think he was hiding it from himself most of all. In the last months of his life he seemed remarkably cheerful and calm, at peace with himself, and pain-free.

While at Burning Man, I often thought about my father. I wondered what he would make of the spectacle. My dad was an abstract painter. He and his friends were New York survivors. Born in England, he had arrived in New York in 1960, part of the second wave of Abstract Expressionism. My dad never made it in the art world. An idealist, he was incapable of strategizing about his work or playing art-world politics. In any case, after the rise of Pop and Conceptualism, sincere abstract art was seen as slow-footed and retrograde. Stranded outside of the art world, he worked constantly—obsessed with painting, a diehard believer in the transcendent value of art. I often despaired when I thought of his canvasses—of the decades of work in his loft, of his solipsism and his gift, his love of the craft, and his solitary pursuit of the ideal.

. . .

AFTER FINDING my father's body in his loft, after fighting through the city's nerve-racking bureaucracy of death, which is its own special punishment of the living, after clearing out decades of junk, after recovering from the initial shock of grief, I spent a lot of time with his works. He had left over 230 paintings and 50 sculptures in his loft on Greene Street—the relics of his lifelong investigation. Some of them were enormous, as much as 10 or 15 feet long. One rolled-up canvas measured 25 feet.

His earlier paintings were hard-edged and geometrical. His later works suggested cosmic chaos, night-lit abysses, fever dreams, the existential confinement of the self in its prison tower. They expressed awkwardness and grace, radiance and revelation, mystical hope and existential horror. They reminded me of Henry Miller riffing for pages on any subject—on a walk he took as a child, on a long-lost friend, or flourishing some metaphysical conceit. Miller's passages skate toward the edge of collapse with careless abandon, but circle back to ensnare his meaning with precision. Scuffed, bohemian, almost abject yet oddly redemptive, my dad's paintings had that quality of a crisis confronted, a disaster averted, but just barely.

In his last years he exercised the freedom of someone who had dropped off the map. Escaping all fashions and trends, he gave up following anything except his own solitary path. In the paintings, he was whispering over and over the invisible secret he had carried with him all his life—from his early childhood in Brighton to the money-mad Manhattan where he had become an anachronism—that phantom of meaning and form that had haunted him. Working in solitude, he proved the theorem to himself alone.

His bookshelves were filled with books on physics and philosophy and Buddhism. He read constantly—Blanchot, Derrida, Wittgenstein, Nietzsche. Overviews of black holes and superstrings, extra dimensions and chaos theory. Some of his late paintings could be seen as poetic images of quantum weirdness, molecular transformations, the space-curving force of gravitational fields. His art was his spiritual path. On his desk I found a scrawled note that said, simply: "The need to believe."

Before his death, I somehow hadn't realized how much our interests coincided. The repeated shapes in his later works were explicitly primordial and basic. They called to mind the tilted menhirs of Stonehenge, as well as crude African artifacts. My father was seeking some mystical pathway out of the contemporary cul de sac.

Reading his notebooks, I realized he was ambivalent about living into the new century; he wrote about feeling the society was increasingly depersonalized, inhuman. He never owned a computer, never received an e-mail. He dreaded what he called "the great Robot Empires of the twenty-first century." He suspected that his belief system, the existential and handmade aura of his life and work, were not going to translate into this new era.

. . .

OVER TIME, I found that my psychedelic explorations had residual benefits. For many years I had recalled almost none of my dreams, and those few that came back to me were feeble fragments, gray slivers, and bland voids. After dabbling in mind-expansion, I rediscovered my dream life. Dreams now manifested each night in full color, increasing in length as I began to study them. I stopped going to the movies because I didn't want to interfere with these nocturnal spectacles. The images generated by my unconscious were more compelling than commercial fare. Sometimes I woke up four times a night to scrawl the plots down in my journal before the images faded away.

In the months after my father's death, he appeared to me in a series of dreams. Sometimes he had suffered a heart attack but survived, or he returned home after an absence. In other dreams, both he and I were confused about whether or not he was still alive. He was often worried about the fate of his paintings. Once we met at an old midtown bar and I suddenly realized we were in a dream. I took the opportunity to reassure him that I was taking care of his work, cataloging and storing it as best I could.

In January, a few weeks after I learned that my girlfriend was pregnant, I had this dream:

> My father and I were sitting by a lake and he said, "Look at the light." Out on the water, light was rippling, a green light breaking into halos around the rocks. It looked like an effect from one of his paintings. I realized I was being allowed to have a last visit with him.

I woke up feeling grateful, happy to be with Laura. That we were making a life with each other, and a child together.

Nine months before my father's death, one of my closest friends had overdosed on heroin. Thirty-three when he died, R was a brilliant writer, a magnetic madman, good-looking, strong and strong-willed, heir to a vast family fortune. His great-grandfather had founded a southern newspaper dynasty. But R had an unhealthy fascination with alcohol and drugs; he was fixated on self-destruction. The galleys of his first novel were on his desk when he died.

I never thought he was an addict; I thought he used heroin and booze to escape the terror that was consuming him. He felt, in some way, cursed, fated to die, and he enacted his hysteric vision of his fate. On the blackboard behind his desk he had scrawled a line from Robert Stone: "Pissing and moaning, mourning and weeping, that was the nature of the drug."

In the months after R's death, I had a series of dreams about him that were similar to the dreams I had about my father months later. At first there was a lot of confusion over whether or not R was really dead. I had several dreams where he overdosed but survived. Once, we spoke about this confusion at a party. Another time I visited him in the hospital. A few times I cried to him in my dreams, sorry I hadn't done anything to help him. I told him I hadn't known how. While he was alive, I had even fantasized about taking him to Gabon for iboga, but I knew he wouldn't be open to it.

Almost exactly a year after R's death, I had a dream where I went up into "the spirit world," a kind of gray limbo accessible by rope ladder, to visit him. He seemed much calmer than in our earlier encounters. He was sitting in front of an old typewriter. I asked him what he was doing with himself now that he was dead.

"I'm writing," he said. "I'm writing about my life. I'm trying to understand what happened."

"That's really good. I'm happy to hear that," I told him before I left.

Most people assume that such dreams are manifestations of the personal unconscious. Before my ibogaine trip, I would have thought that as well. After Gabon, I was willing to consider other possibilities.

As time went on and I examined my dreams, I began to suspect that the spirits of my father and my friend were not just phantoms that my mind created. They were visitors from the after-death realm, still confused, sometimes resentful about their loss of human status. Through the transdimensional spirit world of dreams, they were able to reach me. My unconscious psyche (what some traditions call the "astral body"), still attached to the world of the living, could help them understand what was going on.

Communication with the spirit realm through dreams or visions is a commonplace fact of archaic and indigenous cultures around the world. It is only in the "rational" West that we refute the possibility of such contact—blocked by our blind faith in materialism. The shamans of the Tarahumara Indians told Antonin Artaud that the Whites had been abandoned by the spirits. Perhaps we are only abandoned because we push the spirits away.

In contemporary life we do whatever we can to deny intuition of the invisible realms. We clog up our senses with smog, jam our minds with media overload. We drown ourselves in alcohol or medicate ourselves into rigidly artificial states with antidepressants. Then we take pride in our cynicism and detachment. Perhaps we are terrified to discover that our "rationality" is itself a kind of faith, an artifice, that beneath it lies the vast territory of the unknown.

What is the truth of the era in which we live?

Walter Benjamin called capitalism "a religion of destruction." It is a religion because it is based on faith—untested and unproven by the individual acolyte—in materialism and rationalism. It is a passive worldview, a negative theology. Even in the 1920s, Benjamin recognized "the destruction of the world as the real goal of world capitalism—its systemic hope and transcendent ideal."

Disbelief in any spiritual reality is also a belief system. The capitalist mind perceives the world purely in terms of material resources to be used for its benefit, to increase productivity and profit without thought of long-term consequence. If there is still a vague and oppressive sense of guilt, of wrongness and imbalance, this gnawing guilt spurs capitalism on to greater acts of consumption, more violent attempts to subjugate nature, more totalizing efforts to create distractions. To the "rational materialist" mind, death is the end of everything; this thought feeds its rage against nature, which has placed it in this position of despair. The destruction of the world is revenge against a vanished God, and a drastic attempt to invoke the spiritual powers.

Benjamin writes:

> Capitalism is probably the first instance of a cult that creates
> guilt, not atonement. . . . The nature of the religious move-
> ment which is capitalism entails the endurance right to the
> end, to the point where God, too, finally takes on the entire
> burden of guilt, to the point where the universe has been
> taken over by that despair which is actually its secret hope.
> Capitalism is entirely without precedent, in that it is a religion
> which offers not the reform of existence but its complete de-
> struction. It is the expansion of despair, until despair becomes
> a religious state of the world in the hope that this will lead to
> salvation.

If capitalism is a religion of destruction—currently accomplishing
its goal with alarming efficiency, despite hitting the occasional reces-
sional speed bump—then the current degradation of the planet makes
sense. The flaw in our thinking is systemic. Outside of a traumatic
transformation of values, there is no way to stop an assault based on a
deeply unconscious, even metaphysical, yearning for vengeance.

Perhaps it is only through parsing out the metaphysical rationale
hidden within the modern myth of "rationality" that we can grasp
why there is no coherent attempt to control the catastrophic processes
we have set in motion. These processes—global warming, the punctur-
ing of the ozone layer, the disruption of the electromagnetic spectrum,
nuclear waste that remains radioactive for tens of thousands of years,
the risky bioengineering of new organisms and viruses, the short-term
greed and monotonous moral blindness—increasingly threaten the
very fabric of our being. The individual is intuitively aware of the seri-
ousness of these threats. Our intuition is denied by our leaders and
technocrats, puppets for the corporate interests. They have no vision
for the future.

Benjamin's definition of capitalism clarified the meaning of heroin
in the lives of R and other people I know, the friends and acquaintances
who died from overdoses as well as those who ruined their lives
through addiction. Heroin suffuses the body with pleasure and temporarily nullifies the mind. It is an enjoyable high but not much
more—even that enjoyment is tempered by grimness, by the psychic

vacuity the drug creates. It is true that heroin is physically addictive, but according to treatment counselors the physical effects of breaking that addiction are about equal to a three-day flu. The synthetic narcotic methadone that the government gives to heroin addicts is, alarmingly, far more addictive than heroin. In fact, it was created by the Nazis as a tool of social control.

Heroin addiction, or overdose, is often a response to an inexpressible spiritual emergency. My friend R, as well as other friends who died from heroin, suffered from a spiritual crisis, a moral abyss. R turned to heroin because it was a way out, a simple, straightforward means of escape from the labyrinth created by his wealth, his terror, and his desperation. It was a capitulation to the ideology of destruction. Like me, he had no access to any kind of faith. He had no means of expressing a transcendental impulse—except self-obliteration. Like many users of the drug, inspired by the nihilist background noise of our culture, he romanticized the agent of his doom.

Chapter 15

THE TEMPLE OF TEARS

The best sculpture at Burning Man 2001, one of the best works of contemporary art I have ever seen, was the "Temple of Tears," perhaps six stories high and entirely constructed from carved wooden pieces. The Temple's intricate spires resembled sacred Hindu sanctuaries I once visited in Nepal. The wooden panels used in its construction were the cutout molds from a factory that made dinosaur models for children. Requiring painstaking months of labor, the temple was built in memory of a friend of the artist who had killed himself. It was a commemorative shrine open to all to remember the dead. Over the week, the walls were entirely covered with scrawled names and remembrances. Some people created entire shrines—with photos, mementoes, long letters—for those they had lost. Whenever I entered the space, day or night, it was full of people of all ages, many weeping quietly, praying, burning incense, remembering. Butoh dancers made silent performances, crawling along the ground outside of the entrance. I added the names of my father and R to the walls.

On Sunday night, the last of the festival, the Temple was torched. On the way to it, I got lost in a dust storm with three strangers. For what seemed a very long time, we wandered across the playa, our way illuminated only by the full moon, a white glowing orb overhead, magnetizing the earth. We were surrounded by grayness, by deep nothing. A sparkling rocket exploded in showering white sparks. In the distance, we saw three red taillights define a vehicle as pure geometric form. The three strangers seemed to know each other well. I think they came from some hippie paradise hidden in the backwoods of Oregon. Ignoring me, they were continuing an old conversation. With little context, I understood it was about the overall sense of life, its poetry and pornography and poison, refracted in that Beckett-like moment.

One of them said to the others, "Here's an idea for you: What if it's always been exactly the way it is now?"

I wanted to know what he meant, but I lost them before I could ask. I found my way to the crowd. Thousands of people were massed in a huge circle around the Temple. There was half an hour of hushed silence before the structure was torched, burning majestically, giant flames sinking down to gold embers, wooden ornaments suspended for a moment like ghost faces before crackling into ash and soot and gray smoke.

The Temple revealed the festival's hidden undercurrent of sadness, of mourning. Disguised by its ridiculous excesses, public orgies, art car rallies, and all-night raves, Burning Man also has a sorrowing streak. As they dance, the revelers also grieve (or is it only a projection of my own gloomy nature?) for everything spiritless and vacant—the hideous Medusa mask of our culture—that needs to be torn off and fed to the flames. Sometimes I also intuit, in the midst of that masked and manic carnival, reverberated by techno beats, a kind of ambivalence over the human state; a sense of insufficiency, a yearning for transcendence.

The greatest party in the world is also a wake for this world.

. . .

THE NEXT MORNING I woke up at dawn and stepped out of my tent. I looked to one side of the desert, and one half of the full moon was still visible as it plunged out of sight, beyond the mountains, over the gray flatland. Turning around, I saw exactly one-half of the red-tinged fireball of the sun rising up, 180 degrees opposite, over the playa. Sun, moon, and earth were like three spinning gyres in a cosmic mechanism.

At Burning Man, I was introduced to the ideas of Georges Ivanovitch Gurdjieff, a mysterious occultist from the early part of the twentieth century, by someone I met at the cafe—it was my habit, in that supercharged now-here, to seek out daily conversations with strangers. In this way, I learned many things I hadn't known before.

Originally from the Caucasus, Gurdjieff founded a school near Paris, where he died in 1949. In Gurdjieff's system, students perform movements and dances in a state of heightened self-awareness. At his school, he used ritualized gestures to break apart dead habits—old postures, moth-eaten ideas—and release new forces. Some intellectual defenders of the Rave movement have adopted Gurdjieff's system as a way of explaining the innate mystical rapport Ravers feel while dancing. Gurdjieff thought the purpose of human existence is to transform and transmit certain cosmic energies. Clearly, the all-night exuberance of Burning Man, its playing with the elements of heat and light—fire, laser, and lightning—is an attempt, in Benjamin's phrase, to "commingle with the cosmic powers."

Gurdjieff had many visionary ideas that seem quite strange. He believed that a soul was not something you simply had but something you had to work to acquire. He called this work "intentional suffering" and "conscious labor." He believed the earth and the moon were living, evolving beings—also a shamanic concept—and that humanity was designed to serve the evolutionary purposes of the earth and the moon. Human beings are, in his theory, the "organs of sense perception" for the earth, and in their continual transformations of this planet they serve the planet's needs, not their own. "Humanity, like the rest of organic life, exists on earth for the needs and purposes of the earth. And it is exactly as it should be for the earth's requirements at the present time."

In his system, there are many finer gradients of matter that science does not register—not only ideas and thoughts but even a substrate of the human spirit are types of material. After we die, according to Gurdjieff, the moon consumes the fine matter of human spirits. It is like a magnet that draws our psychic corpses into it: "Everything living on the earth, people, animals, plants, is food for the moon. The moon is a huge living being feeding upon all that lives and grows on the earth." Someday the earth would evolve into a being like the sun, while the moon would transform into a second earth. Humanity was simply a stage in this process.

Only through an intensive effort of conscious evolution—what he called "self-remembering"—is it possible for an individual to escape being eaten by the moon. "The liberation that comes with the growth of mental powers and faculties is liberation from the moon." He argued that humanity was not truly conscious, that man's actions were entirely mechanical: "Everything 'happens,' he cannot 'do' anything. He is a machine controlled by accidental shocks from outside." The influences of the other planets determine wars, revolutions, technological breakthroughs, and environmental catastrophes on the earth's surface. The rapid proliferation of cellular technology, for instance, would be a way for the earth to change its electromagnetic sheath. In his system, progress is an illusion for most of humanity: "Everything is just the same as it was thousands, and tens of thousands, of years ago."

Most of my life, I have been chained to cities where night is, for the most part, a muted void and the elements are reduced to abstractions. On the other hand, in Manhattan, it is very easy to have the uneasy awareness of being a miniscule cog in a vast machine, a "cybernetic pulse engine," accelerating outside of human control. Thinking about Gurdjieff in the Black Rock desert, it was amusing to suspect that the cosmic apparatus of swirling constellations and planetary bodies and radiating moon might exert a direct and causal influence on human destiny, that those forces might be responsible for the running of the entire mechanism. In a sense, it seemed a strictly logical idea.

I returned to New York City. Ten days after the spectacular burning of the "Temple of Tears," Laura and I were caring for our three-week-old baby when we heard the loud thrust of a low-flying airplane and then a sickening thud. We opened the blinds to see one of the World Trade Center towers in flames, a black crater in its side. By the time the first tower fell, dazed crowds were streaming uptown below our window. Before the second tower collapsed, I went out and walked south toward the catastrophe, passing crowds of frightened Wall Street financiers and secretaries, shell-shocked college students, stunned janitors. Some were covered in soot. Many were babbling on their cell phones. Outside the court buildings, newscasters broadcast emergency updates. Policemen tried to control the crowds.

As I watched the chaos, Gurdjieff's poetic visions ran through my mind. "What is war? It is the result of planetary influences," he said. "Everything that happens on a big scale is governed from outside, and governed either by accidental combinations of influences or by general cosmic laws."

It was past eleven A.M. Up in the blue sky, between two towers, a two-thirds wedge of lunar opal was clearly visible, beaming over the city. I was surprised by its brightness so late in the day.

Suddenly, I realized what was happening, if Gurdjieff was right: The moon was feeding.

Part Four

SHAMANISM AND MODERNISM

Chapter 16

WALKING IN MYSTERIES

What if the origin of culture, what Carlo Ginzburg called "the matrix of all possible narratives," was the shamanic journey? Then art and literature, dance and theater would be elaborated or degraded forms of the original impulse to reach the "other worlds" through trance and ritual.

Perhaps modern culture and faith-based religion is a short-term experiment within the larger context of shamanism and its untold millennia of continuity: an experiment in turning away from actual visionary knowledge in favor of cathartic spectacles, symbolic codes, and the mimetic techniques of literature and film; in substituting personal knowledge of sacred realities with faith, and finally, in the secularized West, extinguishing faith entirely in favor of nonbelief in any spiritual dimension of human existence.

The "rediscovery" of shamanism is not just a New Age phenomenon. The Western world has made repeated attempts to understand shamanism, often seeking to reduce it to simple quackery. The process of forgetting and rediscovering, reevaluating and dismissing, shamanism has continued for centuries. From the sixteenth through the eighteenth century, explorers in Siberia and the New World wrote reports of jugglers, conjurers, and tribal sorcerers that were avidly studied by the intelligentsia of Europe. The tone of these accounts ranged from sneering attacks on fraudulent practices and shrill denunciations of devil worshiping, to objective and even compassionate studies of shamanic healing practices.

"While some Europeans continued to ridicule what they considered public trickery and ignoble credulity, others began taking shamanistic practices very seriously," writes the historian Gloria Flaherty in her book *Shamanism and the Eighteenth Century.* "Shamanism seemed to them to epitomize a grand confluence of ageless human activities the world over." Flaherty suggests the evolving cult of the genius, the magic powers of enchantment attributed to Mozart or Goethe, arose out of Europe's fascination with shamans.

The archetypal figure of the eighteenth-century Enlightenment, Goethe amassed information on magic and ghosts, rejected Newton's mechanistic view of nature, believing that nature was animated by spiritual forces. "We all walk in mysteries," the poet and scientist wrote to a friend. "We are surrounded by an atmosphere about which we still know nothing at all. We do not know what stirs in it and how it is connected with our intelligence. This much is certain, under particular conditions the antennae of our souls are able to reach out beyond their physical limitations." Goethe incorporated many aspects of the shaman archetype—contact with ghosts during Walpurgisnacht, drug-induced trance, journeys into the world of the dead, etcetera—into the figure of Faust, the modern magician.

In the nineteenth century, Romantic poets like Samuel Taylor Coleridge, Edgar Allan Poe, and Percy Bysshe Shelley obsessively explored their dreams as a bridge between the unconscious and conscious mind. "I should much wish, like the Indian Vishnu, to float about along an infinite ocean cradled in the flower of the Lotos, and wake once in a million years for a few minutes—just to know I was going to sleep a million years more," wrote Coleridge, whose most famous poem, "Kubla Khan," was reconstructed from an opium revery.

Like shamans, the Romantic poets were practical technicians who investigated their own dreams and trance states, using drugs among other methods to probe the far reaches of the mind. They trained themselves to produce hypnagogic imagery—the semi-controllable hallucinations that can rise up just at the edge of sleep. Thomas De Quincey, who founded the modern genre of drug testimony with *Confessions of an English Opium-Eater,* described these visions as "heraldries painted on darkness." The dream lyricism of the Romantics was an act of resistance to rational empiricism and the Industrial Revolution.

While the Romantics sought to linger in their dreamworlds, the Modernists explored the moment of awakening as the model for a new type of consciousness that could fuse rational and irrational processes. For writers like Marcel Proust, James Joyce, and Virginia Woolf, the effort made by the sleeper to awake from the dream served as a metaphor for the disconnect between the progressive scientific and social thought of their era, and the primordial, ritualistic slaughter of the First World War. "History is a nightmare from which I am trying to awake," announces Stephen Daedalus, near the beginning of *Ulysses,* a book that includes a one-hundred-page play that takes place in "Night Town," a transcript of a semi-coherent nightmare or ghost trip that reads like it was dreamt by the book itself.

In Search of Lost Time begins with Marcel Proust's protagonist lying in his bed, sorting himself out from confused and vivid dreams of the past. Proust's opening reveals the moment of waking up as a mystical transgression between the self and the not-self:

> . . . when I awoke in the middle of the night, not knowing where I was, I could not even be sure at first who I was; I had only the most rudimentary sense of existence, such as may lurk and flicker in the depths of an animal's consciousness; I was more destitute than the cave-dweller; but then the memory—not yet of the place where I was, but of various other places where I had lived and might now very possibly be— would come like a rope let down from heaven to draw me up out of the abyss of not-being, from which I never could have escaped by myself: in a flash I would traverse centuries of civilization, and out of a blurred glimpse of oil-lamps, then of shirts with turned-down collars, would gradually piece together the original components of my ego.

Each night, Proust's narrator journeys from psychic dissolution to self-possession, from dismemberment to remembrance. The image of a "rope let down from heaven" is akin to the shamanic motif of a ladder from the sky, leading between this world and the other realms. The vast undersea kingdom of sleep called into question the solidity of the waking reality: "Perhaps the immobility of the things that surround us is forced upon them by our conviction that they are themselves and not anything else, by the immobility of our conception of them." The sickness that exiled Proust to a cork-lined room, out of contact with other human beings, in a kind of living afterlife, was like the shaman's initiatory sickness and nervous disorder, his celibacy and his compulsion to separate from his tribe while exploring the spirit realms.

The Modernist writers and artists, consciously or not, borrowed elements from the shamanic archetype. Like tribal shamans, the artists saw themselves, in Ezra Pound's phrase, as "the antennae of the race." In a secular culture, they were the ones who journeyed into the land of the dead, who crafted images of an elusive sublime, who went into ecstatic states of inspiration. They believed their icons and testaments, like magic fetishes, contained the power to heal the culture's spiritual maladies. Writers like Gertrude Stein, Tristan Tzara, or James Joyce explored private languages or languages explicitly made out of non-sense—similar to the shaman's common practice of glossolalia, speaking in tongues, during trance. The shaman's songs were taught to him by the spirits; the chants of the Modernist poet were expressions of alienation from a dehumanized and demystified world.

Chapter 17

I AM NOT HERE

In the last centuries of capitalism, industrial progress and rationalism were mirrored by a cultural history of frantic visions, symbolic excursions, and narcotic escapes. Artists and intellectuals searched for antidotes to the suffocating materialism of the West. The exploration of chemically induced altered states was one extreme limit, one essential element, of the Modernist quest. The poet Arthur Rimbaud called for "a systematic derangement of the senses," and in the 1920s the Surrealists, following his lead, found inspiration in psychic disorder and extravagant shock effects. Writing on the Surrealists, the critic Walter Benjamin noted:

"In the world's structure, dream loosens individuality like a bad tooth. This loosening of the self by intoxication is, at the same time, precisely the fruitful, living experience that allowed these people to step outside the domain of intoxication." Altered states allowed thinkers to escape, temporarily, from the overwhelming, and intoxicating, dreamworld of capitalism.

Modernist artists pursued the deviant and disgraced, sought out what had been refused, tossed aside, made alien by the West. The resurgence of interest in the sacred tribal medicines, which began with a few dedicated and often desperate seekers, opened a new phase of

the Modernist exploration of cultural otherness: an attempt to make
direct contact with the visionary knowledge of "primitive" societies.

The writers of the twentieth century who first took the psychedelic voyage out—Antonin Artaud, Henri Michaux, Aldous Huxley,
and William Burroughs among them—found that the tribal sacraments, off-limits and little known in the West for many centuries, had a
split identity. On the one hand, the substances opened vast domains of
perceptual awareness, sparked new ideas, and unleashed visions that
seemed to unfold from the Jungian collective unconscious, or from the
mind of a supernatural trickster. But the experience was also one of
abjection and anxiety and helplessness.

Artaud traveled to Mexico in 1936 to take part in the peyote rituals
of the Tarahumara Indians, a remote mountain tribe living on barren
peaks a few days' journey from Mexico City. The tormented poet went
to the mountains of the Tarahumara out of desperation. He yearned
to recover "that sense of the sacred which European consciousness has
lost . . . the root of all our misfortunes."

Artaud suffered internal exile from his own mind, his own
thoughts, "a fundamental flaw in my psyche." In his writings, he returned, over and over, to this inner separation, felt as terror, as rupture,
as yearning for connection to some reality.

"I am not here," he wrote to a friend. "I am not here, and I never
will be."

Poet, actor, founder of the Theater of Cruelty, inspiration for generations of embarrassing pseudotransgressive spectacles performed in
liberal arts colleges and fringe theaters around the world, he has a de-
served reputation as a radical and histrionic figure who once declared,
"All literature is pigshit." Some of Artaud's writing is mad ravings and
some is extremely tough going, but he was also capable of great lucidity. Seeking clues to his condition, he probed among mystical traditions, alchemical processes, the fragmentary shards gleaned from his
own inner world: "There is a secret determinism based on the higher
laws of the world; but in an age of a mechanized science lost among
the microscopes, to speak of the higher laws of the world is to arouse
the derision of a world in which life has become a museum." His life
was a quest for those higher laws.

For a time, Artaud belonged to the doctrinaire Surrealist party:

"Surrealism has never meant anything to me but a new kind of magic. The beyond, the invisible, replaces reality. The world no longer holds." Surrealism was, for Artaud, a system of techniques for exploring irrational, mystical, and dissociative states—those domains of consciousness that a materialist culture discards as useless. Surrealism showed how, "Out of the right use of dreams could be born a new way of guiding one's thought, a new way of relating to appearances."

He split the Surrealists when they turned to communism. For Artaud, the fact that the Surrealists joined the communists only proved that their revolutionary impulse had not penetrated deeply enough. "The revolutionary forces of any movement are those capable of shifting the present foundation of things, of changing the angle of reality." Communism was doomed to failure because it didn't recognize, didn't transform, "the internal world of thought."

To reach the Tarahumara, Artaud passed through a primordial landscape inscribed with symbols, numbers, and images—blasted trees like crucified men, demonic faces peeking from rocks. Later he saw the shamans of the Tarahumara weave these symbols into a living cosmology that expressed the essence of their mystical science. "This dark reassimilation is contained within Ciguri (peyote), as a Myth of reawakening, then of destruction, and finally of resolution in the sieve of supreme surrender, as their priests are incessantly shouting and affirming in their Dance of All of the Night." Like the Bwiti, the Tarahumara had a symbiosis with their magical root. When the shamans danced, Artaud realized, "they do what the plant tells them to do; they repeat it like a kind of lesson which their muscles obey."

European Modernists like Pablo Picasso and André Derain were fascinated by "Primitivism." Cubists, Fauves, and Futurists took their formal innovations from African masks and Eskimo totems. Despite this interest in the exotic and tribal, only Artaud, of all the European Modernist artists, had enough desperation or courage—often they are the same thing—to venture into the tribal reality and eat the visionary sacrament for himself. Only for Artaud was achieving this knowledge a matter of life or death—or even beyond. He was not looking for any other reward: "I had not conquered by force of spirit this invincible organic hostility . . . in order to bring back from it a collection of moth-eaten imagery, from which this Age, thus far faithful to a whole system, would at the very most get a few new ideas for posters and models for its fashion designers." Thirty years ahead of his time, Artaud presciently conjured the late 1960s, when psychedelia turned mass market, producing much "motheaten imagery" for the machinery of advertising, TV, and design.

. . .

The Peyote Dance, Artaud's text on his voyage, worked and reworked over many years, while its author suffered in mental hospitals, is a fractured narrative made up of stops and starts, convulsive revelations and tormented cries. A unique mytho-poetic masterpiece, his text is shot through with Christian images of crucifixion and redemption, the pressure of his madness, his yearning to reenchant the world. "For there is in consciousness a Magic with which one can go beyond things. And Peyote tells us where this Magic is, and after what strange concretions, whose breath is atavistically compressed and obstructed, the Fantastic can emerge and can once again scatter in our consciousness its phosphorescence and its haze."

The Tarahumara, far from being savage or backwards in their beliefs, were actively seeking answers to the deepest questions of philosophy. "Incredible as it may seem, the Tarahumara Indians live as if they were already dead. They do not see reality and they draw magical powers from the contempt they have for civilization." The Indians pursued metaphysical knowledge in a direct, visceral way, through dance, ritual, and, above all, through Peyote. "The whole life of the Tarahumara revolves around the erotic Peyote root."

The Tarahumara shamans fooled with Artaud at first, as shamans like to do. "They thrust on me these old men that would suddenly get the bends and jiggle their amulets in a queer way," the poet complained. "I saw they were palming off jugglers—not sorcerers—on me." At first the Indians did not want him to participate in the *ciguri* rituals: "Peyote, I knew, was not made for whites. It was necessary at all costs to prevent me from obtaining a cure by this rite which was created to act on the very nature of the spirits. And a White, for these Red men, is one whom the spirits have abandoned."

But Artaud was tenacious. He waited them out. He also learned that the Mexican government was trying to stop the peyote rituals; he confronted the local schoolmaster about it. Later he learned the Tarahumara knew their tradition was coming to an end. The spirit was abandoning them—and all men. "Time has grown too old for man," a priest told him.

He made friends with a tribesman who explained, at least in Artaud's recollection: "Peyote revives throughout the nervous system the memory of certain supreme truths by means of which human consciousness does not lose but on the contrary regains its perception of the Infinite."

Eventually the real shamans arrived. He was allowed to join their all-night peyote ceremony. He was the first white man, the first Western intellectual, to do so.

He ate a fistful of the powdered root, received those "dangerous disassociations it seems Peyote provokes, and which I had for twenty years sought by other means." He watched primordial symbols rise from his inner organs: "The things that emerged from my spleen or my liver were shaped like the letters of a very ancient and mysterious alphabet chewed by an enormous mouth, but terrifying, obscure, proud, illegible, jealous of its invisibility." He witnessed the fiery letters *J* and *E* burning at the bottom of a void—an immense void that was somehow contained within his own body.

"Peyote leads the self back to its true sources," he wrote. "Once one has experienced a visionary state of this kind, one can no longer confuse the lie with the truth. One has seen where one comes from and who one is, and one no longer doubts what one is. There is no emotion or external influence that can divert one from this reality."

As powerful as they were, these revelations could not cure his inner divisions. They could not heal him. Artaud spent the last twelve years of his life in mental institutions, treated by electroshock, writing paranoid letters and increasingly incoherent rants, and revising the text of his revelations among the Tarahumara. Like some of the psychedelic martyrs of the 1960s, Artaud's quest for shamanic knowledge ended in self-destruction. But what other fate was possible or even conceivable for the modern Western artist, compelled beyond any worldly ambition to cross the spiritual wasteland, to resacralize himself and his culture?

Chapter 18

AN ORGY OF VISION

The Wassons introduced the magic mushrooms to the modern world in the 1950s, but the West had known about peyote for centuries. Artaud made his pilgrimage to the mountains of the Tarahumara four hundred years after Spanish explorers and overseers first encountered native use of the cactus. The Spanish Franciscan friar Sahagun wrote about the cactus producing "visions either frightful or laughable" as early as 1560. "It is a sort of delicacy of the Chichimecas," Sahagun observed, "it sustains them and gives them courage to fight and not feel fear, nor hunger, nor thirst, and they say it protects them from any danger." Early chroniclers such as Francisco Hernandez also noted the medicinal benefits ascribed to it: "Ground up and applied to painful joints, it is said to give relief."

Early European travelers and monks did not taste peyote for themselves, or if they did they didn't write about it, and the ceremonial use of the cactus was soon dismissed as a savage custom and demonized. In 1620, the "Inquisition against heresy, depravity and apostasy" in Mexico City prohibited Indians from imbibing this delicacy, "reproved as opposed to the purity and sincerity of the Holy Catholic Faith." The visions produced by the plant were attributed to "the suggestion and assistance of the devil, author of this abuse. . . ." Despite the dangers of persecution, Indian groups such as the Huichol and Tarahumara secretly preserved their relationship with the cactus—to end the connection would have been to destroy their cultures entirely. Assaulted by the fanaticism and ignorance of the Spaniards, the Indians adopted Christianity, but they learned to pursue their old religions in secret, and they saw no contradiction in this.

Mescaline, the essential alkaloid in peyote, was the first psychedelic compound to be isolated by Western scientists. In the 1880s, the German scientist Louis Lewin isolated the active alkaloids. In the next decade, the hard, gray, bitter buttons of the cactus, which are distinguished by tufts of hair and spiraling geometric patterns on their tops, made the rounds of elite intellectual circles in Europe and the United States. Among the luminaries who tried peyote in the 1890s were William James, who suffered stomach pains without getting visions, and W. B. Yeats, who found it similar to hashish. The well-known psychologists S. Weir Mitchell and Havelock Ellis also tested the compound on themselves. They wrote long descriptions of the peculiar visions that resulted.

Anticipating the paintings of Salvador Dali, Weir Mitchell found himself facing a "huge cliff" with a "bird claw of stone" gripping it. From the leg of this bird "hung a fragment of some stuff. This began to unroll and float out to a distance which seemed to me to represent Time as well as the immensity of Space. Here were miles of rippled purples, half transparent, and of ineffable beauty." Green birds fluttered down into the abyss, and he saw "clusters of stones hanging in masses from the claw toes, as it seemed to me miles of them, down far below into the underworld of the black gulf." After the trip, he suffered headaches and "a smart attack of gastric distress." The experience "was worth one headache and indigestion, but was not worth a second," and he doubted there was much therapeutic potential in it.

Havelock Ellis described his trip as "an orgy of vision." At one point he saw himself "as though I were inside a Chinese lantern, looking out through my cheek into the room." Weir Mitchell and Ellis were intrigued by their lugubrious hallucinations, which resembled the most elaborate opium fantasies of De Quincey, but they did not find them especially meaningful. Weir Mitchell predicted "a perilous reign of the mescal habit when this agent becomes attainable." Ellis thought the drug, while "an unforgettable delight," was too intellectual in its character to have a wide appeal.

Louis Lewin, author of the book *Phantastica,* an early attempt to classify the effects of various mind-altering plants, realized that the colorful hallucinations produced by peyote were less meaningful than the plant's other effects: "The most important fact in the whole mechanism of the cerebral cortex is the modification of the mental state, the modification of psychological life," he wrote in the 1920s. Peyote caused "hitherto unknown spiritual experiences compared with which the hallucinations lose in importance." Lewin was far ahead of his time in suggesting that the transcendent sense of unity, of connection to the world and dissolution of the ego, often imparted by peyote and LSD, was more meaningful than any psychedelic fireworks.

Although a handul of artists and occultists experimented with mescaline, the discovery did not create general interest in Europe at that point, or in the decades to follow. I suspect that the European consciousness of that era, from the late 1890s through the Second World War, wasn't prepared for the hard-core surrealism, the sci-fi sensorial ruptures, of psychedelic drugs. The Europeans who experimented with peyote, or mescaline, the hallucinogen's purified and crystalline form, had no context for understanding what they were seeing, and the main effect on them was psychic estrangement. The dream agitprop of Surrealism, the birth of montage in film and the trauma of two world wars opened the Western mind to the psychedelic shock as visionary catalyst.

For those who tried the tribal hallucinogens without proper preparation, the results could be disastrous. Jean-Paul Sartre, for example, took mescaline in Paris during an experimental clinical trial in 1935. For over a week, long after the physical effect of the drug had worn off, Sartre found himself plunged into a lingering nightmare of psychotic dread and paranoia; shoes threatened to turn into insects, stone walls seethed with monsters. He was bewildered, terrified—the physical sickness and psychic anguish may have inspired his novel *La Nausée,* in which the writhing bark on a single tree reveals what he saw as the mechanistic horror of nature.

.   .   .

"THE EARTH HAS HAD all the exoticism washed out of it," the young poet and painter Henri Michaux lamented during a 1928 visit to Ecuador. "If in a hundred years we have not established contact with some other planet (but we will), or, next best, with the earth's interior, humanity is finished. . . . We are in mortal pain, both from the dimensions as they now stand, and from the lack of any future dimensions to which we can turn, now that our tour of the earth has been done to death." Like many intellectuals, Michaux sought an escape from the West after the senseless carnage of World War I.

If not another planet, Michaux discovered an interior escape a few decades later, when he started dosing himself with mescaline. It was in the early 1950s, a time when mescaline was again making the rounds of Western intellectuals, artists, and well-heeled mystics. "A rape, an atrocious voltage . . . annihilating the machinery of the mind" is how Michaux described his mescaline journeys. "Mescaline multiplies, sharpens, accelerates, intensifies the inner moments of becoming conscious," he wrote. "You watch their extraordinary flood, mesmerized, uncomprehending." Images repeated endlessly, like psychic wallpaper—a face, a glass staircase, a pink hippopotamus. "With your eyes shut, you are in the presence of an immense world. Nothing has prepared you for this. You don't recognize it."

Over and over again, in books such as *Miserable Miracle*, in his abstract drawings and paintings, Michaux sought to capture the infinite divisions, the ego-splittings and imagistic explosions, he found on his trips: "I shone, I was shattered, I shouted to the ends of the earth. I shivered, my shivering was a barking. I pressed forward, I rushed down, I plunged into transparency, I lived crystallinely."

He used the chemical to dissect the interior regions of his consciousness, describing incredible accelerations, slowdowns, repetitions, psychic dispersions. He struggled to grasp the drug's alien meaning, its character, but he could not make sense of it. Michaux's study of mescaline was aestheticized, utterly alienated from the shamanic knowledge of the Huichol and Tarahumara. The Indians took peyote as medicine for the body and soul and had cognitive maps of the spirit realms it revealed. Michaux explored the psychedelic experience primarily as an artistic stimulus, and could therefore relate to it only as something exotic and impersonal, inspirational but sinister. "That world is another consciousness," he wrote. But the essence of that otherness eluded him.

Chapter 19

A SEA OF SPIRITUAL PROTOPLASM

Artaud and Michaux recounted their hallucinogenic forays in fractured Modernist style. The British novelist Aldous Huxley narrated the account of his 1953 mescaline trip with the dry wit and clarity of an English detective novelist or a boy's adventure writer. In the introduction to *The Doors of Perception,* the most influential work of Western psychedelic literature, Huxley announces his intent to join "the sleuths—biochemists, psychiatrists, psychologists"—on the trail of mescaline.

Huxley undertook his mescaline journey in 1953, the same year the Wassons first tried psilocybin. The author of numerous novels and literary essays, as well as the best-selling work of predictive science fiction, *Brave New World,* he had long been fascinated by mysticism. This fascination was in spite, or perhaps because, of the fact that his own tendency as a thinker and a writer was toward a prolific but slightly inert rationality. "There was something amoeboid about Phillip Quayle's mind," Huxley wrote in the novel *Point Counter Point,* describing his alter ego. "It was like a sea of spiritual protoplasm, capable of flowing in all directions, of engulfing every object in its path, of trickling into every crevice, of filling every mold." Huxley's almost stifling lucidity compelled him to push toward domains of the irrational and unknowable. He once wrote to a friend, "My primary occupation is the achievement of some kind of over-all understanding of the world . . . that accounts for the facts."

Long before he knew of psychedelics, Huxley was fascinated by mind drugs as potential agents of personal liberation and social control—his thinking toggled back and forth between the two extremes. Recognizing the ambivalent potential of these substances, he invented Soma, a narco-hallucinogen, for *Brave New World,* his prescient vision of a high-tech authoritarian future. Soma was the entheogenic beverage described in the *Rig Veda,* inspirational source of the Hindu cosmology. In Huxley's book, Soma was far from a benign intoxicant. Combining euphoric, sedative, and hallucinogenic powers, Soma functioned as a precisely calibrated tool of "repressive tolerance," keeping the citizens of Huxley's designer dystopia doped and docile, hooked and happy.

Around the time he wrote *Brave New World,* Huxley also penned an essay in which he admitted yearning for a mind drug that could alleviate the boredom, the daily drudgery, of ordinary consciousness. "If I were a millionaire, I should endow a band of research workers to look for a new intoxicant," he wrote in 1931. His discovery of mescaline, and then LSD, were the answers to his prayers. He devoted the last decade of his life to exploring these chemicals and proselytizing on their behalf. Unlike his fictional Soma, and despite the CIA's best attempts, mescaline and LSD had the added benefits of being ineffective agents of social control. Yet he anticipated the development of culturally sanctioned mood-lifting drugs such as Prozac and Ritalin, which would be mass-prescribed: "They may help the psychiatrist in his battle against mental illness, or they may help the dictator in his battle against freedom," he wrote. "More probably (since science is divinely impartial) they will both enslave and make free, heal and at the same time destroy." Huxley died in 1963. On his deathbed, his wife injected him with a sizable dose of liquid LSD—a trip that perhaps evaded even his capacity for rational analysis.

In *The Doors of Perception*—the title is taken from William Blake's lines, "If the doors of perception were open / Everything would appear, as it is in reality, Infinite"—Huxley's manner remains self-assured, his style clear. Even when he approaches the prospect of collapsing

into incoherence, he does it in limpid prose. Looking at a chair and seeing an intensity of actuality comparable to the Christian Last Judgment, he noted: "It was inexpressibly wonderful, wonderful to the
point, almost, of being terrifying." In a flash, he realized what it would
be like to go insane, to plunge into the hells and also the paradises of
schizophrenia. He analyzed the fear "of being overwhelmed, of disin-
tegrating under a pressure of reality greater than a mind, accustomed
to living most of the time in a cozy world of symbols, could possibly
bear." Huxley is admitting his own limits. He was not constitutionally
capable of straying far beyond his "cozy world of symbols." He could
never approach the fever pitch of Artaud, who croaked his peyote revelations from the edge of chaos and dread.

The Doors of Perception was propaganda promoting mystical perception as lifestyle choice. Although Huxley's personal approach to
psychedelics was more mandarin than midcult, The Doors of Perception
paved the way for Timothy Leary and the debasement of the subject
into pop-cultural fodder. Huxley suggests that mescaline or a psychedelic relative of it could be employed within Christianity to give direct
access to transcendent reality: "To be shaken out of the ruts of ordinary perception, to be shown for a few timeless hours the outer and
the inner world, not as they appear to an animal obsessed with survival
or to a human being obsessed with words and notions, but as they
are apprehended, directly and indirectly, by Mind at Large—this is an
experience of inestimable value to everyone and especially to the intellectual."

With an overlay of references to Blake, Aquinas, Goethe, The
Tibetan Book of the Dead, and so on, The Doors of Perception alienates the
mescaline trip from its indigenous and shamanic origins. For the Indians in the Native American Church, peyote is "grandfather." The
bitter-tasting cactus is, itself, a spiritual emissary from the "Green Nation" of the plant world. The Indians use the cactus only within the
context of a carefully structured ritual. Peyote reveals that the natural
universe is entirely animated by spiritual forces, and the vegetable vehicle of this message is inseparable from its meaning.

Fifty years after the fact, Huxley's central argument remains entirely valid. He realized the modern world was increasingly trapped in
its habits of mediation, its almost desperate effort to pursue any subject other than personal revelation:

A catalogue, a bibliography, a definitive edition of a third-rate versifier's *ipsissima verba,* a stupendous index to end all indexes—any genuinely Alexandrian project is sure of approval and financial support. But when it comes to finding out how you and I, our children and grandchildren, may become more perceptive, more intensely aware of inward and outward reality, more open to the Spirit, less apt, by psychological malpractices, to make ourselves physically ill, and more capable of controlling our own autonomic nervous systems—when it comes to any form of non-verbal education more fundamental (and more likely to be of some practical use) than Swedish drill, no really respectable person in any respectable university or church will do anything about it.

As a form of societal shock therapy in a world increasingly threatened by the technology it was unleashing, Huxley advocated large-scale use of mescaline or a similar agent as a tool of consciousness evolution, a chemical shortcut to "direct perception, the more unsystematic the better, of the inner and outer world into which we have been born."

Chapter 20

A HANDFUL OF ASHES

While modern artists sought an exit from the modern wasteland, the new discipline of anthropology gave itself the task of studying the nonliterate tribal societies as the colonial powers hurried to contaminate and destroy them. The history of anthropology is made up of a series of misunderstandings and projections, deliberate obfuscations, outright blunders, sell-outs, and criminal acts. From Franz Boas to Margaret Mead, from Claude Lévi-Strauss to Napoleon Chagnon, anthropology has functioned as a distorting mirror into which the West has gazed, pretending to learn about "the other" while studying endless reflections of itself. Onto the native societies we projected our prurient obsession with sexual relations and the incest taboo; our fascination with violence and the "survival of the fittest." We studied magical practices in order to demystify them or reveal them as frauds. Through our anthropological emissaries we enacted our compulsion to consume the exotic and, in the act of consumption, annihilate it.

In his memoir *Tristes Tropiques,* Lévi-Strauss mused on the folly of the anthropological quest—the impossibility of contacting an uncorrupted civilization. He imagines going backward in time. With each jump back, he realizes he would regain lost customs while he forefeits the ability to interpret them: "I can be like some traveller of the olden days, who was faced with a stupendous spectacle, all, or almost all, of which eluded him, or worse still, filled him with scorn and disgust; or I can be a modern traveller, chasing after the vestiges of a vanished reality." For the stern patriarch of structuralism, this vicious circle proved that anthropology can never reach its object.

In his darkest moments, Lévi-Strauss gives himself over to nihilism. "Journeys, those magic caskets full of dreamlike promises, will never again yield up their treasures untarnished," he mourns. The achievements of the Western world, its "order and harmony" were based on contamination and pollutants emitted on a global scale: "The first thing we see as we travel round the world is our own filth, thrown in the face of mankind." Everywhere he looks he finds apocalyptic squalor, entropy—The Wasteland. He redefined anthropology as "entropology," the study of a world running down.

Lévi-Strauss equates the vogue for travel writing—for popular narratives of visits to exotic cultures—with the "quest for power" of adolescents undergoing initiation rituals in tribal societies. The "dazed, debilitated, and delirious" initiates go into the wilderness, believing "that a magic animal, touched by the intensity of their sufferings and their prayers, will be forced to appear to them." This "absurd and desperate attempt" to contact the spiritual world by breaking away from the social world, Lévi-Strauss believes, finds its structural parallel in the young travel writer of the West who briefly exposes himself to an extreme situation and returns "endowed with a power which finds expression in the writing of newspaper articles and bestsellers . . . its magic character is evidenced by the process of self-delusion operating in the society and which explains the phenomenon in all cases."

Lévi-Strauss's work, his effort to "recapture the master meaning," is animated by a feverish urge to demystify. "Can it be that I, the elderly predecessor of those scourers of the jungle, am the only one to have brought back nothing but a handful of ashes? Is mine the only voice to bear witness to the impossibility of escapism?" His demythifying "science" takes part in the work of destruction, what he calls the irrevocable result of human history: "Mankind has opted for monoculture; it is in the process of creating a mass civilization, as beetroot is grown in the mass," he writes. "Henceforth, man's daily bill of fare will consist only of this one item."

His memoir is the triumphant lament of the maniacal rationalist who will not be taken in by any ruse, any mystical vibration or fleeting hope, who allows us no possibility of escape. But this nightmarish vision of triumphant mechanization is, it must be said, also a myth.

In a central chapter of *Tristes Tropiques,* Lévi-Strauss studies the intricate body painting of the Caduveo Indians of Brazil: "Their faces, and sometimes even their whole bodies, were covered with a network of asymmetrical arabesques, alternating with delicate geometrical patterns." Lévi-Strauss is fascinated by these patterns, which look to him like the backs of European playing cards. The Indians, however, refuse to elucidate the reason for their decorations. Ultimately, he decides that the body paintings have a purely "sociological function." The Caduveos lacked complex social institutions (no Académie Française, no Bibliothèque Nationale), and the "mysterious appeal and seemingly gratuitous complexity" of the patterns were therefore "the phantasm of a society ardently and insatiably seeking a means of expressing symbolically the institutions it might have, if its interests and superstitions did not stand in the way."

His patronizing attitude toward the Indian spiritual culture reflected five hundred years of colonial repression and European snobbery. Lévi-Strauss barely alludes to the use of psychoactive plants among the Indians, although this use is the likely origin for the ornaments that fascinate him. He does not suspect that the body patterns might be a form of communion with a sacred reality that the Indians knew through their own visions, a knowledge they chose to hide from foreign interlopers.

When psychedelic drugs suddenly erupted as a force in Western consciousness in the 1960s, anthropologists began to wonder about their use in aboriginal societies. A few field-workers tentatively started to look deeper into the meaning of the hallucinogenic revelations known to the Indians. Some of them even tried the plants and potions for themselves as part of their fieldwork, but this testing was always done as an aside, a footnote appended to the real work they were doing. When these anthropologists interpreted what they saw, they mapped the visionary dimension back onto the sociological models they had learned in universities. Invested in the ideology of social science, they needed to prove that social codes always structured the visionary experience—they needed to prove it, and so they did.

In 1969, the anthropologist Gerardo Reichel-Dolmatoff wrote a paper on the Tukano Indians of Colombia and their use of *Banisteriopsis caapi* (a.k.a. ayahuasca or *yagé*): "For the anthropologist it is most intriguing that the Indians maintain that everything we would designate as *art* is inspired and based upon the hallucinatory experience." According to the Indians, their entire culture was based on ayahuasca: "They do not simply witness visual hallucinations but also hear music and see dances." Reichel-Dolmatoff tried the Tukano potion. He saw streams of constantly changing images: "like microphotographs of plants . . . like stained glass windows. . . . These things drawing near are like bodies . . . now they are like caterpillars with a lot of quills and fur . . . like certain ties in bad taste."

Reichel-Dolmatoff was able to deftly describe and analyze native customs and spiritual beliefs, but he was unable to find validity in his own visionary experience. Despite a trip that seems astonishingly transcultural, worthy of careful analysis, Reichel-Dolmatoff asserts, "in a state of hallucination the individual projects his cultural memory on the wavering screen of colors and shapes and thus 'sees' certain motifs and personages." Noting how the Tukano describe their visions to each other, the anthropologist is quick to add, "This open communication of experiences could lead to a consensus, to a fixation of certain images; in this manner, no matter what the vision, its interpretation could be adapted to a cultural pattern."

Around the same time, Marlene Dobkin de Rios studied rituals of ayahuasca healing among Mestizos in Iquitos, Peru, for her book *Visionary Vine*. During her own ayahuasca trip she saw "very fast moving imagery almost like Bosch's paintings . . . a series of leaf-faced visions . . . followed by a full-length colored vision of a Peruvian woman, unknown to me, but sneering in my direction." Afterward, she wrote, "No jungle creatures filled my visions. . . . The visions I had contained symbols of my own culture." Were "leaf-faced visions" really a part of her culture? The anthropologist's insistence that ayahuasca visions can only be a projection of "cultural memory," a reshuffling of "symbols" from one's own background, neatly conveys an impression of scientific objectivity while ignoring her actual experience.

In the late 1950s the anthropologist Michael Harner worked with the Jivaro Indians in the Amazon. At that point, "I did not fully appreciate the psychological impact of the *Banisteriopsis* drink upon the native view of reality." He did not appreciate it because he did not try it. A few years later, he drank a whopping dose of ayahuasca for himself, with a different tribe, the Conibo, in the Peruvian Amazon: "For several hours after drinking the brew, I found myself, although awake, in a world literally beyond my wildest dreams. I met bird-headed people, as well as dragon-like creatures who explained that they were the true gods of this world. I enlisted the services of other spirit helpers in attempting to fly through the far reaches of the Galaxy." The next day, he told a blind shaman about the dragons who said they had created the world. The shaman smiled knowingly. "Oh, they're always saying that. But they are only the Masters of Outer Darkness."

Harner had encountered an overwhelming alternate reality that could not be ignored, explained away, or sociologically pigeonholed. "Transported into a trance where the supernatural seemed natural, I realized that anthropologists, including myself, had profoundly underestimated the importance of the drug in affecting native ideology." Ever since that night, Harner has devoted himself to understanding shamanism. He started an Institute of Shamanic Studies in the United States, attempting to teach shamanic techniques of drumming and healing to Westerners.

Harner was a modern anthropologist who went into the field armed with all of Lévi-Strauss's tools of analytic distancing. While Lévi-Strauss preserved his flawless ironic detachment and outsider status, Harner, animated by the inquisitive spirit of a different generation, took the professional risk of testing the native's sacred reality for himself. There he found something much stranger and more astonishing than a "handful of ashes." He found a magical theater within his own mind where the supernatural was performing a spectacle that was as real as waking reality, more tangible than any dream. This spectacle had no connection to his expectations or his beliefs—it was not a product of his personal identity, his Freudian unconscious. It was not the faulty wiring of his synapses blowing a fuse. It was the revelation of a different order, a profound and arcane otherness. The revelation spun around the entire compass of Harner's thought. It transformed his life.

History is a process of awakening, of bringing into awareness the "not-yet conscious knowledge" of what has been. The plants that produce visions can function—for those of us who have inherited the New World Order of barren materialism, cut off from our spiritual heritage by a spiteful culture that gives us nothing but ashes—as the talismans of recognition that awaken our minds to reality.

Part Five

THE MEDICINE

The purpose of taking [yagé] is to return to the uterus . . . where the individual "sees" the tribal divinities, the creation of the universe and humanity, the first human couple, the creation of the animals, and the establishment of the social order.
—GERARDO REICHEL-DOLMATOFF,
Flesh of the Gods

We have drunk the Soma; we have become immortal; we have gone to the light; we have found the gods. What can hatred and the malice of a mortal do to us now, O immortal one?
—*Rig Veda* (C. 1000 B.C.)

Chapter 21

THE PURGE

"I was on all fours convulsed with spasms of nausea," William Burroughs wrote to Allen Ginsberg, describing a *yagé* session. "I could hear retching and groaning as if I was someone else. I was lying by a rock. Hours must have passed."

The year was 1953. Burroughs went down to Colombia searching for *yagé*. At that time, the drug was virtually unknown in the West. The thirty-nine-year-old Burroughs had heard rumors of it as "the ultimate kick" and as a potential cure for heroin addiction.

Burroughs was a desperate man. An aging trust-fund brat, heroin-addicted, homosexual, Burroughs had killed his wife several years earlier, drunkenly shooting her through the head at their home in Mexico City. It was a party trick gone wrong, but Burroughs knew it was more than that. He felt he was possessed by evil spirits, that he was damned. He went to the Amazon in search of *yagé*, hoping his visions could redeem or exorcise him somehow, that the hallucinogen would free him from his dependence on junk. In Bogotá, he met the legendary Harvard botanist and Amazonian explorer Richard Schultes. The two Harvard alumni hit it off. Burroughs attached himself to one of Schultes's botanical expeditions.

He took the plant brew with several *brujos* in the Amazon jungle.

After some misfires, Burroughs was given his visions—not visions of light and life and self-regeneration, but visions of dark mergings and dissolutions and horror. "Larval beings passed before my eyes in a blue haze, each one giving an obscene, mocking squawk (I later identified this squawking as the croaking of frogs)," he wrote to Ginsberg after an early session in which he vomited six times.

"*Yagé* is space time travel," he wrote from Peru, after many misadventures and traumatic trips. "The room seems to shake and vibrate with motion. The blood and substance of many races, Negro, Polynesian, Mountain Mongol, Desert Nomad, Polyglot Near East, Indian— new races as yet unconceived and unborn, combinations not yet realized passes through your body."

The drink gave Burroughs entry to the "Composite City where all human potentials are spread out in a vast silent market. . . . The city is visited by epidemics of violence and the untended dead are eaten by vultures in the street." Although he only took *yagé* a few times, it is possible to argue that the *yagé* visions had a much deeper effect on his fiction than his use of heroin. His Amazonian visions of a sleazed-out "composite city" became the atmosphere of *Naked Lunch,* written a few years later, with its dissolutions of identity; urban wastes of festering plagues, sex manias, and sadistic control freaks. Even the montage-like breaks that characterize his mature style call to mind the overlapping hallucinations of the Amazonian brew.

The infinite murmuring vista of urban sleaze and cheap kicks and blank death that Burroughs discovered on *yagé* was probably not the vision he wanted. But it was the vision he needed.

. . .

I THINK THAT, even before I tried ayahuasca, I had some intuition about what it was. In the Amazon, *yagé* is "the medicine," "the purge," "the vine of souls," "the rope of death." It is the substance that reveals the Amazonian Indian cosmology, source of indigenous wisdom. The shamans of the Amazon say that all of their knowledge, of the plants and the spirit world, comes from ayahuasca.

We live in a culture where everything is designed for our comfort or entertainment but nothing satisfies. At our core, we remain insatiable, constantly on the prowl for new commodities and pleasant sensations to fill the void. "Life tastes good," proclaims an ad for Coca-Cola. *Yagé*, on the other hand, tastes extremely bad. It is a bitter concoction, made of the bark of a vine and the leaves of a shrub. The flavor is like the distilled essence of forest rot. *Yagé* drinkers vomit and shit, shiver and sweat, and at the same time receive outrageously beautiful visions. The potion is an antidote—following Benjamin, I am tempted to say a dialectical cure—for our current condition. As a hipster shaman told me at Burning Man, "White man medicine make you feel good first, bad later. Indian medicine make you feel bad first, good later." Many people report feeling both physically and psychically recharged after *yagé*. I certainly do.

I first drank the brew with strangers, wearing Adult Depends diapers and a blindfold, sitting in a small, drab apartment overlooking the East River. New Age–sounding tribal music played on a tape deck. Initially, I saw, as Burroughs had, images of gray squalor—corpses lying in the gutter of an anarchic slum, pigs gnawing on them. I had a momentary vision of bright emerald-green vines waving in front of a blue waterfall. Afterward, for a long time, there was nothing else. I listened to the gasping and retching of the woman sitting across from me. She was horribly sick for hours. The guides tried to help her, but to no avail.

The Indians revere ayahuasca for its healing powers. The purging of parasites and toxins is part of the healing process. I felt as if an alien intelligence was coursing through me, examining my organs and nerves and cellular processes, making subtle adjustments. It was like I was a computer and ayahuasca was a program performing scans and repairs. When it had done its work, I threw up—the vomiting was like the beep at the end of a program.

My thoughts drifted off. I watched a scene taking place within my mind. Particles, like little flares of light, gathered into clouds that floated upward—when they arose, the focus of my awareness would suddenly shift to a different subject. I realized I was watching a model of thinking, of the neurochemical process of my subconscious creating thoughts. These clouds were synaptic concentrations, neural nets; one after another, they floated to the surface of my consciousness. When the information reached a sufficient density, "I" would be presented with a new perception.

This vision was a small revelation. I realized that most thoughts are impersonal happenings, like self-assembling machines. Unless we train ourselves, the thoughts passing through our mind have little involvement with our will. It is strange to realize that even our own thoughts pass by like scenery out the window of a bus, a bus we took by accident while trying to get somewhere else. Most of the time, thinking is an autonomous process, something that happens outside of our control. This perception of the machinelike quality of the self is something many people discover, then try to overcome, through meditation.

· · ·

AYAHUASCA is highly sophisticated jungle chemistry. The Amazonian potion usually consists of two ingredients, the bark of the ayahuasca vine (*Banisteriopsis caapi*, which grows in thick double-helix-shaped coils around rain forest trees) and the leaves of *Psychotria viridis* or some other plant. The vine contains a class of psychoactive and sedating drugs called beta-carbolines, which includes harmine and harmaline. The leaves have dimethyltryptamine (DMT) in them, a highly potent hallucinogen that is also produced within the human body, found in the base of the spine and the brain. Although powerful when extracted and smoked, DMT is not orally active. Monoamine oxidase (MAO) enzymes in the gut break it down before it reaches the brain. You can eat pounds of the stuff without feeling any effect. However, the beta-carbolines in the vine are natural MAO inhibitors, which means they allow the DMT to work. The ayahuasca brew, according to Santo Daime, a Brazilian religion that takes *yagé* as its sacrament, is a combination of the "force" of the vine and the "light" of the leaves.

DMT, smoked alone, creates a rapid-fire visionary experience, an overwhelming immersion in an extremely alien world that lasts less than ten minutes. The beta-carbolines, taken alone, create subtle, monochromatic hallucinations that are soft, warm, and humanized. A friend of mine described seeing compassionate maternal faces floating above him after a strong dose. Mixed together in the ayahuasca brew, the beta-carbolines seem to have a pacifying and humanizing effect on the DMT visions, acting like an interface, and they stretch the experience out from a few minutes to a few hours. It is unknown how Indians, living among hundreds of thousands of plants in the forest, learned to combine these botanical ingredients, which are usually boiled together for several hours. The Indians say that the ayahuasca vine taught them how to do it.

. . .

THE MORE I learned about it, the more I was fascinated by ayahuasca. Even the taste seemed to change in my memory from something simply horrible to something horrible that I yearned to taste again. But the opportunities to find it in New York were few and far between. Finally, a year after that first session, I found the right ingredients and cooked up a brew for myself and two friends. I used plants that differed from the traditional Amazonian sources. In the last decades, many other plants have been found with identical chemical compounds, sometimes in much more concentrated amounts. Botanists have discovered DMT, especially, in a wide range of flora, including some common grasses. My brew was made from the reddish DMT-containing bark of *Mimosa hostilis* and a black powdered extract of Syrian Rue (*Peganum harmala*), a Near Eastern plant that produces a mixture of beta-carbolines, like the ayahuasca vine. Syrian Rue has an ancient history of ritual use in the Near East. Some researchers have suggested that the reddish geometrical-patterned hallucinations caused by ingesting Syrian Rue may be the historical origin of the patterns on Arabian carpets, as well as the source of the Arabian myth of flying carpets.

I followed the recipes of Jonathan Ott, whose book *Ayahuasca Analogues* describes how to make ayahuascalike compounds using plants from every hemisphere. "I hope the simple home technology described in this book will drive the last nail into the coffin of the evil and hypocritical . . . crusade to eliminate this class of drugs from the face of the earth," he writes in his introduction. "May the Entheogenic Reformation prevail over the Pharmacratic Inquisition. . . ."

Cutting up the plant matter, grinding it into powder, and boiling it down took an entire afternoon. The woodsy aroma of the broth permeated the apartment. Within an hour of drinking the vile stuff, both of my friends threw up violently and repeatedly. They thought I had poisoned them.

Soon enough, shuddering, I followed them to the bathroom and threw up. Afterward I felt, spreading through me, a magnificent sensation. I felt cleansed and strong as the *yagé* opened my visionary capacity. I lay on the couch as my psychic periscope rose into the imaginal realms.

Images coiled around the sounds from the stereo. We played Javanese gamelan, Ravi Shankar, Ornette Coleman, Bach. The dead skin around perception was peeled away to reveal new levels of sensory subtlety. Music was like a physical event permeating the cells, opening new pathways through the psyche with every change in phrase.

Images crowded into my mind—faint, fragmentary, flickering. I entered viny jungles, shot through the abandoned reaches of outer space. Pictures formed and dispersed at high speed. Geometric mandala patterns appeared and faded. I watched twisting forms that were tubular, tentacular. Suddenly I seemed to be on a spaceship. The creatures piloting the ship shook their long spindly limbs at me in greeting. They were plantlike, undulating their stalks and blossoms to show me their otherworld comedy.

I removed my blindfold and looked around. The room was shimmering, pulsing with waves of light. I felt I was inside the liquid material, the flowing invisible currents, of my dreams. The hallucinations seemed to happen in a psychic space between willing and letting go. If I tried to force the visions, they evaporated. If I didn't pursue them, they also disappeared. There was, I realized, a skill to perceiving them, an internal effort that required utilizing a form of visionary seeing that was disconnected from normal sight.

I held a metaphysical dialogue, unsure if I was conversing with some higher aspect of myself or the plant-spirit or both. I tried to interrogate that elusive "other" about the nature of life and death, the holographic universe, the spirit realms. The response was something like a suppressed giggle.

The thought came to me that human consciousness is like a flower that blossoms from the earth. The stem and the roots are invisible cords, etheric filaments that lead back to a greater, extradimensional being. Our separation from that larger being was only a temporary illusion. The universe was, we would know if we could perceive its workings, purposeful and good.

Then I was looking up from my grave as dirt was thrown on my coffin. Yet this horror-movie vantage point didn't bother me. It made me feel calm.

We were listening to Ravi Shankar play the sitar, a woman singing with him. The music was a seductive whispering tale. Each slow melodic riff announced itself, then insinuated its message like a teasing sexual possibility. Images and ideas licked out like tongues of shape-shifting flame. There were rainbow-tinged tunnels drawing me forward, visual echoes of cartoon carnivals, and sideways entries to schizoid paradises of paradox. At the end of the night I saw, very clearly, a multiarmed Shiva dancing before me. He broke apart into flimmering octopus arms, writhing plant forms. Soon after that, the visions ended.

That night, my two friends had little to report besides extreme nausea and an expansion of their senses. Later, after other successful and failed trips, I understood that that is part of the deal with ayahuasca. Compared to other psychedelics, *yagé*'s effects are extremely unpredictable, depending perhaps on the weather, the dream you had the night before, the position of the stars. It can unveil the shamanic rainbow, access the universal serpent-power, or it can leave you vomiting and visionless. In a perverse way, for me at least, that is part of what makes the brew so appealing. Unlike LSD or mushrooms or ecstasy, *yagé* cannot be commodified or consumed recreationally; its gnosis must be earned.

Chapter 22

MY SHAMANIC VACATION

In October 2000, two months after Burning Man, I visited the Secoya Indians, a small tribe of 750 in the Ecuadorean Amazon. The Secoya live on the Rio Aguarico, a river winding through the largest unroaded stretch of rain forest left in the world. Later I learned that the Secoya are respected among the neighboring Indian groups for the purity of their ayahuasca tradition. Like many Amazonian tribes, the Secoya have been decimated over the last century by disease and forced acculturation. Their last great shaman is Don Caesario, a small and frail man in his eighties.

"The Secoya culture is based on communion with the 'heavenly people' who live along the river and in the sky," said Jonathon, the ethnobotanist who organized my trip. "They drink *yagé* to see them."

Don Caesario usually maintained the distanced but regal demeanor of someone with command over the deep mystical realms. He resembled a high Tibetan lama, with Asiatic features and the large ears of the spiritually advanced. He was often seated quietly on a hammock, wearing crisscrossing necklaces made from painted seeds, a knee-length white tunic, and a yellow crown—the traditional garb of the Secoya.

On my first morning in the jungle, Don Caesario stood inches away from me in a long dugout canoe. He did not radiate calm. He was shaking with rage, brandishing a loaded shotgun. A few days ago, Don Caesario's personal canoe and outboard motor—worth about $4,000, a lifetime's wages for the average Secoya—had been stolen. The shaman demanded vengeance.

The expedition included a group of male Secoyas ranging from elders to young boys. Also a few of the assistants employed by Sentient Experientials, the tour group, as well as four foolish tourists including myself. At the helm of the boat, John Bella, a gung-ho rain forest activist and junior member of the Sentient staff, held a hunting rifle that I hoped he wouldn't try to use. The Sentient staff was a nebulous group that included a healer from California, a sullen masseuse from Colombia, a shaggy-bearded cook, others whose roles I never figured out, and some Quechua Indians. Also traveling with us was Pablo Amaringo, a painter known for his wonderful and intricate renderings of ayahuasca visions. A gentle man and art teacher, Amaringo had been a Peruvian *ayahuasquero* for many years, drinking *yagé* every day. He said he started to have visions of a witch who was trying to kill him every time he took *yagé*. He realized that he would have to kill her if he wanted to remain a shaman. He decided to give up his practice instead.

I was sitting next to Mark Miller, a psychologist in a tie-dyed T-shirt.

"What am I doing here?" Mark asked, as the canoe churned the waters of the Aguarico River, a muddy channel flowing from Ecuador to Colombia. "I've got a wife and baby back home."

Don Caesario raised his gun. In Spanish he shouted, "I will kill the thieves when I find them."

Mark and I had been invited along by Jonathon Miller-Weisberger, a Berkeley-born, Ecuador-raised, Jewish botanist with a penchant for quoting the Tao. He had organized this tour. He was also the founder of Grupo Osanimi, an organization that works on cultural-revival projects with Ecuadorean tribes. Most of the profits from this trip would go to benefit Grupo Osanimi's projects. During our two weeks in the jungle, Jonathon wanted us to get a full dose of Amazonian life. He explained that theft along the Aguarico, once almost unheard of, was becoming common as conditions deteriorated: Mestizos were settling on isolated plots of land between the territories belonging to the Siona, the Secoya, and the Quechua. They eked out a living by growing coffee beans and corn, and the most unscrupulous among them tried to take advantage of the Indians.

Meanwhile, the U.S. government was pouring $1.5 billion into Plan Colombia, making war on the guerrillas, and attempting to annihilate the coca fields hidden along the Ecuadorean-Colombian border. From planes, they were spraying massive amounts of Round-Up, a deadly poisonous herbicide developed by Monsanto, that apparently laid waste to large swathes of the jungle, destroying uncountable species including ayahuasca—and poisoning the fish in the rivers, according to the Indians. It was unknown to what extent the underground coca industry was damaged by this indiscriminate eco-cide. The Secoya feared Colombian guerrillas sneaking into Ecuador—in fact, the guerrillas may have stolen the canoe. To add to the anxiety, we were in a region where desperadoes had been kidnapping American and European oil-company workers with alarming regularity. The tension thickened to match the equatorial humidity as we scanned the silent, sticky jungle for enemies.

After several hours we came upon the canoe chained in front of a ramshackle homestead. A path from the riverbank led up to thatched huts shaded by the shiny leaves of coffee bushes. Families—a few scared men, mothers, children, blacks, and Mestizos in cheap Western clothes—watched us hesitantly from the shore. It was impossible to read their faces. Were they guilty and ashamed? Cunning and deceitful? Were other settlers, rifles drawn, targeting us from behind the trees?

Don Caesario and some of the Secoya jumped into the canoe and cut it loose. Heated words were exchanged. The shaman's lips trembled in fury as he raised his shotgun and pointed it at the frightened leaders of the homesteaders.

Mark and I looked at each other. We were caught between our shaman's sight line and his enemies. It did not seem like a safe place to be.

Jonathon leapt out of the boat and stepped in front of the settlers. The Secoya gunned the motor and piloted Don Caesario away. Shots rang out—the sound of our spiritual leader emptying his chambers into the air.

We met Jonathon in Quito, Ecuador's capital, where the country's sudden switch to a U.S.-dollar economy, due to an IMF-engineered debt crisis, was spurring massive inflation and riots. Our group was booked at Casa del Sol, a small hotel staffed by Quechua Indians, on Avenida José Calama. Calama was *turista* central, a street of hotels, bars, and hostels. Recently wired to the Net, it was home to an alarming number of new cyber cafes—pool.net, papaya.net, earth.net—blaring pop music and selling multihued fruit drinks. Young backpackers, ranging from the hip and dreadlocked to the preppy and generic, sat before banks of terminals, e-mailing their friends back home about their romantic hook-ups, visa problems, and stomachaches. But the multicultural buzz of the cafes was muted by the black-uniformed guards who stood in the street with dogs and automatic weapons, protecting the gringos from the ever-present threat of kidnappers and thieves.

Jonathon had rented a bus to take us from Quito. We drove through the cloud forests of the Andes, descending into the Amazon in a bumpy twelve-hour ride. This ride tattooed on our eyeballs the devastation wrought by the oil industry. The roads built by the oil companies had opened up the jungle to loggers and poor, desperate Mestizo settlers. All thoughts of visionary Indians and mystic revelations were wiped away by the blunt reality of the pipeline running inexorably beside the road, surrounded by recently clear-cut land, like a snake sucking the marrow out of the jungle.

We spent the night at Lago Agrio, the Dodge City of Ecuador, population 25,000 and growing. It was a ragged boomtown of two industries: oil and prostitution. Ten years ago, the area was virgin rain forest; now it was slashed-and-burnt scrub. Once it is destroyed, the rain forest does not regenerate, and the local climate quickly becomes too hot and dry for farming. The land, for all practical purposes, becomes useless.

Our bus driver and his buddy returned with sheepish grins from a night on the town. They bragged about the teenage prostitutes who could be had for two dollars at the local whorehouses. I thought of the chain of dehumanization and exploitation beginning with the oil company's quest for profit, the American consumer's avidity for cheap gas to fuel SUVs, the corrupt governments of bankrupt Third World countries seeking payoffs, ending with despoiled rain forests and teenage

Mestizo girls contracting AIDS from drunk ditch diggers in Third World backwaters. Benjamin's "religion of destruction" was performing its good works.

The next day we rode for four hours on motorized canoes, on the mud-brown Rio Aguarico, ever-deeper into the jungle, surrounded by its secretive green density. We passed through the territories of neighboring Indian tribes. As night fell, we were brought to the rough stone steps leading up to the house of Don Caesario.

· · ·

OVER THE LAST 300 years, the Secoya have lost their ancestral homeland and 98 percent of their population. Decimated by the diseases of the Spanish conquerors, enslaved and forced to work on rubber plantations, a tribe of more than 30,000 has been reduced to a paltry 750. Almost half live on the Rio Aguarico, the rest in the remote jungles of Peru.

Across the Amazon, Indian cultures have been compromised and quickly destroyed through contact with the West. Vast treasures of botanical knowledge and linguistic and spiritual traditions are already gone. As the force of the colonialists and their Christian missionaries overwhelmed the Indians, followed by ruthless rubber tappers and then even more ruthless oil corporations, the tribal shamans lost their authority. Many were accused, often by missionaries, of witchcraft. Shamans have even been murdered by Indians looking for scapegoats to blame for the collapse of their world.

In the United States and Europe, shamans have been reappropriated as heroic figures by anthropologists, psychedelic avatars like Terence McKenna, and New Age populists. But the fact is that ambiguity hovers over shamanism wherever it appears. The magical powers acquired through disciplined use of ayahuasca can be turned to good or evil. *The Yagé Drinker* is the autobiography of the famous Secoya shaman Fernando Payaguaje, compiled from interviews with his grandsons. Payaguaje spoke about the temptation of sorcery: "Some people drink yagé only to the point of reaching the power to practice witchcraft; with these crafts they can kill people. A much greater effort and consumption of yagé are required to reach the highest level, where one gains access to the visions and powers of healing." Michael Harner, studying the shamanism of the Jivaro (or Shuar) Indians of the Amazon, noted that Jivaro shamans wielded magical darts, *tsentsak,* that could be used either to cure or kill. The Jivaro, like most tribal groups, lived in constant fear of witchcraft. Sorcery is the inescapable shadow side of shamanism.

The modern West, engaged in a neoshamanic renaissance, has so far ignored the ambiguous aspects of shamanism. The American anthropologist Michael F. Brown finds it unsettling "that New Age America seeks to embrace shamanism without any appreciation of its context. For my Santa Fe acquaintances, tribal lore is a super-market from which they choose some tidbits while spurning others." Among the Indians, "Shamanism affirms life but also spawns violence and death. The beauty of shamanism is matched by its power— and like all forms of power found in society, it inspires its share of discontent."

Westerners who have rediscovered magic and spirit as living facts of human existence, transformed in their own inner being by the knowledge, yearn to reintroduce these forces to the contemporary world. Yet these elemental forces cannot be divorced from ambiguity, from danger. Magic shades into witchcraft, communicating with the spirit realm is a step away from occult invocation. Bringing this knowledge back into contemporary life requires reckoning with dark forces, a delicate balancing act that is intrinsic to shamanism.

"Ayahuasca tourism," a growing phenomenon throughout South America, reflects the surge of underground interest in ayahuasca in the United States. Precise figures are hard to come by, but one could estimate that there are hundreds of shamans, ranging from authentic to ambiguous to fraudulent, receiving thousands of Western visitors annually. Websites devoted to the vine keep multiplying, along with new books: *The Cosmic Serpent,* by Jeremy Narby; *Ayahuasca: Human Consciousness and the Spirits of Nature,* edited by Ralph Metzner; and *Ayahuasca Visions,* by Pablo Amaringo and Eduardo Luna, to name only a few. Magazines like *Shaman's Drum* promote group tours to visit Mestizo shamans across the Amazon for a few weeks of fasting and "journeying."

Some critics attack these excursions for marketing native spirituality and further degrading Amazonian traditions. The anthropologist Marlene Dobkin de Rios, author of *Visionary Vine,* a book on *yagé* healing in Peru, believes that Americans are driven to shamanic adventures by the syndrome of the "empty self," the inner void left by our materialistic culture. In the introduction to his book *Ayahuasca Analogues,* Jonathan Ott bemoans ayahuasca tourism in the Amazon, "which can only disrupt the evanescent remnant of preliterate religiosity struggling to make a place for itself in the modern world, while attracting the wrong kind of political attention to ayahuasca."

It seems to me that these perspectives are shortsighted, not only because the shamans themselves have the vision of sharing their knowledge with Westerners, but also because *yagé* tourism, if it is done conscientiously, is a force that can help to preserve indigenous traditions at this point. This is what seems to be happening with the Secoya. There are not going to be any "pure" Indian cultures anymore, certainly no illiterate ones. After decades of seeing their cultures trashed by missionaries, assaulted by Western governments, overrun by corporate greed, the Indians need to know that certain groups of rich Westerners value their knowledge and history. The *yagé* tours are, in fact, beneficial to both sides: The shamans desperately need the revenue, and we, equally desperately, need the revelations.

Sentient Experientials did not explicitly use *yagé* to promote their journeys to Secoya territory. Don Caesario was not paid for his shamanism; instead, he was compensated for his hospitality with gifts, such as his house and canoe. Beholden to no one, he could skip the ceremonies entirely if he did not like the attitude of the group.

I fervently hoped he wouldn't do that to us.

. . .

AFTER THE RECOVERY of the boat, we settled in for a twelve-day stay. The women set up tents while most of the men slept on hammocks under the shaman's thatched roof, where the elders and an ever-rotating number of Secoya families also lived. Several times I returned to my hammock in the afternoon to find a tiny baby sleeping in it.

Among our group of hopeful psychonauts, the largest contingent, surprisingly, was made up of feisty middle-aged women—social workers, therapists, academics, and housewives—some white-haired, most wearing fanny packs and Tevas. Two were graduates of the California Institute of Integral Studies, a kind of New Age think tank. There was also Octavia Martin, a pensive Native American artist who lived on a reservation in Massachusetts. We did not seem likely candidates for a trek into the deep jungle; our campsite was a three-hour canoe trip away from a phone or hospital. I was especially worried about Annie Bush, a psychotherapist whose large body suggested the soft excesses of suburban living (later she outhiked me through the forest). There were two other guys in their thirties following a personal "vision quest."

"I do what the Great Spirit tells me to do," said Mark, the therapist, only half-joking. He had gone on a thousand-mile peyote hunt, the annual rite of the Huichol Indians in Mexico, with a Huichol shamaness. Nervous about *yagé*, he called taking psychedelics "going into 'The Mystery.' "

Andrew Doxer, a rail-thin teacher in a Boston after-school program, regularly visited a Mestizo shaman in Peru to take *yagé* and fast. He wanted to follow the "shamanic path." The first time he drank the brew, Andrew said, he saw a visible current of energy flow up into him from the floor. He realized, in a flash, that he should be working with children. After that, he stopped having visions, which was frustrating. Yet he was ready for another dose.

Our group also included Tamara Swingle, a cheerful twenty-three-year-old botany student from Washington State, small, blond, and muscular. John Emerson, a well-traveled beekeeper from Hawaii, looked like a spy from a Graham Greene novel in his Panama hat and khaki suit. Jean-Michel Taub, a French businessman, reminded me of Pepe Le Peu, the insufferable French skunk from Warner Bros. cartoons. While mocking American consumerism, Jean-Michel brought a handheld global-positioning device to the jungle. (He offered to explain its workings to Don Caesario: "No, thanks," the shaman replied gruffly. "I already know where I am.")

Almost instantly, our group started to succumb to the jungle conditions. On the second day, Tammy, seemingly the fittest of us all, caught a raging stomach bug. Hae Soog Jo, a Korean academic from Berkeley, developed a severe infection on her foot. A few others bumbled into a hive and were attacked by angry bees. The casualties crept back to their tents or hammocks, where they lay, dazed by the intense midday heat, making the rest of us feel lucky.

Chapter 23

MEET THE SNAKE

Jeremy Narby was a young anthropologist studying the Ashaninca Indians in the Peruvian Amazon when he first took ayahuasca in the mid-1980s. The Indians had told him that ayahuasca was the source of their plant knowledge. They called it "forest television." Narby was interested, though skeptical.

He was less skeptical an hour after drinking the brew, when he found himself surrounded by two huge snakes, fifty-foot boas, who spoke telepathically to him, putting him in his place: "They explain that I am just a human being. I feel my mind crack, and in the fissures, I see the bottomless arrogance of my presuppositions. It is profoundly true that I am just a human being, and, most of the time, I have the impression of understanding everything, whereas here I find myself in a more powerful reality that I do not understand at all and that, in my arrogance, I did not even suspect existed." Later, the shaman tells him the snakes are known as "the mother of ayahuasca."

Ayahuasca, as Ralph Metzner noted, is a "gnostic catalyst." It opens the door to those occult dimensions of psychic reality that are vigorously denied by modern rationalism. Like Michael Harner a generation earlier, Narby found himself forced to reevaluate his anthropological stance and his own beliefs after drinking *yagé*. His book, *The*

Cosmic Serpent, is an attempt to interpret the visionary realms opened by ayahuasca in a way that might fit with a scientific worldview. He finds that the motif of snakes, especially twin serpents—the caduceus of Hermes and the sign of Western medicine—appears worldwide in archaic myths of creation, and as kundalini, the Hindu occult symbol of the life force. Narby links the serpent or tangled snakes often beheld through ayahuasca with the twisted and twinned coils of DNA. He theorizes, "In their visions shamans manage to take their consciousness down to the molecular level." Shamans, according to Narby, receive images and information from DNA. DNA, a snakelike string of coded data, is also an aperiodic crystal, four atoms wide, that beams out photons. "The global network of DNA-based life emits ultra-weak radio waves, which are currently at the limit of measurement, but which we can nonetheless perceive . . . in hallucinations and in dreams," he writes. He theorizes that this transmission is the "vegetable gnosis" and collective consciousness of the natural world.

Detouring into molecular biology, Narby explores genetics and the Darwinian theory of natural selection. He finds that Darwin's theory does not seem to fit the development of the genetic code, an incredibly complex language packaged with a high-tech transcription program that appeared with the first bacteria 3.5 billion years ago. The theory of natural selection also has to be stretched to explain the sudden explosion of animal species that started 543 million years in the past.

"Throughout the fossil record, species seem to appear suddenly, fully formed and equipped with all sorts of specialized organs, then remain stable for millions of years," Narby writes. Other psychedelic avatars share Narby's suspicion that what is going on in evolution is more than the result of endless chemical reactions. As pioneering LSD psychoanalyst Stanislav Grof wrote, "The probability that human intelligence developed all the way from the chemical ooze of the primeval ocean solely through random sequences of random mechanical processes has been aptly compared to the probability of a tornado blowing through a gigantic junkyard and assembling by accident a 747 jumbo jet."

Even Francis Crick, one of the discoverers of the DNA double helix, found it necessary to advance the thesis that the building blocks of organic life arrived on meteorites to explain how the gene code could have developed. Of course, like the theory that extraterrestrials bred us for experimentation, such a hypothesis resolves nothing and only adds to the mystery.

Narby suggests that the scientific adherence to the theory of natural selection is a form of faith. His book falls within "the blind spot of the rational and fragmented gaze of contemporary biology." Against the postulates of reductive materialism, Narby believes that "DNA in particular and nature in general are minded. This contravenes the founding principle of the molecular biology that is the current orthodoxy." He suspects that the ayahuasca vine may be exactly what the shamans say it is: The sentient spirit of nature, the mind of the forest, which directly communicates with human beings through this chemical interface.

Narby makes a laudable effort to study ayahuasca by accepting that the *ayahuasqueros* possess real knowledge, rather than assuming, as most Westerners have for centuries, that the shamans were either schizophrenic, deluded, fakers, or at best fabulators. It is increasingly clear that shamanic practices have validity—for healing, for spiritual regeneration, and telepathic communication, among others. It remains difficult for scientists to approach the subject rationally because shamans work with invisible psychic currents, "supersensible" forces, and the existence of such forces, such as the subtle currents recognized by Eastern traditions, are beyond the perimeters of what our tools can measure at this point. The existence of what cannot be quantified is not only ignored but vehemently denied by Western scientists, who forget that "absence of evidence is not evidence of absence." How can the rational perspective of the West comprehend a technology that makes use of invisible and seemingly unmeasurable forces? That will be a subject for the new century to explore. As Terence McKenna wrote, "Shamans speak of 'spirit' the way a quantum physicist might speak of 'charm'; it is a technical gloss for a very complicated concept."

The Cosmic Serpent is only one of many recent efforts by Western thinkers to reinterpret the meaning of ayahuasca shamanism for the new world order. In *Shamanism, Colonialism, and the Wild Man,* anthropologist Michael Taussig interprets *yagé* shamanism in Colombia, where ancient rituals have taken on new meanings in the wake of the cruel excesses of colonialism. Taussig's indigenous sorcerers exorcise the legacy of colonialist terror through laughter and improvisation, "building and rebuilding neocolonial healing rituals wherein fate is wrested from the hands of God and transcribed into a domain of chance and perhapsness." Most anthropologists believe that all religious rituals work to order and unify society. Taussig finds the opposite with *yagé*: The ceremonies open up a transcendent space for chaos. He quotes from Roland Barthes's *Image, Music, Text* on the idea of a "third" or "obtuse meaning," outside of what can be expressed in language or defined by cultural analysis:

> . . . the obtuse meaning appears to extend outside culture, knowledge, information; analytically it has something derisory about it; opening out into the infinity of language, it can come through as limited in the eyes of analytic reason; it belongs to the family of pun, buffoonery, useless expenditure. Indifferent to moral or aesthetic categories (the trivial, the futile, the false, the pastiche), it is on the side of the carnival.

For Taussig, shamanism preserves a place for knowledge that can heal because it falls outside of any system. *Yagé* visions open up constellations of the unknown, obtuse meanings, and "chance and perhapsness."

Narby collected some of the more nuanced accounts of shamanic practices in an anthology, *Shamans Through Time*. Read chronologically, the essays in the book make it clear that terms for studying spirituality, shamanism, and mysticism are starting to shift radically. Recent texts include one from the anthropologist Edith Turner, who recalls seeing "a spirit form" during an exorcism ritual in Zambia:

"I saw with my own eyes a large grey blob of plasma emerge from the sick woman's back," she writes. "Then I knew the Africans were right, there is spirit affliction, it isn't a matter of metaphor and symbol, or even psychology. And I began to see how anthropologists have perpetrated an endless series of put-downs in regard to the many spirit events in which they have participated—participated in a kindly pretense." Transformed by her own experiences, Turner decries the "religious frigidity" of modern anthropologists.

The anthropologist Françoise Barbira Freedman studied the Lamista Indians in the Peruvian Amazon. In the book *The Ayahuasca*

Reader, she tells how she apprenticed herself to a tribal shaman, taking ayahuasca and learning about the local tensions between sorcerers and shamans. "As I progressed in my apprenticeship, the increased awareness that there was no neutral position within reach frightened me," she writes. "I was now in the game." During one ayahuasca trip, she experienced animal transformation firsthand. She became a jaguar stalking through the forest. The elder shaman visited her in the form of an eagle, communicating telepathically. "Nothing I ever read about shamanic animal metamorphosis could have prepared me for the total involvement of my senses, body, mind, in this process." This vision was a sign of acquisition of certain shamanic powers, but she was told by the shaman that it also carried dangers with it. From then on, if she continued learning, she would have to constantly protect herself from sorcerers and malevolent spirits by magical means. Freedman decided to end her apprenticeship at this point. "There was no longer any possible vantage point for me as an anthropologist other than that of the shamanic rainbow," she notes. She wonders how the moral structures of Western culture can absorb or adapt this ancient and ambiguous practice.

For his part, Narby thinks ayahuasca could be a valuable tool for the modern biologist, who could use the substance to interrogate the "mind of nature" directly. Recently, Narby brought three European molecular biologists down to visit an Amazonian shaman. During their trances, they attempted to ask direct questions of the ayahuasca spirit relating to their areas of research. All received answers to their queries. For example, one genetic researcher found herself transformed into a protein flying above a long DNA strand, and was able in this way to understand the meaning of certain patterns in what had previously been considered "junk DNA":

> She saw DNA sequences known as "CpG islands," which she had been puzzling over at work, and which are found upstream of about sixty percent of all human genes. She saw they were structurally different from the surrounding DNA and that this structural difference allowed them to be easily accessed and therefore to serve as "landing pads" for transcription proteins, which dock on to the DNA molecule and make copies of precise genetic structures.

All of the biologists were intrigued by what they found, and two of the three felt they had communicated with an "independent intelligence."

When Dennis McKenna, Terence's botanist brother, drank ayahuasca with the Uniao do Vegetal, a Brazilian syncretic religion that uses ayahuasca as its sacrament, he was turned into a sentient water molecule in the jungle soil, pulled up through a vine's roots to experience the miraculous molecular processes of photosynthesis in its leaves. "Somehow I understood—though no words were involved—that the *Banisteriopsis* vine was the embodiment of the plant intelligence that embraced and covered the earth," he recalled. At the end of his vision, a voice told him, "You monkeys only think you're running things."

Yagé opens up a playful zone of "chance and perhapsness," yet it seems to convey particular messages about the biological world, and often creates specific models of natural processes. More than other psychedelics, ayahuasca seems to dissolve the rigid categories that modern culture has erected between poetry and science, medicine and magic, knowledge of the self and knowledge of the universe. If the "Vine of Souls" was a trademarked brand, I would have wanted it as this book's official sponsor.

Chapter 24

ALL THE ENERGY
IN THE UNIVERSE

Jonathon Miller-Weisberger met Don Caesario seven years ago at a conference held in the Secoya's ancestral homeland, La Garta Cocha, near the headwaters of the Amazon. "I had such a fun time with this old guy," said Jonathon, who could sound like a West Coast dude at one moment, deeply serious mystic explorer the next. "I spent three weeks with him at his home, laughing all the time, sleeping under the same mosquito net. His house had fallen down and he was living with his son. He asked me to help him build a new house."

Jonathon had learned about the Secoya when he was a kid growing up in Quito, where his mother ran a vegetarian restaurant. He found a postcard of a Secoya at a bookstore. "I saw this totally rad-looking Indian wearing this yellow crown, with flowers around his arm, strings of beads, and I thought, Wow, I would love to meet that guy," he recalls. Years later, he heard a story about a Secoya who got lost in the forest one night and slept at the top of a tree: "During the night, an evil spirit started to cut the tree down. The Secoya started to sing. He sang to the flowers that blossomed on the tree. The flowers turned into heavenly beings that stopped the evil spirit from hurting him."

Now thirty, he wore blue jeans, beat-up Keds, and a T-shirt embroidered with the "Om" insignia. He practiced tai chi and discoursed earnestly on Eastern wisdom and indigenous mysticism. He was about the same age as Daniel Lieberman, my guide in Gabon. Like Lieberman, he was Jewish, dark-haired, thin, an idealistic outsider with a Buddhist orientation. Encountering Lieberman and then Weisberger, it seemed as if I had stumbled across some contemporary archetype—the young ethnobotanist as wandering Jewish sage.

Jonathon called Don Caesario "a saint of *yagé*" who had "achieved spiritual immortality." He told us that Don Caesario is the tribe's last great shaman, a once-prestigious leader who lost his authority. With the exception of a few elders, the tribe has stopped following shamanism over the past thirty years. Even Caesario's son, Caesar, was an evangelist, converted by the missionaries. Although Caesar was the tribe's community president, like most of the younger Secoya he wore Western clothing. He never drank *yagé*.

At an evening ceremony we met the last upholders of the tradition, the tribal elders, a coterie of dignified gentlemen in colored tunics and yellow crowns who averaged under five-foot in height. Don Esteban, nicknamed Magico, is a Cofan Indian who married into the Secoya. Esteban wore a traditional feathered headdress and an iridescent parrot feather through his nose. Don Augustine, nicknamed Tintin, was the apprentice shaman. Tintin rarely said a word—he kept approaching me and then dissolving in mischievous laughter. Don Emilio, we were told, was the master of the forest, with an encyclopedic knowledge of plants and plant remedies. Meeting the elders, I knew I had found what I was looking for, what I had wanted as I pounded the familiar pavement of New York City: As much as they were perfectly present, the elders also had the eccentric aura of mystics, of sages who traveled far into distant visionary realities and returned to giggle about it.

Don Esteban stood up and told us the story of his life. He had been a shaman in his youth, but when the missionaries arrived he assumed that Christianity had greater power. He abandoned his traditional spiritual culture and became a Christian, working with the missionaries. They told him not to take ayahuasca, so he didn't. But as time went on, he realized that, as a Christian, he was no longer able to heal anybody. A nephew of his died, and he knew that with ayahuasca he would have been able to heal him. He decided that Christianity didn't have all the answers and he returned, after a thirty-year hiatus, to ayahuasca. I he also said he had tried LSD, given to him by a tourist, and that he could use it to heal as well. "LSD is strong medicine," he said. He promised to help us reach the "deep spiritual realms."

I was ready.

But on the day scheduled for our first *yagé* ceremony, Don Caesario announced he didn't feel well. Worse yet, he had suffered from bad dreams during the night. Dreams are part of the shaman's professional equipment. The ceremony was postponed.

Shamanism is a delicate enterprise. Thick coils of the ayahuasca vines grew near the ceremonial lodge. Early that morning, a few of us, myself included, walked up to the vines and looked them over. We even touched them. At breakfast, we learned that our examination gave Don Caesario, who wasn't watching us, a splitting headache. Menstruating women also disturbed the shaman—Caesario is married, but to keep his spirit pure, he has been celibate for decades—and about half the women in our group were having their "moon." These women were forbidden from going anywhere near the *yagé* or participating in the ceremonies.

Some of us consoled ourselves with a long hike led by Don Emilio, the forest maestro. In the humid, vine-canopied jungle, my fellow tourists and I, in rubber boots and hiking gear, blundered along like enormous marshmallows next to our quiet, barefoot guide. Don Emilio showed us the dragon blood tree, cutting the bark with his machete to let blood-red sap run out. He carved a thick vine into a wooden eyedropper that slowly dripped sap into our eyes—the jungle version of Visine. He pointed out healing plants clinging to the trees.

That night I could not sleep. The hike was my first venture into the depths of the rain forest, and the jungle was its own trip. Images of endless plant forms and swaying vines flashed on my closed eyelids like photo prints. Meanwhile, six miles from my hammock, Occidental was drilling an exploratory oil well.

The tiny remnant of the Secoya tribe was struggling to survive. Thieves were only one threat among many: The Indians feared Colombian guerrillas and the mass quantity of herbicides that the U.S.

government was spraying along the border. The biggest fear of all, however, was the encroaching oil company.

In a scene straight out of *Apocalypse Now*, a large square of land had been cleared in the midst of deep jungle, with helicopters whirling over a two-hundred-foot drilling platform as they dropped supplies into the camp. The drilling, which had been going on since late last year, was currently 8,700 feet deep, and the company had yet to strike oil. If they do indeed find oil, Occidental will build a road straight to the site. The destruction of the surrounding forest and the Secoya culture will soon follow.

Pressured by Occidental and the Ecuadorean government, the Secoya agreed to give access to their land for $700,000, a paltry sum considering the hundreds of millions a successful oil prospect could yield. Even so, the bribes handed out by the oil companies are often enough to destabilize Indian groups who have no practice in economic planning. It is obvious that indigenous groups who up until fifty years ago were strangers to the modern world—who still have a completely different, communal conception of land and property than we do, and no tradition of using money—should not be negotiating with legal teams from the oil companies. But that's been the practice for some time.

In the early 1990s, Jonathon worked on boundary demarcation with the Huaorani, a tribe of twelve hundred hunter-gatherers given title to two million acres of Amazonian rain forest. "Nobody ever treated me the way the Huaorani treated me," he said. "They were the most proper people I ever met." For Jonathon, the Huaorani seemed to exist in a zone of spiritual perfection: "They were totally detached from everything. Even from their own lives." He befriended Wepe, a one-hundred-year-old Huaorani who had killed a hundred men. Wepe told him, "The tip of my spirit cuts through everything." The Huaorani were the only Indians in the region who didn't use hallucinogens—they didn't need them.

At the time, the land title seemed like a major victory for the Huaorani, but when the government of Ecuador grants land to indigenous groups, it forces them to forfeit subsoil rights. The once-pristine Huaorani territory was now crisscrossed by roads built by the oil companies, followed by the timber companies. The tribe was living in company-built shacks.

Over twenty years, the wells will produce enough oil to sate U.S. demand for, at the most, two weeks.

"I wept for four days straight about the Huaorani," Jonathon said. "I wept until I couldn't weep anymore."

The jungle surrounding the Secoya is facing the same process of shortsighted pillaging. The systematic destruction of the Amazon rain forests, formed over millions of years of evolution, the living lungs of the planet, means ever-accelerating climate change. I have read that some Indian tribes in North America would consider the consequences of their actions seven generations into the future. Our "advanced" society, on the other hand, seems unable to envision the consequences of its actions even a few years ahead.

. . .

TWO DAYS LATER, when tensions had subsided, Don Caesario announced we would drink *yagé* that night. At breakfast I told Pablo Amaringo my dream of the night before. I dreamt that I was drafted to fight in a war. Parts of the dream took place in bootcamp, but it was all quite friendly. Amaringo smiled. "Your dream means that you are being conscripted into the army of the spirits," he told me.

At sunset we gathered in the lodge, a long thatched building with posts set up for stringing rows of hammocks. The shaman lay in the center of the room, attended by his assistant, Tintin. The Secoya, in their crowns and beads and twined flowers, lay in rows on one side of him, the visitors on the other. There were thirty of us altogether, swaying in our hammocks. Several young Secoya were drinking *yagé* for the first time, including Caesario's teenage grandson. For one night, anyway, they traded in their basketball shorts and sneakers for old-school Secoya tunics and crowns.

I felt bad for Annie and the other women having their "moon." They had come all this way only to be denied the chance to try *yagé*. Jean-Michel, the Frenchman, backed out, perhaps fearing the psychedelic might undermine his rigid Gallic prejudices.

One by one, we were called up to Don Caesario, who gave us a coconut cup full of *yagé*, first blowing soft prayers into it. I chugged the bitter brew, suppressing shudders. Eager to push myself as far as

possible, I forced myself to go back to the shaman for two more cup-
fuls of jungle murk later in the night, overcoming spasms of revulsion
each time.

I lay back in my hammock as the activity behind my eyelids slowly
intensified. Coldness enveloped me. I felt like a caterpillar in a cocoon,
immobilized, receptive, fighting the turbulence in my stomach. Time
seemed to slow down and distend.

Eyes closed, I saw a grid stretching in all directions. Geometrical
forms of strobing spheres and pyramids arose on all the points of the
grid. These forms gave way to shape-shifting geometrical patterns,
then more explicit imagery. I saw the vague form of a Mayan-like deity
with an animal snout and Indian headdress. I tried to follow him, but
he vanished into the ether. I looked into a swirling snake pit at the center of my visual field, where serpents slithered and coiled around each
other. The snake pit turned into a field where plants were growing at
an incredible velocity, blossoming and then decaying, again and again
and again. An endless profusion of botanical forms rose up, swooned,
died, and rotted away. There seemed to be a message to this—that a
plant, like every living being, was actually made of energy, the form we
see just a temporary snapshot, an illusory interruption of the constant
flow, the movement of the spirit.

Every now and then the images were interrupted by the spas-
modic gasps of somebody vomiting in the bushes. I didn't throw up. As
I noticed when I took *yagé* in New York, there was a bizarre humor to
the visions. At one point I watched a line of black spacemen slowly fil-
ing into a black spaceship. It was a somber, melancholy vision. Suddenly I understood the meaning of this spaceship. My bowels
sputtering, I needed to find the outhouse. I staggered out into the jungle. The stars were merry and bright overhead, the banana palms and
hovering trees seemed to be welcoming me into the spiritual universe
as I sent off my spacemen.

The Secoya sang incredible melodies through the night. Songs of
healing magic, chants in a language taught to them by the spirits.
Sometimes the songs humorously copied gurgles of nausea or the roar
of a wild boar. Don Esteban stood up and let loose with long, unwinding whoops that had the manic ferocity of archaic war cries. A shiver
was passing through reality—when I opened my eyes I could see it, like

electric pulses—and the songs matched the fast, stuttering rhythm of that shiver.

It was as if the ceremonial lodge had become a boat or a spaceship, gliding across dark water, with Don Caesario calm at the helm. The music was like the rudder setting our course. I felt tingling vibrations in my teeth, and throughout my body I could sense currents like a magnetic pull following the directions where the songs were carrying us.

The hallucinations started to deepen into a realm that I could not recognize, that I lack language to describe. I found myself wandering across a shimmering space with beings that never stopped changing— porcupine-quilled, tusked, multitongued, amoebic, but even those words are only approximations of entities that could be compared to the darker imaginings of H. P. Lovecraft. The shaman and the elders seemed to be inhabiting this space with me. Glowing in the light cast by the fire, their features seemed animated by an almost nonhuman intensity. They sang, their words unintelligible, to these creatures, interacting with them, in mystical communion. It seemed that this was the goal of the ayahuasca ceremony, the arrival point. These were "the heavenly people."

Don Caesario drank another cup of the bitter brew, prepared for him by his assistant Tintin. Then he sang alone. His song seemed to be the wildest and most private ode, a psalm of solitude, unveiling the secret knowledge of his soul. He barely whispered. He breathed into the stars. Then the melody returned, his voice rose up. To my augmented ears, he seemed to be weaving a subtle discourse on reality, describing the victory of form over emptiness. As he sang, he seduced a spirit-creature that started to grow, spinning cotton candy filaments around itself. Then Tintin started to sing as well. But he seemed to challenge the shaman's metaphysical viewpoint, arguing that emptiness ultimately triumphs over form. Don Caesario sadly concurred, and the cotton candy creation was released to fall back into the void. Startled by the concreteness of these hallucinations, I did a quick reality check, opening my eyes to the night. The shaman lay back, illuminated by the flames, the other tourists breathed or slept near me in their hammocks.

I had no more doubts that the Secoya engaged in extradimensional exploration, using ayahuasca as their psychic telescope and transport.

This was what Jonathon called the "spiritual science of the Amazon." For the Indians there was, I realized, no difference between the natural and the supernatural worlds. Their songs were the chants of spirits calling out to other spirits and elemental forces, weaving through the astral realms.

Later I learned that the Secoya elders say that, through *yagé,* they can sometimes sing new plants into being. At the end of a long night of pure trance, Don Caesario may look down at his fist to find he is holding a seed or sapling in his palm. He buries that gift from the heavenly people in his garden. In a few months it grows into a medicinal herb, a new remedy to add to their extensive herbarium.

.   .   .

IN THE MORNING we compared notes on our journeys. Some of the travelers were disappointed. Some felt healed or rejuvenated. Tammy, no longer sick, just giggled at the "weird stuff" she had seen during the night—abstract forms, geometrical swirls, trembling entities. "It was totally fun, but I don't know that it meant anything," she said.

Mark and Andrew suffered interminable (you have to take *yagé* to fully appreciate the meaning of "interminable") nausea and vomiting, and received no visions. Due to some last-second failure of will or nerve, they hadn't pushed themselves to drink more. "It's not my drug," shrugged Mark. He chalked it up to the elusive ways of the "Great Spirit" and seemed relieved to be done with it, ready to go home. Andrew, however, struggled to laugh off his frustration over failing, yet again, to have visions. Like a secretive magician willing to reveal only one trick, the plant refused to show him anything new. Each time he drank, it attacked his guts with more violence.

Octavia said she rocketed through visionary realities. She was led around a museum of archaic artifacts to a small cube of glowing white light. "Pick it up," the spirits urged her. "What is it?" she asked. "It is all the energy in the universe." She decided to leave it alone.

Barbara Nelson and Kerry Locklear, a psychologist and social worker, shared a vision of a small owl watching them. Three others, including a Quechua Indian, saw dolphins spiraling in a blue ocean. (Such "transpersonal" sightings are common on *yagé*; when the drug was discovered by Westerners in the 1920s, scientists gave it the name telepathine.)

When I tried to tell Don Esteban about my night, he laughed. "Your soul was flying outside your body," he said. "When your soul is flying like that, you can go anywhere you want to go. You can see anything you want to see."

Jonathon burst into the ceremonial lodge with tears in his eyes. Even without partaking of the *yagé*, he had been up all night, tormented by images of encroaching oil companies, murderous guerrillas, the doomed tribe.

"Where else are you ever going to find old dudes like this who stay up all night to sing for you and heal you?" he asked. "Anyway, nothing ever really goes extinct. We might think it does, but there are a million billion universes out there. Everything that disappears from our world gets reborn somewhere else."

Part Six

LSD AND THE 1960S

*"Do you believe that drugs are a spiritual form
of gambling?"*
"Yes, I do."

—FROM THE FILM *Sympathy for the Devil,*
BY JEAN-LUC GODARD

Chapter 25

THE MULTIPLE MILLION-EYED MONSTER

The disease is striking in beachside beatnik pads and in the dormitories of expensive prep schools; it has grown into an alarming problem at UCLA and on the UC campus at Berkeley. And everywhere the diagnosis is the same: psychotic illness resulting from the unauthorized, nonmedical use of the drug LSD-25.

—*Time,* MARCH 1966

I was born in 1966, too young to catch the electric crackling of that era's social, sexual, and neurochemical turmoil except as a vague childhood flashback—I seem to have some shadowy memory of a protest march or two, and a vivid impression of watching my baby-sitter excitedly peeling the static-clinging plastic wrap from the Beatles' new album, *Abbey Road.* I think I must have been continuously bathed in the Beatles' sonic waves as a child, for even today I find their harmonies, like familiar lullabies, instantly pacifying. For the first few years of my life, my parents lived on Saint Mark's Place, in the midst of counterculture chaos, although they were a generation older than the hippies. My mother, a former Beat, was an editor at McGraw-Hill, where she slipped Abbie Hoffman's first book, *Revolution for the Hell of It,* as well as "Movement" works by black revolutionaries, feminists, and Marxist organizers, onto an otherwise conservative list. Yet she wrote in her memoir *Minor Characters*:

> The sixties were never quite my time. They seemed anticli-
> mactic, for all their fireworks. Some culmination had been
> short-circuited. I saw hippies replace beatniks, sociologists re-
> place poets, the empty canvas replace the Kline. Unenthusias-
> tically, I observed the emergence of "lifestyle." The old
> intensities were blanding out into "Do your own thing"—the
> commandment of a freedom excised of struggle. Ecstasy had
> become chemical, forgetfulness could be had by prescription.

The year of my birth was the year that the government outlawed LSD and other psychedelics after a series of emergency Senate hearings, dominated by a mood of panic. At the same time, mainstream opinion, informed by the exaggerated horror stories broadcast by the mass media, turned against LSD, which went from "wonder drug" to "horror drug" in a few brief years. Although earlier studies had shown LSD to be "astonishingly safe," now every crisis, every emergency room visit or suicide attempt, that could be linked to use of the drug was front-page news. And of course, the media made no attempt to put such data in the context of much-more damning statistics of fatalities and crimes caused by socially approved substances such as barbitu-ates, cigarettes, and alcohol.

As Jay Stevens writes in *Storming Heaven*, "By the autumn of 1966, opponents were hinting that LSD probably caused long-term brain damage. Their evidence? The fact that so many kids, post-LSD, showed little desire to adjust to the corporate-suburban lifestyle embraced by their parents." Another scientific study, quickly picked up by news-papers around the country, suggested that LSD damaged chromo-somes—although this study's evidence was quickly refuted, the image stuck in the public's mind. Norman Mailer, who could have known bet-ter, harps on it repeatedly in *Armies of the Night*, envisioning the hippies with "twenty generations of buried hopes perhaps engraved in their chromosomes, and now conceivably burning like faggots in the secret inquisitional fires of LSD." Even today, many people believe that LSD and other psychedelics damage either brains or genes, although there is no evidence to support either position. It seems the only serious danger of LSD use is that it may reveal a preexisting psychotic condition. Despite alarmist reports, flashbacks seem to be chimeras—rarely encountered and hardly dangerous. But of course, like all powerful tools, LSD, even if it were legalized, should only be used with caution.

Two excellent books have been written on the history of LSD and the counterculture: Stevens's *Storming Heaven: LSD and the American Dream,* and *Acid Dreams: The Complete Social History of LSD: The CIA, the Sixties, and Beyond* by Martin A. Lee and Bruce Shlain. *Storming Heaven,* for the most part, follows the adventurous antics of Aldous Huxley, Timothy Leary, Ken Kesey, Allen Ginsberg, and other psychedelic avatars who spread the LSD gospel, escaped from police and federal agents, sought personal enlightenment, and tripped and skipped across the globe. *Acid Dreams,* on the other hand, reveals a darker undercurrent, exploring the close relationship of the CIA to LSD through the secret mind-control program, MK-ULTRA. *Acid Dreams* makes it clear that the CIA and the military were responsible for the large-scale dispersion of LSD to research hospitals and academic studies—Ken Kesey and Allen Ginsberg, among others, first tried LSD under the auspices of government-funded studies.

The shortcircuited sixties were polarized between extremes: on one hand, the political and personal experiments of the young; on the other, the wars and new systems of social control pursued by the government; on the one hand, the populist struggle of guerrilla insurgents in Third World countries; on the other, the ever-increasing reach of global capitalism.

In his essay "Periodizing the Sixties," the critic Frederic Jameson shows how the utopian fervor and counterculture of the era masked, and in a sense mirrored, the unleashing of new forms of repression and new economic forces. Jameson dates the start of the 1960s "with the great movement of decolonization in British and French Africa," and the successful revolutions of the Third World, especially the Algerian war and the Cuban revolution of 1959, which announced that the sixties would be an era of radical breaks and rapid innovations.

And yet, Jameson writes, "The conception of the Third World 60s as a moment when all over the world chains and shackles of a classical imperialist kind were thrown off in a stirring wave of 'wars of national liberation' is an altogether mythical simplification." During the 1960s, there was a transformation from one mode of First World dominance to another—from direct colonization to a new, subtler, but ultimately more effective neocolonialism. Today, that transformation is symbolized by institutions such as the World Bank and the International Monetary Fund. This process turned much of the Third World into permanent debtor nations. The "Green Revolution"—the industrialization of agriculture, disrupting local economies and indigenous cultures—forced the creation of guerrilla insurgents and resistance movements.

While the hippies were tuning in and turning on, capitalism did not retreat during the 1960s. It was expanding and mutating rapidly, discovering new means of production, carving out new markets, refining its methods of control:

> Late capitalism in general (and the 60s in particular) constitute a process in which the last surviving internal and external zones of precapitalism—the last vestiges of noncommodified or traditional space within and outside the advanced world—are now ultimately penetrated and colonized in their turn. Late capitalism can therefore be described as the moment when the last vestiges of Nature which survived on into classical capitalism are at length eliminated: namely the Third World and the unconscious. The 60s will then have been the momentous transformational period when this systemic restructuring takes place on a global scale.

In the cultural field (what Marxists call the superstructure, compared to the economic infrastructure), the "sixties" were marked by the sense that anything was possible, that the world worked on magical and mystical principles as well as rational ones. This temporary return of "marvelous intuition," to borrow a Shakespearean phrase, was partially fueled by the transformative surges of LSD. In Jameson's terms, "this sense of freedom and possibility . . . can perhaps best be explained in terms of the superstructural movement and play enabled by transition from one infrastructural system or systemic stage of capitalism to another. The 60s were in that sense an immense and inflationary issuing of superstructural credit."

The transition between world economic systems opened a temporary gap of ideological uncertainty, and in this gap, the mirage of the cultural and social revolution of the sixties spread its rainbow. The sixties ultimately reveals itself as a "properly dialectical process, in which 'liberation' and domination are inextricably combined." Jameson wrote this essay in the 1980s. Today it is even clearer how the explosive potential of the sixties led "to powerful restorations of the social order and a renewal of the repressive power of the various state apparatuses." The thirty-year War on Drugs, begun under President Nixon, has been one potent agent of that repression (1.6 million Americans were arrested for drug violations in the year 2000 alone, more than 600,000 for possession of marijuana). The new War on Terrorism, allowing centralized domestic intelligence-gathering, may well turn out to be another one.

Jameson, of course, like most Marxists, has no interest in drugs. The fact that physical matter, plants and chemicals, can radically transform human consciousness falls outside the scope of traditional Marxist analysis (even though Marxist dialectics have a mystical streak). Jameson ignores the part that LSD might have played in transforming the superstructure, even though Nature and the unconscious, those last aspects of traditionalism to be eliminated by capitalism, are the particular forces revealed, in mythically transfigured form, by psychedelics. Only a renegade mystic-Marxist like Walter Benjamin could allow himself to explore the relationship between intoxication and social reality, showing how the repressive mechanisms of modern society depend on enforcing the trance of modern life.

The Politics of Ecstasy promoted by Leary, Ginsberg, and others only confused the straight-edge radicals of the 1960s, who worried that LSD created false consciousness and sapped energy from the political struggle. "We feared that utter frivolity would short-circuit American youth's still tenuous sense of moral obligation to the world's oppressed," wrote Todd Gitlin, former president of Students for a Democratic Society, in his book *The Sixties: Years of Hope, Days of Rage.* "The hip-youth-drug thing, whatever it was, was beyond our control, and we must have sensed that the disciplines of politics (including our own) were in danger of being overwhelmed." On the other hand, many movement supporters became radicalized after trying marijuana and LSD. The fact that the government quickly prohibited use of these substances was proof to many that the rulers did not have their best interests at heart.

Acid Dreams shows that liberation and domination were never more wedded than in the story of LSD's rise and fall. With little romanticism, the writers describe LSD as a "non-specific amplifier of psychic and social processes." When CIA agents and the military became fascinated with the drug in the 1950s, dosing themselves as well as unsuspecting victims, most of them did not have mystical revelations. They tripped out on baroque James Bond scenarios instead, such as putting chemicals in Castro's shoes to make his beard fall out, assassination plots, or envisioning bombing patterns through North Vietnam. LSD may have had a permanent distorting effect on the tactical mind-set of the CIA. Long after its love affair with LSD ended, the CIA remained fascinated by mind-control drugs, and for many years they maintained a secret project in extrasensory perception.

Acid Dreams suggests that, by the end of the 1960s, the CIA worked covertly to ensure that a cheap supply of LSD remained available to the radicals of the counterculture: "According to a former CIA contract employee, Agency personnel helped underground chemists set up LSD laboratories in the Bay Area to 'monitor' events in the acid ghetto. . . . A CIA agent who claims to have infiltrated the covert LSD network . . . referred to Haight-Ashbury as a 'human guinea pig farm.' "

Along with the CIA, the ideologies of radical Leftist groups—such as the Weather Underground, the White Panthers, and other organizations—turned increasingly militant, paranoid, and megalomaniacal under the effects of LSD. "The delusions of grandeur [the Radicals] entertained were amplified to the point that some felt themselves invested with magical powers," Lee and Shlain write in *Acid Dreams*. "They wanted to change the world immediately, or at least as fast as LSD could change a person's consciousness." They suggest that the CIA anticipated—welcomed, aided, and abetted—LSD's penetration into the Radical Left: "In their stoned hubris the Yippies, the White Panthers, and the Weather Underground misread the depth of the cultural revolution and its impact on the political situation in America. Their delusions about the omnipotence of the Movement derived in part from their experience with psychedelic drugs."

. . .

FOR MORE THAN a decade after LSD was discovered, its potential use eluded the attempted categorizations of scientists, spooks, and shrinks. Psychologists couldn't fathom its meaning for psychology any better than the CIA could figure out how to use it in the spy trade. Acid did not fit any of the existing parameters. Tasteless, odorless, with doses measured in micrograms, LSD was the most powerful consciousness-altering substance ever found by many magnitudes, but its effects were completely unpredictable and unrepeatable.

Psychologists first used it as a "psychotomimetic," a training tool that would allow them to temporarily experience psychotic or schizophrenic states. But this proved untenable; since the altered mindscapes of LSD can be enjoyed and comprehended with full knowledge of the changes caused by the drug, its effects are radically different than psychosis. By trial and error, psychologists slowly learned what any shaman could have told them: "set" and "setting"—the environment and the mental attitude of the user at the start of the trip—determine the individual's experience of the LSD trip. In the late 1950s, some psychologists started to use LSD in therapy with astonishing results.

Up until the mid-1960s, when the drugs were restricted and then outlawed, the psychedelic compounds were considered the most promising tools for exploring the human mind that psychology had ever found. Many of the best and most inquisitive minds in the field embraced this new direction enthusiastically. Before LSD was made illegal, more than a thousand papers were published covering some forty thousand patients, recording amazing successes and profound challenges to the prevailing models of the human psyche: "Every type of madness, every type of parapsychological phenomenon, every type of mystical, ecstatic illumination, Jungian archetypes, past lives, precognition, psychosis, satori-samadhi-atman, union with God," writes Stevens in Storming Heaven, "it was all there in the scientific record."

By 1968, the FDA had forbidden any more research in psychedelics. All around the world, an impregnable barrier was placed around the subject, putting it outside the domain of legitimate science. As Dr. Stanislav Grof, a pioneer in LSD psychotherapy and theory, noted, "Psychedelic research clarified . . . many previously puzzling historical and anthropological data concerning shamanism, mystery cults, rites of passage, healing ceremonies, and paranormal phenomena involving the use of sacred plants. . . . The experimentation with psychedelic drugs has shattered the conventional understanding of psychotherapy, the traditional models of the psyche, the image of human nature, and even basic beliefs about the nature of reality."

Not only modern society, but also modern psychiatry was simply unready for such a paradigm shift. Since then, we have seen a retrenchment and a retreat into an increasingly narrow and normative model of the psyche. Today, most psychiatrists assume that mental illness almost always has a biological or genetic basis rather than a social or psychological or even spiritual origin.

The interrupted history of LSD and psilocybin therapy includes treatment programs in which alcoholics were given single large doses of LSD, resulting in a high rate of cure—as much as 50 percent, according to Dr. Humphrey Osmond, a scientist who had discovered the structural similarity between the mescaline molecule and adrenaline in the 1950s, and who conducted clinics for psychedelic therapy at several hospitals. Even Bill Wilson, the founder of Alcoholics Anonymous, recognized the tremendous potential of LSD as a treatment for compulsive drinkers. Leary's Harvard project gave psilocybin to prisoners at Massachusetts Correctional Institute in Concord, a maximum-security prison. This experiment seems to have been similarly effective. During the Concord program's brief life, it cut the recidivism rate for prisoners who tried the drug from 80 to 25 percent, at least according to Leary's calculations.

Leary chronicles this episode in his autobiography, *Flashbacks*. In prison for the first time, tripping on psilocybin with a bank robber, he writes, "I could see him much too clearly, every pore in his face, every blemish, the hairs in his nose, the horrid green-yellow enamel of his decaying teeth, the glistening of his frightened eyes, every hair on his head looking big as a tree-branch." Leary told the convict, "I'm afraid of you," and the convict answered, "Well, that's funny, Doc, 'cause I'm afraid of you." "Why are you afraid of me?" Leary asked. "I'm afraid of you 'cause you're a fucking mad scientist." At that point, Leary and the prisoner both laughed—a connection had been made, "a bit of pagan magic had occurred." From there on, according to Leary, the prison sessions were a success.

A typical manifesto of the psychedelic therapy movement of the early 1960s described the therapeutic model as follows: "The subject constantly works off repressed material and unreality structures, false concepts, ideas, and attitudes, which have been accumulated through his life experiences. Thus a form of psychological cleansing seems to accompany the subjective imagery. . . . Gradually the subject comes to see and accept himself, not as an individual with 'good' and 'bad' characteristics, but as one who simply is." The authors of this manifesto, like other psychedelic therapists, did not shy away from the spiritual aspects of the LSD encounter:

> The central perception, apparently of all who penetrate deeply in their explorations, is that behind the apparent multiplicity of things in the world of science and common sense there is a single reality, in speaking of which it seems appropriate to use such words as infinite and eternal.

After a patient reached this deep perception of eternal unity, the therapists discovered, nine out of ten times his or her other problems disappeared. The transcendent dimensions of the LSD trip alarmed most mainstream scientists, who were trained to consider mysticism and science as separate categories that should not overlap.

Much like Prozac in the 1990s, LSD was the psychological "wonder drug" of the early 1960s. LSD therapy inspired instant best-seller accounts, similar to the memoirs of life-changing encounters with antidepressants popular in recent years. Constance Newland published *Me, Myself and I*, a confessional account of her LSD therapy for sexual fridgity, in 1962. Newland, a middle-aged woman emerging from the sexual repression of the 1950s, used LSD to find her erogenous zones (the first hallucination she has in her twenty-three sessions is of herself as a "closed-up clam," alone on the ocean floor) and break her neurosis.

Through LSD hallucinations, Newland plumbed the depths of her stereotypically Freudian unconscious. Backtracking through early traumas, she learned, "in addition to being, consciously, a loving mother and respectable citizen, I was also, unconsciously, a murderess, a pervert, a cannibal, a sadist, and a masochist." These discoveries had a cheering effect on her psychic life. She got rid of her neurosis. "I also achieved transcendent sexual fulfillment." After therapy, her life had "new savor, new meaning, new mystery." Newland's mass-market memoir makes for surprising reading today, when both LSD and the Freudian unconscious have been marginalized.

. . .

IN THE EARLY 1960s, the avatars of the nascent psychedelic movement believed that LSD could radically change the individual—and, by extension, the world—by "deconditioning" patients from limiting beliefs and neuroses. The supporters of psychedelics thought that they had a chance to shape public perception of these new compounds, an opportunity they soon lost. Gordon Wasson, the investment banker who discovered the Mazatec mushroom cult, snobbishly decreed that use of these sacraments had no place at all in the modern world (except when he took them with his friends). Aldous Huxley, Al Hubbard, Alan Watts, and Myron Stolaroff, among others, favored a mandarin approach. They planned to discreetly distribute the drugs to influential and well-connected people in business, the arts, and government. "In the relative privacy of learned journals, the decent obscurity of moderately highbrow books," according to Huxley, the mandarins would shape the discourse, then let the information slowly filter down through the society. Before they could undertake this top-down indoctrination, events overtook them.

Chapter 26

A PATHETIC CLOWN ACT

The most efficient way to cut through the game structure of Western life is the use of drugs. Drug-induced satori. In three hours under the right circumstances the cortex can be cleared.

—LEARY SPEAKING AT THE CONGRESS FOR APPLIED PSYCHOLOGY, COPENHAGEN, DENMARK, 1961

A Harvard psychology professor on a tenure track, Timothy Leary was almost forty years old when he tripped for the first time while on vacation in Cuernavaca, Mexico. It was the summer of 1960. "I had run through and beyond the middle-class professional game board. There were no surprise moves left. I had died even to the lure of ambition, power, sex. It was all a Monopoly game—easy to win but meaningless," he wrote later. Since the Wassons' visit to Maria Sabina, knowledge of *teonanacatl*, the "flesh of God," had spread. An anthropologist friend of Leary's tracked some down in a village market. Leary was less than enthusiastic. "The smell was like crumbling logs or certain New England basements, and it tasted worse than it looked." Yet that first trip pushed him down the evolutionary ladder— "snake-time, fish-time, down-through-giant-jungle-palm-time, green

lacy fern-time"—and convinced him that his carefully constructed ego
and his academic career were nothing but shams:

> For most people it's a life-changing shock to learn that their
> everyday reality circuit is one among dozens of circuits which,
> when turned on, are equally real, pulsing with strange forms
> and mysterious biological signals. . . . Since psychedelic drugs
> expose us to different levels of perception and experience, use
> of them is ultimately a philosophic enterprise, compelling us
> to confront the nature of reality and the nature of our fragile,
> subjective belief systems. . . . We discover abruptly that we
> have been programmed all these years, that everything we ac-
> cept as reality is just social fabrication.

He had found the cure for his jaded disillusionment and boredom
in a fistful of foul-tasting fungus. When he returned to Harvard that
fall, he began the Psilocybin Project with his fellow professor Richard
Alpert (who would later change his name to Ram Dass), giving the
synthesized chemical, purchased through Sandoz, to hundreds of graduate students, housewives, poets, and other test subjects. The purpose
of the experiments as well as the methodology were already under investigation by the administration at Harvard in 1962, when Leary was
visited by a pot-bellied Englishman, Michael Hollingshead. Hollingshead was carrying a jar of mayonnaise loaded with ten thousand doses
of LSD. For a while, Leary resisted the lure of the mayonnaise jar, but
finally he took a spoonful. Propelling him far beyond the realms of
"cozy know-thyself psilocybin," LSD detonated his ego:

> All forms, all structures, all organisms, all events were televi-
> sion productions pulsing out from the central eye. Everything
> that I had ever experienced and read about was bubble-
> dancing before me like a nineteenth-century vaudeville show.
> My illusions, the comic costumes, the strange ever-changing
> stage props of trees and bodies and theater sets . . . I have
> never recovered from that ontological confrontation.

After LSD, Leary realized later, "it was inevitable that we would leave
Harvard, that we would leave American society."

I have always considered Leary a central villain in the psychedelic saga. He was certainly naive, charismatic, sloppy, self-promotional, and out of control. Other researchers and psychologists—Stanislav Grof, Myron Stolaroff, and Oscar Janiger among others—many of whom had worked with psychedelics for years before Leary jumped into the fray, had intentionally maintained a low profile. They recognized the potentially revolutionary and paradigm-shifting nature of their work, and realized that they had to go slowly or face expulsion from the mainstream. Leary, a latecomer to psychedelic research, made that cautious strategy impossible.

Inspired by Allen Ginsberg but above all following his own flashy temperament, Leary chose to mass-market chemical mind expansion, using the media to spread the LSD message as fast as possible. Like the other psychedelic therapists, he envisioned using psychedelics in a professional and government-sanctioned context. He advocated government restrictions on psychedelic use, and the training of official guides, both mystics and therapists. In a sense, Leary and his supporters envisioned a new type of professional shaman, one who would be trained to utilize the psychedelic drugs as tools for psychic transformation.

Could psychedelic shamanism flourish in a modern bureaucracy, as a regulated profession? Could the West institutionalize psychedelic exploration rather than forbid it? Perhaps we will never know if such an effort might succeed—or perhaps we will. Currently, European drug laws are being liberalized at an astonishing rate. Even in the United States, the Food and Drug Administration has recently approved a pilot study using ecstasy in treatment of post-traumatic stress disorder, along with trials of psilocybin for treating obsessive-compulsive disorder.

Or is the true shamanic impulse too anarchic to be expressed in that intricate "social fabrication" that is our postmodern world? As Ken Kesey put it, "The purpose of psychedelics is to learn the conditioned responses of people and then to prank them. That's the only way to get people to ask questions, and until they ask questions they're going to remain conditioned robots." Kesey's approach was more radical—less therapeutic but perhaps more shamanic—than Leary's. For Kesey, who first tasted LSD as a research subject, and his Prankster followers in their magic bus, taking LSD had a "revolt of the guinea pigs" antiauthoritarian edge. Their motto was "freak freely." When the Merry

Pranksters visited Leary and his acolytes at the luxurious Milbrook estate, they found Leary's use of Bach, meditation rooms, and the pseudoreligious vibe distasteful. They dubbed his brand of high-brow psychedelia the "crypt trip."

In the years after Harvard dismissed him, Leary's pronouncements became increasingly strident. His ego amped-up by excessive exploration of LSD, he used the mass media to disseminate frightening and radical messages that caused a predictable panic reaction: "I would say that at present our society is so insane, that even if the risks were fifty-fifty that if you took LSD you would be permanently insane, I still think that the risk is worth taking, as long as the person knows that that's the risk," he told an interviewer at the height of his infamy.

As the self-appointed power-tripping "high priest" of LSD, Leary used the same mechanisms of game-playing and image manipulation that allowed him to flourish in the prepsychedelic buttoned-down ambience of 1950s Harvard. Unsurprisingly, whenever Leary took LSD, he said he relived a "recurring science fiction paranoia. Suddenly I am on camera in an ancient television show. . . . All my life routines a pathetic clown act."

Leary insisted that young people across America use the LSD trip as programmed ego destruction, with the aid of his superficial rewrite of *The Tibetan Book of the Dead*. He confidently proclaimed a reductive six-word motto as a directive for confused teenagers and college students: "Turn on, tune in, drop out." Intoxicated by his sense of self-importance, Leary failed to recognize that there was a difference between a forty-year-old Harvard psychologist choosing to abandon his societal role, and a sixteen-year-old kid making the same decision.

The smashing of the ego that Leary advocated was, for many trippers, a viciously nihilistic quest. Leary's slick, superficial constructs lacked the deep framework of separation, transcendence, and reintegration that shamanic cultures had developed over 75,000 (give or take) years. The "high priest" of psychedelia led his acolytes astray, abandoning them to float in a mind-blown void. John Lennon was one of Leary's casualties. Lennon tripped on LSD over a thousand times in the late 1960s, leading to a long period of inactivity. "I got a message on acid that you should destroy your ego," he admitted later. "I was reading that stupid book of Leary's and all that shit. We were going through a whole game that everyone went through, and I destroyed myself."

Leary, like most of the avatars of the early psychedelic movement, saw the value of psychedelics as deconditioning and deprogramming agents. Psychedelics allow users to "unhook the ambitions and the symbolic drives and the mental connections which keep you addicted and tied to the immediate tribal game." They break the trance of the consensus culture. But neither LSD nor Leary could provide answers to the most profound issue exposed by the LSD trip: Once the individual ego was liberated from its social role, from the well-worn grooves of Western society's game machinery, what was it supposed to do?

This agonizing question is refracted, reverbed, and wa-wa pedaled through the psychedelic rock of that era. Psychedelic rock oscillates between contrasting impulses. There is the Dionysian desire to pulverize all the boundaries of space and time—Jimi Hendrix's yearning to kiss the sky, or chop down a mountain with the side of his hand. But the feeling of magic super-potency is countered by its opposite, a childlike helplessness, found in the nursery rhyme pastoralism of Pink Floyd's "See Emily Play" or the Beatles' "Mother Nature's Son."

Psychedelic rock reached its unfortunate endpoint in distorted soundscapes of psychic disintegration, pretentiously adolescent fantasias such as the Beatles' "Revolution Number Nine," late-1960s Pink Floyd, and The Doors. The music traces the sorrowful process of psychic decay, swirling down toward what Freud called "the oceanic," a zone of preinfantile undifferentiation. The records describe failed attempts at initiation—short-circuited blow outs, made without road map or guide, except for Leary's dangerous manual.

Perceived as avatars of a new and potentially revolutionary Romanticism, the rock stars of that era eagerly embraced their role. Sid Barrett, Jimi Hendrix, Janis Joplin, Brian Jones, Jim Morrison, and Brian Wilson were among those who destroyed themselves, physically or psychically, through messy orgies of narcotic excess and shamanic regress. In their public flame-outs, they acted out the crisis of their generation. They used drugs to push their perceptions, decondition their egos, but found themselves unable to return to "consensual reality."

The 1960s pursuit of shamanic knowledge was too shallow, too uninformed, to succeed. Products of a consumer culture, the hippies and flower children tended to treat psychedelics and spirituality as new commodities. Fooled by the immediate psychic transformations of LSD, they thought enlightenment could be quickly achieved. Instead, tripping without shamanic support, and for kicks, some of them induced in themselves what the Mazatecs call "mind shadows"—negative spiritual energy—and these mind shadows, like destructive demons, compelled them into dark phantasmal realms.

The psychedelic culture flourished for a few short years, leaving behind a chaotic legacy of short-circuited brilliance and schizoid tragedy. Some figures—Allen Ginsberg, Bob Dylan, and Abbie Hoffman—captured the hallucinatory moment in all its carnival urgency. Ginsberg's synesthetic wordplay—"reality sandwiches," "hydrogen jukebox," etcetera—mimicked the sensory distortions of hallucinogens. Dylan's LSD-inspired songs from the mid-1960s present mental dreamscapes or stage sets, where mythic figures and archetypes interact with floating fragments of the real world. On peyote, Ginsberg saw visions of a world-destroying Moloch; on LSD he met a million-eyed monster. Dylan's psychedelia was equally caustic and hard-edged. He described drinking a potion, a mixture of "Texas medicine" and "railroad gin":

> An' like a fool I mixed them
> An' it scrambled up my mind
> An' now people just get uglier
> An' I have no sense of time

Abbie Hoffman's LSD-inspired insight was to take the logic of Ginsberg's surreal poetry and transform it into direct actions, media events that mocked and undermined the structuring logic of capitalism. Acid taught him that "action was the only reality." When the Yippies burned money on Wall Street it was a reverse magic trick in which they took the dollar's symbolic value and nullified it, turning bills back into paper scraps, mocking money's occult power.

LSD sparked genius—Ken Kesey's *One Flew Over the Cuckoo's Nest* was inspired by trips, the black humor of Pynchon had a distinct psychedelic tinge, the cartoonist R. Crumb found his signature style under the influence of "fuzzy acid"—and it also ruined minds. The era left behind a number of stark psychoanalytic self-portraits, anatomizing the phases of psychedelic breakdown, paranoia, and regression.

The late 1960s were the apotheosis of the paranoid strain in American life. As Thomas Pynchon put it, the era induced "a delirium tremens, a trembling unfurrowing of the mind's plowshares." By the end of the decade, hallucinatory hysteria and consensual reality merged into an indissoluble whole, and they have never separated since. It was an era of messianic fantasies, violent acts, and adolescent rages, of surges toward liberation and fizzles into madness. The thrust of it was a quest for initiation—an attempt, in Ginsberg's words, "to resurrect a lost art or a lost knowledge or a lost consciousness." The goal was to restore a living knowledge of the sacred to the dazed and alienated denizens of a desacralized modern world.

Psychedelics inspired the dream of a mass social rewiring, toward a new order based on spirituality, sexuality, and a return to Arcadian nature (the Yippie movement demanded "Compulsory unemployment for everyone. Let the machines do it."). The failure of this idealistic vision of social transformation was a temporary victory for the commodity culture, which co-opted the mesmerizing imagery of hallucinogens into its techniques of marketing and promotion, repackaging psychedelia as another selling tool, stripped of all content. It is still visible in the swirling graphics used in endless car and e-commerce advertisements today.

Hunter S. Thompson's *Fear and Loathing in Las Vegas* captured and helped to define the post sixties hipster attitude toward drugs: "What sells, today, is whatever Fucks You Up—whatever shortcircuits your brain and grounds it out for the longest possible time," he wrote in 1972. "The ghetto market has mushroomed into suburbia." Thompson inspired generations of preppy self-abusers. He defined the new era's jaded attitude toward chemical mind-expansion:

> This was the fatal flaw in Tim Leary's trip. He crashed around America selling "consciousness expansion" without ever giving a thought to the grim meat-hook realities that were lying in wait for all the people who took him too seriously . . . but there is not much satisfaction in knowing that he blew it very

badly for himself, because he took so many others down with
him.

   Not that they didn't deserve it: No doubt they all Got
What Was Coming To Them. All those pathetically eager acid
freaks who thought they could buy Peace and Understanding
for three bucks a hit. But their loss and failure is ours, too.
What Leary took down with him was the central illusion of a
whole life-style that he helped to create . . . a generation of
permanent cripples, failed seekers, who never understood the
essential age-old mystic fallacy of the Acid Culture: the desperate assumption that somebody—or at least some force—is
tending that Light at the end of the tunnel.

Thompson's cynicism was cool and proto-punk, an easy attitude for
future generations to cop. But the fault in his argument goes far deeper
than Leary's.

   If we don't explore the nature of our minds as deeply as possible,
using whatever tools are available to us, what kind of world can we
hope to create?

   What kind of world are we creating now?

Chapter 27

THE LIGHT AT THE
END OF THE TUNNEL

*Those who use (LSD) frequently or chronically almost
inevitably withdraw from society and enter into a solip-
sistic, negativistic existence. These individuals, color-
fully described by their confreres as acidheads, engage
perpetually in drug-induced orgies of introspection and
are no longer constructive active members of society. . . .*

—TESTIMONY FROM SENATE
SUBCOMMITTEE HEARING, 1966

One night in late spring I had a vivid dream in
which I took a bracing dose of Albert Hofmann's special recipe at an
all-night outlaw "psychedelic trance" party under the George Washington Bridge, near the northern tip of the concrete island of soaring
greed and steel-and-glass monoliths I have been, all my life, both privileged and cursed to call home.

Hypnotized by the water swirling like a river of shimmering jew-
els beneath the lights of the Manhattan skyline, which glowed in the
purple distance like a euphoric nightmare vision or fairy-tale Oz, I in-
dulged in a private orgy of introspection, jotting down the profound,
or perhaps pointless, revelation:

"The universe is the pattern in the process of coming-to-
consciousness of itself."

In other words, I thought I understood, for a brief moment, how I was also the pattern in the act of awareness, that the cosmos was knowing itself through me. By this act of perception, I felt as if I were performing a useful but impersonal function. I also wrote, "As if every moment is recorded and played back infinitely—and it never even happened."

In the predawn hours, sitting beneath the vast orange-colored limbs of the bridge, hearing its deep electric reverberations, I continued to stare, as if mesmerized, at the sliding surfaces of silver water, the luminous whirls and tumbles, while in my thoughts I reviewed the patterns and forces, psychic and impersonal, geological and anthropological and mystical, the old and new currents of history and fate that had brought me to that point in time—all of these forces represented by the currents shifting across the river like rippling glass, the graffiti-strewn rocks below, the expanse of steel above—until the totality of the awareness snuffed me, for one moment, like a candle flame blown out by the wind.

This sudden satori was a beautiful shock. I merged with the fullness, the emptiness—then came back into myself again. For the first time I realized the Buddhist paradox that expansion of awareness to a higher point was simultaneously the vanishing of awareness, the fusing of self into cosmos.

At another point I was aware—shades of the rapid DMT transport—of the Entire Sentient System running me. With the merest flick of a switch it could turn me on or off any time it wanted. It warned me of this. Humbled and grateful, I thanked the Self-Weaving Cosmological Firmament for allowing me, puny strand of spirit-stuff, to be spun in its loom. I often pass through such an Old Testament God phase of the LSD trip—a program running before or after the swarming, multi-tentacled, million-eyed Hindu/Buddhist wrathful deity section, which is also standard fare.

I closed my eyes and hallucinatory realms swarmed into view. Japanese pagoda dragons shook their rainbow-colored manes and iguana tails. I spied into strange 1960s-feeling white-molded plastic and wall-to-wall mirror scenes of inhuman sex transgressions, resembling Italian porn produced by an alien race—succulent pink and red organic forms fusing and undulating. I visited an extradimensional switchboard, like the silicon interior of a computer's memory, where, every second, a million wires were slotted into new sockets.

I requested some ancestral Judaic wisdom, and suddenly, on cue and as if in mockery of my desires, a high-speed stream of sacred Hebrew letters poured forth from a funnel-shaped geometric mandala. The letters were followed by Jewish Stars, Trees of Life, streams of golden light. Suddenly, the mystical signs vanished to be replaced by a horde of black cats, each perfectly rendered with identical glittering eyes. The black cats filled up everything until I was looking at black cat wallpaper, a universe of black cats.

I opened my eyes. LSD throws open the gates to the Pleroma, the Gnostic realm of cosmic superabundance. The amount of material that pours through those gates is overwhelming and, at the same time, annoyingly trivial and soulless.

Having finished my introspective orgy, I returned to my plan: an attempt to fathom the nature of LSD from inside the LSD trip.

I walked back toward the dancers, their movements a spindly robot poetry in the crisp predawn. They were swaying to scritchy-scratchy patterns of trance music underneath a screen of projected video showing swarming rhizomes and flimmering scenes from the collective psychedelic unconscious—the visual kitsch of the trance world. I lay down on a blanket and closed my eyes again. Immediately, multicolored geometries overlaid my interior view screen, spinning and changing at hyperspeed.

What was the meaning of these patterns and hyperreal hallucinatory forms? The pallid scientific thesis—that they were simply self-generated by-products of an overstimulation of the neocortex—does not account for their organized precision. They were as fully realized as the data seen in the eyes-opened world.

While tripping, I reviewed the events surrounding the discovery of LSD. In 1938, a Swiss chemist, Albert Hofmann, was working for Sandoz, a pharmaceutical company. Hofmann's assignment was to synthesize a series of derivatives of ergot, a fungus growing on wheat—in other words, a mushroom. Sandoz was looking for compounds that induced muscular contractions. Ergot has a long history of human use. For thousands of years perhaps, midwives and wise women have used ergot for its ability to induce labor. But ergot was also the source of

Saint Vitus' Dance, a violent disease causing descents into madness and death that struck like a plague when a village or region unsuspectedly ate bread made from ergot-infected wheat. In other words, like the history of LSD itself, ergot's interaction with humanity had positive and negative aspects. LSD and ergot were ambiguous tools.

Lysergic acid diethylamide was LSD-25, the twenty-fifth in a series of syntheses that Hofmann made from ergot. The compound was tested on animals. It seemed to have no useful effects, and it was shelved, along with thousands of other useless compounds, seemingly permanently. Hofmann, however, could not forget this particular chemical. He had dreams about it and what he recalled as "a peculiar presentiment." Something about its molecular structure compelled him to remake it—the only time he had resynthesized a compound that showed no promise. Five years later, in 1943, he made a new batch of LSD-25 in his laboratory in Basel. Somehow, he does not know how it happened, he either ingested a small amount of the substance or got some on his skin, and he was propelled on the first acid trip. Lying on his couch, he watched a "stream of fantastic images of extraordinary plasticity and vividness and accompanied by an intense kaleidoscopic play of colors." He assumed he had gone mad. A few days later, he decided to intentionally test LSD's psychopharmacological properties and ingested what he thought would be a minute amount—too little to affect him—but was, in fact, a whopping dose: 250 micrograms. After a now-legendary bicycle ride back to his home, he found himself hovering on his ceiling, staring down at his own body, convinced that he had died.

Why would a chemist go back and resynthesize, five years after the fact, one of thousands of compounds he had made, one that his company had already dismissed as having no value? And how strange that this would happen in 1943, in the center of Europe, as the Nazis geared up for the systematic deployment of the Final Solution. Most peculiar, perhaps, is that the discovery of LSD would happen only a year after nuclear fission was demonstrated, and as the first atomic bombs went into development.

Before he returned to it, Hofmann dreamt repeatedly of the molecular structure of LSD-25. In the annals of science, it is notable that many scientific insights first appear in dreams and visions. The

German chemist Friedrich Kekule, for instance, dreamt of a snake with its tail in its mouth, and understood that the molecular structure of benzene was a closed carbon ring. The French mathematician Jules-Henri Poincaré, during a sleepless night, saw mathematical symbols colliding until they coalesced into equations. These intuitive levels of insight, whether scientific or artistic, function like the prophetic dreams of shamans, or like the teachings, the "mind treasures," that Tibetan lamas sometimes receive from predecessors who have been dead for hundreds or thousands of years, through conscious dreams. According to the physicist David Bohm, the nature of insight remains beyond our understanding. "The insight is probably from immense depths of subtlety—perhaps even beyond the organism for all we know," he said. "The reflex of thought is continually resisting and defending against it, because the insight may be seen as a threat to the structure which you want to hold." Hofmann's discovery of LSD was that kind of insight—a flash from a deeper order of the self or, perhaps, from outside the self entirely.

When I arrived in Gabon, I had asked Lieberman how the Bwiti thought of iboga. I was told they considered it "a superconscious spiritual entity that guides mankind." At the time, of course, I dismissed this as impossible. Later, I was not so sure. During the iboga trip, it seemed that something—something I could only describe as a force or even an entity—took me by the hand and led me through my entire life up to that point. This being seemed able to navigate through time and to organize the data from the holographic index of my memories as easily as I might walk around the art in a museum hall. I recalled the fact that I had seen a golemlike statue carved from wood, and a Bwiti shaman had assured me that this was the spirit of iboga itself, "coming out to engage you in conversation."

What if it was literally true?

What if iboga was a sentient being, a spirit, or an extradimensional intelligence involved in human affairs?

Terence McKenna, in his book *Food of the Gods,* explored the history of the relation between human beings and psychoactive plants. He described hallucinogenic plants as "repositories of living vegetable gnosis." Like the Bwiti, he accepted the shamanic notion that these plants are ways of contacting higher dimensional entities disposed, in a more or less friendly fashion, toward the human attempt to develop higher consciousness. He wrote; "By entering the domain of plant intelligence, the shaman becomes, in a way, privileged by a higher dimensional perspective on experience."

Perhaps eating the iboga bark somehow linked me to a "spiritual entity" able to access and expose the hidden matrix of my life with such intentionality because it was, in some way, an extradimensional being, therefore not bound by our laws of space and time. Psilocybin and mescaline were also chemical catalysts of this kind—the Indians even said that "peyote was a plant that sees in six dimensions."

McKenna suspected that an archaic partnership with hallucinogenic mushrooms might have catalyzed the human acquisition of language, as well as being the basis of the religious impulse in man. He also speculated that the alkaloids extruded by these plants might be something like "exopheromones," chemicals created by one species to modify the behavior of another. Perhaps various psychoactive agents appeared—and vanished—at different times in history to push human beings to develop certain faculties.

If I could suspend disbelief, even for a moment, over the possibility that there were such extradimensional beings involved in human affairs, then it seemed sensible to understand the timely appearance of LSD as an interpolation into our realm. The chemical catalyst was a connective cord or something like a dial-up connection to a higher-dimensional entity of enormous intelligence, somewhat cold but essentially empathic, dispensing foresight and catalyzing knowledge. The "other" had used Hofmann as a means of getting into our world.

As I lay on the blanket with eyes closed, listening to the skittering beat of the trance music, ignoring the cheerful glow-stick-waving freaks dancing nearby, I hypothesized that the timing of the "discovery" of LSD in nearly the same moment as the Final Solution, the Holocaust, and the construction of nuclear weapons might be far from coincidental. Perhaps this exact sequence of events has happened many, many times in the history of the cosmos. Perhaps there are numerous planets sprinkled across the universe's starry voids where a sentient, tool-using species rises up from the evolutionary muck to discover instrumental reason, mechanistic science, then sprints straight to the perilous point where they unleash the force of the atom. Perhaps, time after time, this intoxication with mechanical rationalism requires, in a kind of dialectical process, temporary amnesia, the loss of connection to archaic spiritual knowledge. Precisely at that dangerous and difficult transitional moment, a probe is sent down from the extra dimensions. This probe takes the form of a molecule with the power to radically transform the nature of consciousness. Unlike the local plant spirits that have spurred evolution over thousands of years, this new catalyst has to be mass-producible, simple to synthesize and distribute, and extremely powerful. The molecular probe or catalyst allows the recovery of lost levels of awareness, reveals gaps and flaws in the mechanistic worldview, and forces a reconsideration of the nature of reality, as well as the relationship between "subjective" awareness and "objective" world, from inside the domain of the narrow "rationality." LSD reveals reality as more supple, more capable of being reshaped and reinvented, than anyone can begin to know.

McKenna wrote, "The suppression of the natural human fascination with altered states of consciousness and the present perilous situation of all life on earth are intimately and causally connected." Beyond all of its other messages, the LSD trip supports the core truth of that statement. Although Western science continues to dismiss and ignore the possibility, the subjective perspective of human consciousness remains the only conceivable link—or, if you will, escape hatch—to other realms and higher dimensions. LSD and the other psychedelics suggest, with remarkable persistence, that humanity has more to learn about its place in the cosmos—discoveries that can only be made through inner experience and study of the self.

But if LSD was such a transformative tool, then why had the sixties ended in ruins? Why had human beings failed to be transformed in their essence?

LSD pushed the West to rediscover the mystical impulse and it helped to launch mass movements of personal liberation and ecological consciousness, but at the same time it inspired the covert control apparatus of the intelligence agencies to turn its most terrifying fantasies into "meat-hook realities." In other words, LSD catalyzed and accelerated both sides of the liberation/domination dialectic. LSD has caused creative breakthroughs and unleashed latent psychoses. It is an ambiguous tool.

There is a secret history of scientists exploring psychedelics that remains to be uncovered and studied. Among scientists and engineers, LSD and other psychoactive chemicals continue to be used as tools to catalyze insights. For instance, the genetics researcher Kary Mullis, winner of the Nobel prize for his discovery of polymer chain reactions, used LSD for visualizations and problem-solving. Mullis has been one of the few to proclaim his psychedelic use. Mark Pesce credits his contributions to writing VRML, a virtual reality programming language, to insights he received from psilocybin. Many of the computer programmers and technical engineers responsible for creating the personal computer and the Internet were devout acidheads in their youth, and the younger generation has followed in their footsteps. That the brain trust of Silicon Valley descends annually onto the hallucinatory carnival of Burning Man demonstrates the close connection between psychedelic perception and cutting-edge computer science.

Watching the dancers at the trance party, I thought of an idea of Henri Bergson, a philosopher of the Industrial Age. Bergson suggested the universe "was a machine to create Gods." The mechanistic metaphor was jarring, but the underlying idea—that despite surface appearances, humanity, as a mass, is accelerating toward some particular end—seems plausible, although one-dimensional. By revealing the gaps in the materialist worldview and undermining every certainty with secret laughter, LSD makes it abundantly clear that our current civilization is not "the end of history," not the final form our evolution will take.

Psychedelics revealed to Terence McKenna "a curious literary quality running across the surface of existence." A poem, to a formalist critic, is "a machine made out of words," designed to create a certain effect. According to McKenna, the shamanic perspective is that the world, ultimately, is made out of language, woven from myth—in other words, an objectified expression of consciousness.

The notion that the world of matter is actually a densified form of consciousness is intrinsic to Buddhism. For Buddhists, physical reality is only relatively real, and matter ultimately has as much or as little intrinsic reality as the objects we might encounter in a lucid dream. As Lama Anagarika Govinda writes in *Foundations of Tibetan Mysticism*, the body is "the coagulated, crystallized, or materialized consciousness of the past." It is the manifestation of accrued karma, constructed by subtle levels of the mind. While tripping, I could easily perceive my own life—and everybody else's—as a kind of cosmic fable, a gnostic comic book, or a passion play that we were all writing. More and more, I suspect that Buddhists and shamans are correct. We live in a world made out of language, woven from consciousness, whether we ever allow ourselves to know it or not.

Part Seven

ΕΝΤΗΕΟΒΟΤΑΝΥ

*Other echoes
Inhabit the garden. Shall we follow?*

—T .S. ELIOT

Chapter 28

WHITE BLOSSOMS

One night, sitting outside a bungalow of the serene Chan Kah Hotel in Palenque, Mexico, I met Douglas, a traveler from British Columbia. Tall and long-limbed, Douglas had black dreadlocks, wide heavy-lidded eyes, and an appealingly attenuated goat face. He was not enrolled in the symposium I was attending, the last annual Visionary Entheobotany Conference after a thirteen-year run. "Entheobotany" is an eccentric coinage, merging ethnobotany with "entheo" to create a new discipline: the study of god-releasing plants. This week-long gathering used to be a major source for cutting-edge knowledge of obscure intoxicants, art historical clues, archaeological discoveries, and plant recipes, but the Internet has absorbed some of those functions. It was attended by a well-heeled audience of enthusiastic psychonauts. Douglas was visiting from Pan-Chan, a popular low-budget hang-out along the road to the nearby Mayan ruins. With two restaurants, three campgrounds, hostels, and bungalows, as well as nightly entertainment of fire dancers and didgeridoos, Pan-Chan is a hippie institution, where college kids and broke wanderers rent small huts or sleep in collective circles under huge tents. The Chan Kah Hotel is a palace of luxury by comparison.

Douglas told me how, when he was twenty, he had hitchhiked

down to Florida with his girlfriend. She left him in Key West, where he ran out of money. For several months he lived in a park with other homeless kids, panhandling to survive. One night, a friend of his said, "Dude, we don't have any cash, but I heard about this flower you can eat that gets you really high." They went out on a search. They found a tree growing the flowers his friend had heard about. The white blossoms were long, pendulous, trumpet-shaped. They picked the flowers and ate three of them each.

The tree was datura. Datura, also known as jimson weed, has been used since time immemorial by Indians in North and South America in initiation rituals and other ceremonies. In North America, it was sacred to the Navajo, Zuni, and Algonquin, among many other tribes. In some places, adolescents would take a single massive dose and "unlive their former lives." At the end of the two-week trip, the initiate would describe his visions to the shaman. Based on those visions, the shaman would decide what role the initiate would play in the tribe, as well as the future course of his life.

Datura is equally renowned in Asia. "When Buddha was preaching, heaven sprinkled the plant with dew or raindrops," according to *Plants of the Gods*. "A Taoist legend maintained that Datura metel is one of the circumpolar stars and that envoys to earth from that star carry a flower of the plant in their hand."

In India, the seeds are smoked by yellow-robed ascetics and followers of Shiva—the flower can be found in many statues of Shiva, blossoming in his long hair. Datura contains the same alkaloids as solanaceous plants such as belladonna, henbane, and mandrake, the key ingredients in the "flying potions" of European witchcraft. Datura produces scopolamine and other toxins that act directly on the central nervous system. I have read many accounts of datura trips, and they are remarkably consistent. The effect is long-lasting and terrifying. It is part of the peculiar logic of the War on Drugs in America that datura, which is dangerous and dissociative and can in fact kill you, is legal to own and to use, while marijuana, one of the least harmful of intoxicants, remains illegal and demonized. Unlike ayahuasca or mushrooms or LSD, datura is the real horror-film hallucinogen—those who ingest the plant find themselves in unreal worlds of psychosis that seem totally convincing. The spirit of the plant often appears as a cackling witch or beautiful woman. Dreams of flying, of transformation into animals and satanic orgies are common. Unprepared trippers often end their journeys in straitjackets.

"For three days," Douglas said, "I had no idea what was happening to me. I remember, at one point, I was climbing a mountain, going up rock by rock, hand over hand. Then I came back to myself, and I was actually crawling along the sidewalk on my hands and knees." Continually dry-mouthed and dissociative, he had long conversations with friends, family members, and strangers, but later he found out that none of those talks actually happened. "Luckily, this guy I knew found us. He knew about jimson weed and he figured out what was going on. He brought us to his house and took care of us until the effects wore off." After seventy-two hours, Douglas recovered his senses. A few months later, he returned home to Canada. "One thing that was weird after that," he said, "although I never tried datura again, I kept wanting to do it, thinking of it, and several times I tried to convince friends to take it with me, telling them how cool it was."

Seven years passed before Douglas went down to Mexico to visit another friend. His friend was living with the Huichols, the tribe made famous in the 1960s by Barbara Meyerhoff's book *Peyote Hunt*. The Huichol go on a long sacred pilgrimage every year, traveling to a distant desert and storing up supplies of peyote. His friend was learning the Huichol language, studying their traditions in exchange for his labor. He brought Douglas to meet the tribe's shaman, a small, wrinkled man in his seventies. The shaman looked at him for a moment, then turned to his friend and said one word in the Huichol language, which his friend then translated: "Datura."

Douglas was stunned. Embarrassed by memories of being dissociative and out-of-control and generally uncool, he had never mentioned the hellish trip to his friends. The shaman immediately saw that he had encountered datura, that he had been damaged by the malicious plant-spirit. Datura had wounded his psyche and this wound had never been repaired. The shaman offered to repair the damage. During a ceremony, the old man chanted over his body, sucked at his skin and spat out—the brusque techniques of traditional shamanic healing. For hours, until he was convinced that the healing had taken effect, the old shaman sang, spritzed tobacco juice and mescal over his bare torso, dispelling the evil presence. "I didn't feel different right away, but over time, my life seemed to go better than before," he said. "I don't know if it was that ceremony or not that made the difference."

I heard many stories like that one during my week in Palenque, stories of plants with specific powers, of shamans able to commune with them and perform healings. The Visionary Entheobotany Conference featured several lectures each day. The lecturers were a curious mixture of chemists, psychedelic researchers, hipster anthropologists, ethnobotanists, and art historians. After the 1960s, when psychedelics became so interesting to so many people that they were quickly outlawed and suppressed, the study of mind-altering plants was relegated to the cultural margins. I didn't know it when I first became interested in the subject, but outside of the mainstream the area was never abandoned. A group of brilliant researchers and seekers, independent mavericks, have pursued the subject with single-minded passion and diligence. Many of them self-published their findings in remarkable tomes. I had the opportunity to meet some of them.

Chapter 29

THE QUALITY
OF REVEALING

A Ph.D. chemist in his sixties who started his career working for Dow, Sasha Shulgin has dedicated himself to discovering and analyzing new mind-altering compounds. In person, he is a large man, wearing untucked Hawaiian shirts and projecting a warm, Santa Claus vibe.

"I went to Harvard, didn't fit in there, so I went into the navy," he recalled at Palenque. "In the navy, I first thought about the connection between psychology and chemistry when I was given morphine after an accident. The pain was still there but it didn't bother me anymore. I found that fascinating: How could I have pain and it not hurt?" He first tried mescaline—"gorgeous crystals, long, needle-shaped"—in 1960. He described the experience in his book *PIHKAL*: "More than anything else, the world amazed me, in that I saw it as I had when I was a child. I had forgotten the beauty and the magic and the knowingness of it and me." What remained with him, above all, was the realization that "this awesome recall had been brought about by a fraction of a gram of a white solid." The colors of the world, the reclaiming of childhood sensations, was not inside the powder. The chemical only revealed what was inside of him.

"I understood that our entire universe is contained in the mind and the spirit. We may choose not to find access to it, we may even deny its existence, but it is indeed there inside us, and there are chemicals that can catalyze its availability." He synthesized a mescalinelike chemical, changing the position of one atom. "This time I tore up the flower instead of staring at it." He was amazed that such a small change in a compound could reveal such utterly different aspects of his own mind. Fascinated, he began to synthesize "a whole cascade of white solids"— he had found his field of research.

If the counterculture accorded an equivalent to the Nobel prize, Shulgin would be a shoe-in for the honor. He pulled MDMA, ecstasy, out of the dustbin of ignored old chemicals—it was originally made by a German company in the 1920s, then forgotten. Shulgin resynthesized MDMA in the late 1960s, noted its fizzy, empathic properties—"It was not a psychedelic in the visual or interpretive sense, but the lightness and warmth of the psychedelic was present and quite remarkable. . . . I developed a great respect and admiration for the material"—and launched it on the thirty-year trajectory that would lead to the smiley-faced rave culture we know today, as well as an effective, often obscured, tradition of psychotherapeutic use. But that was just one of Shulgin's accomplishments. He made the long-lasting psychedelic DOM, later given the street name STP ("serenity, tranquillity, and peace," or, Shulgin recalls, "too Stupid To Puke"). As often happened with Shulgin, he found the chemical, self-tested and analyzed its effects, published a paper about it, then found later that dealers had ripped off his formula and distributed it to the street in excessive dosages. STP is a heavy-duty mind warper—Shulgin's unfortunate contribution to the chaos of the late 1960s. It lasts a long time (ten to sixteen hours), and its effects take hours to come on—kids would take a pill, wait a while and think that nothing was happening, then take another pill. When the double dose kicked in, disoriented trippers would end up in emergency rooms. Shulgin discovered what was happening quickly. Ironically, at the same time he was inventing new chemicals, he was also employed by the DEA to analyze new drugs turned up by the police.

With his wife, Ann, Shulgin has self-published two books, *PIHKAL* ("Phenethylamines I Have Known and Loved") and *TIHKAL* ("Tryptamines I Have Known and Loved"), that are thick compendiums of his research and development of hundreds of new psychoactive chemicals. He published his findings because of the example of Wilhelm Reich, the once-esteemed German psychoanalyst, promoter of sexual liberation and the orgasm, who came to the United States to escape Nazi persecution. The story of Reich's later life is tragic and cautionary: Continuing his research in the United States, he believed that he had uncovered a regenerative biological force, which he called Orgone Energy. In the 1950s, Reich, carried away by what may have been crackpot enthusiasm, marketed Orgone Boxes, which looked a bit like telephone booths, as a way of concentrating this life-giving force. He believed his boxes provided protection against cancer and other health risks. The FDA imprisoned Reich for making unproven health claims for his boxes, and he died, brokenhearted, in prison. After his death, the U.S. government, in the grip of cultural McCarthyism, seized Reich's archives of unpublished papers and destroyed them. Shulgin realized such a fate was possible for any scientist working far outside of the mainstream, especially in his much-demonized arena, and he decided to distribute his knowledge as a form of self-protection.

Shulgin's chemical engineering is much more exact than the frothy pseudoscience behind Reich's orgone. In the books, Shulgin split his research into two classes of chemicals, each related to one of the brain's major neurotransmitters: serotonin, which is a tryptamine, and dopamine, a phenethylamine. Tryptamines found in nature include DMT, LSD, psilocybin, and bufotenin. Well-known phenethylamines include mescaline, MDMA, and MDA—the simple molecule, phenethylamine itself, is a major constituent of chocolate.

"A molecule is like a dangling hexagon," Shulgin said. "I ask myself: How many things can I attach to it. It is like putting decorations on a Christmas tree. You can do things in six different ways. I try to test out all of the options. When you find a little something at one level, you don't double the amount, don't leap into a new level. Early on in my research, I tried to find the most potent compounds. Later I backed away from that to search for the most interesting and revealing. The potency is less important than the quality of the revealing."

I have taken the opportunity to sample a few of the concoctions analyzed in Shulgin's books. Most intriguing—so intriguing, in fact, that it is now, alas, Schedule One—was 2CB, a compound described to me, accurately, as a "super-sanity" drug. One of the only creations to be given a "+++++" in Shulgin's version of a five-star rating system, 2CB is known to be very dose-sensitive. A tiny increase of 5 or 10 milligrams in the ingested amount can cause a spectacular increase or radical transformation of effect. In low doses, as I tried it, 2CB increases mental and sensory acuity. Thoughts zing around the mind on high-tension wires. Light reveals itself as precision filaments, as spindly networks of refractions. If 2CB were legally available, it would be, on low doses, an intriguing, highly productive tool for intellectual labor.

For those explorers who are hard core into the psychedelic culture—deeper into it than I care to go—there is a trend called "poly-drugging" in which multiple chemicals are mixed and matched. The professional psychonaut Jonathan Ott calls this process the "bioassay." He sees it as scientific experimenting. In this terra incognita, abandoned by the academies, the only possible territory for the experiment is your own brain and nervous system. Although I am, compared to some, a psychonautical chicken, I did try one such chemical cocktail— a martini-mix of MDMA with a vermouth-sized whisper of 2CB. I will not tell a lie. That combination was a magic meld of warmth, euphoria, and clear light. It is consciousness as an Air Elemental or sylph must enjoy it. I hasten to add, despite the rush of that lucid, limpid state, I felt no compulsion to repeat the trip. There was no addictive pull toward it; it was, as Huxley described mescaline, a "gratuitous grace," with a faint chemical bite. While walking around a mist-shrouded forest on that potion, I suddenly realized exactly who Shulgin is: With his bushy eyebrows, including a few straying strands of prodigious length, and white curly beard, he is the contemporary reincarnation of Merlin, original druid and archaic alchemical genius of the British Isles. Shulgin is an alchemist engaged in the ageless quest for the consciousness-expanding elixir or philosophers' stone.

PIHKAL and *TIHKAL* are texts devoted to Shulgin's singular intellectual enterprise, and not just references but also memoirs, philosophical treatises, essays on the suspect politics of the drug war, meditations on the nature of consciousness, chemistry lessons, and recipe books. Despite FDA scrutiny and government raids on his laboratory, Shulgin has never been arrested and is unwavering in his belief in the inherent importance of drugs as tools for self-exploration. In the introduction to

TIHKAL he describes the entry of psychedelics into the consciousness of the West as a parallel process running beside the discovery of new technologies of destruction—an Eros to the technobureaucractic Thanatos. Shulgin states that radiation was discovered in 1897, one year before Arthur Heffter tried mescaline in Leipzig.

"Since almost all discoveries about the physical world can be used for both benign and lethal purposes, it is essential that we begin to develop a way of exploring and understanding those forces within our unconscious selves which will inevitably make those decisions," he writes. While cautioning explorers to seek veteran guides and be aware of the dangers, Shulgin notes that psychoactive compounds are the swiftest means to self-exploration, and with the ever-increasing dangers of modern technology as well as the rapid growth of authoritarian controls, our own awareness must take quantum leaps to keep pace. "These tools—the psychedelic drugs and plants—offer a much faster method than most of the classical alternatives for the accomplishments of the goals we seek: conscious awareness of our interior workings and greater clarity as to our responsibilities towards our own species and all others with whom we share this planet."

In the books, he diagrams each molecule, describes the process of synthesizing it, then recounts his own self-testing, beginning with a low dose and slowly moving up. If the compounds reached a certain point of evident interest, Shulgin would share them with his wife and a close circle of psychonautical friends—weekend experiments, continued over years, that have become the stuff of underground legend. One of my favorites of these anonymous reports goes as follows: "About 10 seconds or so after inhaling the last of the smoke, it began with a fast-rising sense of excitement and wonder, with an undertone of 'Now you've done it,' but dominated by a sense of 'WOW, this is it.' "

He has found drugs that affect only one of the senses, such as DIPT, which causes changes in hearing, a collapse of any sense of pitch. He has done fascinating experiments with cyclotron machines that showed the surprising path of certain mind-altering compounds through the body—for instance, the long-lasting compound DOB affects the mind although it is absorbed by the lungs. "We saw DOB go directly into the lung, not into the brain. There are neurons in the lung,

and then, while it was there, DOB metabolized into something else."
Shulgin has invented, over the course of his career, a tool kit for exploring consciousness—as well as the senses, the mind, and the emotions.
Due to the prohibition on mind drugs, except for ego-controlling SSRIs
like Prozac, there is no major research facility anywhere in the world
studying the possible uses of these tools in more detail, unless the CIA
has remained covertly on the case.

Shulgin believes that psychedelics are, for the mind, what the telescope was for astronomical research, or the microscope for biology.
They are instruments that create the grounds for new discoveries. He
equates the continued animosity toward exploration of the mind
through chemicals to the Church's reaction to Galileo's theory that the
earth was not at the center of the solar system. Three hundred and
fifty years ago, Shulgin notes, the Church proclaimed, "The earth is the
center of the universe, and anyone who says otherwise is a heretic."
Today, the government proclaims, "All drugs that can expand consciousness are without medical or social justification, and anyone who
uses them is a criminal." In Galileo's time, the authorities said, "We do
not need to actually look through that mysterious contraption." Now
the government says, "There is no need to actually taste those mysterious compounds." In the past, the Church said, "How dare you claim
that the earth is not the center of the universe?" Today the government
says, "How dare you claim that an understanding of God is to be found
in a white powder?"

He quotes Voltaire: "It is dangerous to be right in matters on
which the established authorities are wrong."

Chapter 30

THE FAIRY FOLK

The attendees at the conference were a mixture of hedonists and scientists, public school teachers and English aristocrats, suburban housewives and therapists, promoters of unscheduled drugs and witches, advertising copywriters and apprentice shamans. There was Paul, a precocious nineteen-year-old from Utah, long-haired, pale, and frail, who seemed to have committed to memory entire archives of information about psychoactive compounds, minds, and molecules. For Paul, the world was a multileveled cosmic-gnostic conspiracy. He warned me about evidence of mental deterioration caused by high levels of fluoride in the U.S. drinking water, told me to read a six-volume set of works on earlier civilizations and UFO contact. When I passed him in the dining area, where he was conferring with Shulgin or other experts, Paul always seemed to be making comments such as, "I am really interested in the structure of that benzene molecule when you add that particular indole ring."

There was Psycho Tim, a black-mustachio'd middle-aged chemical engineer working for Monsanto in his real life, building new mood alterers, who broke out subcultural T-shirts of aliens, lizards, and 'shrooms for his week of unbridled psychoactivity. Dara, a witch from Tennessee, had been hired as a gardener by the Catholic Church, then fired for her pagan beliefs, and was now involved in a lengthy lawsuit demanding reinstatement. Dara had a nervous edginess, a recognizably ambiguous witchy twitchiness to her. It was not surprising to learn that her ally of choice was datura. There was the lovely, batty Lady Neipath, wearing colorful designer outfits, with husband, Lord Neipath, in tow. Lady Neipath had achieved a certain amount of shuddery notoriety for her avowed belief in trephination, once common among Aztec nobility. Simply put, trephination is the practice of drilling a not-inconsiderable hole in the top of the skull, thought to increase intelligence and mystical communication by speeding blood flow through the brain. The Neipaths not only put up a Website on the subject, they both underwent the procedure—Lady Neipath had, in fact, trepanned herself in her starry-eyed, bohemian youth.

There was talk at the conference about William Pickard, a Harvard academic and friend of Lord and Lady Neipath. Recently busted in Kansas, Pickard was allegedly responsible for building an LSD factory inside an abandoned nuclear missile silo on private land, producing as much as ten million doses of LSD a month (a third of all the LSD produced in the United States, by one estimate). The silo had been outfitted with a whirlpool bath, Italian marble tiling, and a £60,000 audio system, according to *The Times* of London.

There was only one drug that, if it could be found around the shadowy margins of the conference, I was keen to test-drive. That was the purified form of synthetic dimethyltryptamine. Through plants such as *Psychotria viridis,* DMT is a component in ayahuasca potions. It is also present in the psychoactive snuffs used by tribes such as the Yanomamo of Brazil—famous films of the Yanomamo show the tribesmen, naked except for a penis sheath, blowing powder through long tubes up each other's nostrils, then shaking their heads, wildly entranced, as thick rivulets of green snot pour out. From all I had read, the smokable or injected form of synthetic DMT—no snot involved— seemed to be modern science's greatest contribution to archaic Amazonian spirituality: It was supposed to provide an instant breakthrough into out-of-body visionary experience—you go up like a rocket and splash down in under ten minutes. Over the last decades, smoked synthetic DMT was popularized as the ego-crusher-of-choice by the late Terence McKenna.

McKenna fluently described his DMT flashes as "bursting into a space inhabited by merry elfin, self-transforming, machine creatures. Dozens of these friendly fractal entities, looking like self-dribbling Fabergé eggs on the rebound, had surrounded me and tried to teach me the lost language of true poetry. They seemed to be babbling in a visible and five-dimensional form of Ecstatic Nostratic, to judge from the emotional impact of this gnomish prattle. Mirror-surfaced tumbling rivers of melted meaning flowed gurgling around me." McKenna was the star lecturer and biggest draw of the Visionary Entheobotany Conference up until his death, after which the event seemed to have lost its impetus and its force, and attendance dropped by more than half.

Throughout Central and South America, many Indian tribes settled near sources of potent tryptamines, which influenced their language, cosmology, and shamanic practices over centuries. Submersion in the DMT state was the ultimate spiritual goal. Even though it can be chemically synthesized from numerous botanical sources—commonly available plants such as phalaris grass, acacia, and Mimosa hostilis—there is something oddly inaccessible about pure DMT. Unless I am mistaken, it seems that smokable DMT, the physical stuff as well as the bizarre realms it reveals, has a leprechaunlike quality. Sometimes DMT turns up when you are not ready for it—"instant other world access? Of course I appreciate the offer but you see I have this dentist appointment tomorrow"—and then, when you are finally prepared to blast off, it will vanish. In my search for the stuff I kept meeting people who had it, or proudly announced that they did, but then would begin to mumble or look away when I actually asked for a tiny lump from their stash. Not much is more than enough; a lifetime supply would be smaller than a bar of hotel soap. I know of other DMT-seekers who waited, plotted, finally found it—as well as the proper set and setting, the requisite glass pipe and butane lighter, the shamanic helper and proper astrological alignment—and then found themselves coughing up the precious vapor before they could ingest enough of it to blast off. As Mark Pesce told me at Burning Man, "I've never been able to hold the smoke long enough to get through the glass chrysanthemum."

As DMT did not instantly materialize, I went with another

conferee, a Bay Area lawyer working at a think tank on educational policy, on a hunt for mushrooms, the local specialty. Attempts to buy drugs are always exercises in humiliation. In this case, we had to ask locals, old wizened ladies selling candy on the road, for directions to *los hongos*. They pointed to a dirt trail and we marched along it cluelessly until a young boy rode out to us on a donkey. With a solemn and professional manner, he told us to wait while he fetched plastic bags full of black murk with a slush of mushrooms floating around inside—highly unappetizing. Somehow ashamed by the entire transaction, we forgot to bargain him down from his high asking price.

Before the mushrooms, eaten in a broth of Mexican chocolate, we took a first course of moclobemide, an over-the-counter (in Mexico, anyway) antidepressant containing a monoamine oxidase inhibitor. As with ayahuasca combinations, the effect of this MAO-I was to potentiate the tryptamines in the mushroom. I had never tried such a combination before, and its fizzy chemical ambience disturbed me.

A few years earlier, when I revived my interest in psychedelics, I first went through a merry mushroom-eating phase. I was impressed by the way moderate doses of mushrooms added levels and layers to normal conscious life—colors and sounds deepened, the effect of a pattern of light and shadows could become almost unbearably beautiful, my own empathic and emotional qualities seemed finer-tuned. On higher doses, with eyes closed, I saw those Aztec-patterned sci-fi civilizations flying past me at jet speed, as McKenna described, although I never took the five-gram megadose that, according to McKenna, leads to direct communication with a loquacious "mushroom man." The Aztec futurist imagery still seemed like something that could be an optical effect, a rapid firing of neuronal impulses caused by a drug working on neurotransmitters.

That night, on mushrooms and moclobemide in Palenque, I saw something that I absolutely did not want to see—something so ludicrous, so embarrassing that I hesitate to tell it. Lying on a bed in a darkened room with eyes closed, I watched rapid bands of green and yellow flimmering across my inner view screen, typical optical effects, but these green blobs suddenly sharpened into focus—the knobs of my internal receiver turning—until I found myself staring at a group of laughing green elves standing in a line.

There were many of them. A mob of little people in traditional green outfits and peaked caps. The elves were jumping up and down and they were cheering. When I saw them, I could hear their cheers faintly in my ears—"Hooray!" They seemed to be welcoming me, very happy and excited because I had seen them. What was alarming about this apparition was that it was like a photographic projection: The elves were as clear to my inner vision as film images. How could this happen?

Of course, there are many possible answers. The elves could have been some form of high-resolution delusion. Perhaps my previous psychedelic endeavors were making me susceptible to new forms of nuttiness. *If I am going to hallucinate,* I thought before eating the mushrooms, *show me something related to the majestic Palenque ruins, evoke the cruel and silent Mayan gods.* Instead, here confronting me were a bunch of happy elves. This was leprechaun kitsch, an outtake from a Disney flick. I had no interest in elves and was perturbed to see them. Perhaps some element of my unconscious had glommed onto the "Elf Archetype" and pulled it up from out of my childhood. I knew McKenna's writing on DMT, and I might have been influenced by it, although these elves were not transforming and not at all machinelike. They were just normal, garden-variety fairies.

Another option to consider:

Maria Sabina, the famous Mazatec shamaness, called the mushrooms she used in divination and healing "the sacred children." She said that these children appeared to her when she ate the mushrooms, and they showed her how to heal people, told her what plants to use, and generally helped in all of her undertakings. Perhaps I was being allowed a glimpse of Sabina's "sacred children." Was it my cultural bias or a universal phenomenon that they appeared identical to the traditional "fairy folk" or the "good neighbors"—those archaic spirits of the Welsh and Irish countryside, exhaustively chronicled in a wonderful turn-of-the-century book by Dr. W. Y. Evans-Wentz called *The Fairy Folk in Celtic Countries.* Evans-Wentz took hundreds of testimonies from country folk and local seers who had confronted the fairies—actually, there seemed to be different hierarchies of supernatural locals, including the Siddhi, the "tall shining ones," and pygmy fairies such as gnomes, leprechauns, and "Little People." Contradicting the restrictive dogmatism of modern rationalism, Evans-Wentz argued that because these peculiar dwellers in their sylvan worlds had been encountered by so many otherwise sensible Celts, and appeared as such a universal element in world folklore, they had, in some way, to be real.

Chapter 31

WHY DID YOU EAT US?

A tentative exploration of such "magical" realms leads the seeker beyond the boundaries of the "consensual reality" of Western science and hard materialism with no way to return. Once you have gone through "the door in the wall," the looking glass, the glass chrysanthemum, you are a permanent exile, forever on the other side looking back—exactly like those poor little elves, trapped in my mind, waving frantically to get my attention, trying to tell me that they, too, exist, although in a way we can't fathom. Once you have seen the elves, you might as well trepan your skull to complete the process.

In the sophisticated contemporary world, it seems absurd to propose that the dismissed and disgraced psychedelic compounds might be real doorways to neighboring dimensions, and within those other realms there are beings we can contact who are waiting to welcome us with disconcerting glee. It is even more absurd to suggest that some of those beings resemble our folkloric archetypes, because they are the source for those archetypes in the first place.

Beyond early childhood, most of us learn to keep our minds shut to the possibility that other worlds exist beyond this seemingly solid, deterministic one that we accept as reality. We are trained, indoctrinated, to void those aspects of our being that belong to the realms of insight, intuition, spiritual manifestation, and dream. The narrowed consciousness of "adulthood" is a kind of rigidly defined trance, continually reimprinted on us by the world we have created. If we studied the matter, we might discover that our modern presumptions of rationality rely entirely on secondhand information, on faith in what "experts" have told us. They have no more basis in "reality" than a vivid dream or a child's fantasy.

I watched the excitable elves for a few minutes only. The spectacle was making me too existentially tense. As the effects of the mushrooms wore off, I got up and went for a walk with Robert, my new friend, who wanted to tell me about his life.

I had met Robert on the buffet line at lunch. Gray-bearded, in his early fifties, he looked a bit like a jovial version of the late Hemingway. He told me he had been doing shamanic work in Hawaii and Massachusetts, using the "ayahuasca analogue" of *Mimosa hostilis* and Syrian Rue.

"The ayahuasca vine has a long history in the Amazon," Robert explained. "This other medicine has no history—it was only discovered ten years ago. As Westerners, we can start from scratch. We can create our own tradition."

I told him I didn't think Westerners could become shamans. We lacked the discipline and the traditional training methods, which include long periods of celibacy and fasting, plus nearly fatal ingestions of tobacco juice and various herbal potions. Robert said, quietly, that he had gone through it all in his own way.

Robert grew up in Massachusetts. He said his hometown was the place to which the remaining witches moved after the Salem witch trials drove them undercover, and it preserved a tradition of witchcraft, the European residue of shamanism, until the death of the last witch in 1950. Years after he moved away, he learned that the house in which he grew up had been her home, a local landmark in the town. Robert said his family had lived in Massachusetts since the Colonial era. One of his ancestors even came over on the *Mayflower*. As a young man, he began to experience, through dreams and hints, a "call" toward shamanism.

"I was in my mid-twenties when my wife left me with two small kids," Robert recalled. "She ran away. Later I found the house where we were living was on a Ley line, which probably caused some of our problems. Anyway, one night I had this dream. In the dream, a thunder cloud appeared over my head. It reached down an enormous, muscular arm, grabbed me, and pulled me up toward the cloud. In the dream I struggled and just managed to break free before I was taken inside the cloud. I fell back to earth and, at that moment, woke up. I looked out the window. It was a clear night sky, full of stars, but just outside my window there was one thunder cloud. The cloud let out three claps of thunder—*Boom! Boom! Boom!*—and floated away."

Over the next months Robert discovered two unusual things happening to him at the same time: "First of all, I started to realize that I was becoming a woman. I was growing breasts and my hormones were going haywire. My girlfriend at the time left me because she said I had lost my 'male energy.' "

At the same time he lost his maleness, he was undergoing another confusing and improbable process: He was developing the ability to control the weather.

"Of course I didn't believe it, who would? But I kept testing it and it kept working. If I thought about rain, clouds would gather and it would start to rain. If I thought of the sun, the clouds would go away and the sun would appear."

As he was comprehending this situation, he started to lose his breasts. He returned to manliness, and he could no longer control atmospheric forces. The entire episode lasted five months. "It was maybe five or six years later that I happened to pick up a book about Native American cultures."

Richard read about the Lakota, who had a traditional figure called the Heyoka. The Heyoka was a kind of shaman who lived away from the tribe, on a hill nearby, with the entrance to his tepee pointed in the opposite direction. "The Heyoka always dressed in women's clothing, and traditionally he was thought to have the power to control the weather."

"You were becoming a Heyoka?"

"The Lakota believe there are Thunder Beings who live in the clouds, and they want human beings to take on this role of Heyoka. Now, Thunder Beings look around and they don't see any Indians. They nominated me as a likely candidate." He believes that, if he hadn't wriggled out of the Thunder Being's grasp in the dream, he would have been trapped in the role of Heyoka. "The whole thing makes me wonder how many people are in mental institutions because some spiritual entity was trying to work through them or communicate with them in some way."

When he was in his late twenties, still living in Massachusetts and working as a gardener (he gardened for the Kennedys for a while), Robert had a dream in which he saw a patch of red-and-yellow mushrooms growing in his backyard, and picked and ate them. Several months later, he went into his backyard and he found the same mushrooms growing in the place where they had been in the dream. He looked the mushrooms up in a book and learned that they were an American strain of Fly Agarics, or *Amanita muscaria* (the American strain is red and yellow, while the Asian variety is red and white).

Fly Agarics are the famous red-capped, white-spotted mushrooms of Siberian shamanism. Often characterized as deadly poisonous in mycology guides, the mushrooms are known to cause a range of distortions. They can make objects in the world seem much bigger or smaller, an effect Lewis Carroll had incorporated into *Alice in Wonderland* (it is unknown whether Carroll had personal knowledge of the "bemushroomed" state). Gordon Wasson argued that *Amanita* was the Soma of the *Rig Veda*.

Here is how Fly Agarics inspired the Santa Claus legend: In Siberia, the mushrooms were rare and extremely valuable—apparently one mushroom could cost the same as a reindeer. Ibotenic acid and the other active ingredients of the mushroom concentrate in urine, and up to seven or eight people can share the intoxication by passing along their piss. Many Siberian tribesmen even preferred ingesting the piss as it caused less gastric distress. Reindeer also loved to drink the mushroom-scented piss. All a Siberian nomad had to do was pour a bit of the piss on the ground and reindeer would come galloping over from miles around. This archaic, symbiotic relationship—reindeer, red-and white-capped beings bringing gifts from the other world, the frozen tundra—was incorporated, consciously or not, into the story of Santa Claus.

Robert dried the mushrooms from his backyard and arranged to eat them with a friend. One night they ate three mushrooms each. An hour and a half passed. Absolutely nothing happened. "We were disappointed. I went into the kitchen to get a beer from the fridge," he recalled. "I took out the beer, turned around, and across the kitchen there were three huge mushrooms staring at me—a five-foot-tall, a four-foot-tall, and a three-foot-tall mushroom. The mushrooms were red and yellow and they had little eyes and little mouths. They looked just as solid and real as me or you."

He stared at the mushrooms. The mushrooms stared at him. Finally, the largest of the mushrooms spoke to him.

"Why did you eat us?" it asked.

He thought about it for a moment. "I was just following my dream."

The mushrooms conferred with each other. Finally they seemed satisfied by his answer. "But are you prepared to follow this path?" the tallest Fly Agaric asked.

Robert answered, intuitively and without hesitation, "Yes, I am." Whereupon the mushrooms vanished. Fifteen years passed before Robert realized that the path he had agreed to follow was plant shamanism. He told me a story about a friend who ate Fly Agarics years later. The mushroom spirits showed up in the same surprising manner, and asked the same question: "Why did you eat us?" His friend said, "I was trying to get high." The mushrooms said, "Well, if you ever do this again, we're going to kill you."

Robert now thought the Fly Agarics belonged to some other-dimensional civilization. They were visitors to our world, making their own journey through the cosmos. And to a limited extent, when it suited them, they involved themselves in human affairs. In his book on visionary plant use through history, *The Long Trip*, which was unknown to Robert, Paul Devereux describes common features of *Amanita* intoxication: "the spirits of the mushrooms might appear to the individual and converse with him directly. He might even feel himself turning into a mushroom spirit. The mushroom spirits tend to wear wide hats on heads that sit on stout cylindrical bodies without an intervening neck, and the number seen depends on the number of mushrooms eaten."

I asked myself whether I believed Robert's stories, and I decided that I did. I don't mean that I believed he believed them; I mean I be-

lieved the things he described had actually taken place. My existential
certitudes were being given another twist. It was late at night by now.
We walked around the hotel grounds, sat by a stream where small unfamiliar animals darted along, quicksilver flashes nibbling at the edge
of the black water. Robert turned away from mushroom spirits and
Thunder Beings and started talking about America, its ruthless materialism and its ingrained and unconscious hatred of native spirituality.

"If you compare the U.S. policies against the Indians with their
policy toward the blacks, you can see a difference," he said. "After slavery ended, the blacks were allowed to live as Americans. I think it is because their native spiritual traditions were totally wiped out. They
didn't pose a threat anymore. The Indians, on the other hand, never
lost their direct connection to the spiritual world. I think that is the real
reason our government has tried so hard to destroy them."

Years ago Robert visited a Massachusetts tribe with friends who
were starting an organic farming commune—in the current lingo an
"intentional community"—down south. They wanted to learn about
the sustainable, nondestructive agriculture the Indians have practiced
for centuries. "When we came to meet the tribe, they said right away,
'Oh we know who you are. You're the Tree People!' It turns out they
have a whole series of prophecies about what is going to happen in the
next decades, and they just keep crossing items off their list as they
come up."

Robert accepts the indigenous cosmology populated by realms of
spirits and elemental beings. He thinks that America, despite its proliferation of Christian fundamentalist movements and crackpot cults,
is spiritually bereft. We have been abandoned by the spirits, as the
Tarahumara shaman told poor Artaud.

Shamanism is a phenomenon that comes up through the earth
when human beings are connected to their home. Over time, this natural connection to the land manifests in supernatural ways. Because
Robert's family had been in Massachusetts since Colonial times, he was
offered a shamanic role by the local elemental forces. He was a special
case. By the time they become adults, most modern citizens are so
alienated from themselves and the earth, indoctrinated by media, and
deluded by the "false needs" of the consumer culture that they have little hope of connecting with the other worlds surrounding them.

"I had to give my own son a huge dose of the medicine to wake up his spirit," Robert recalled. "I nearly killed him. He went so far out, I couldn't bring him around for a long time. I pushed him under the cold shower, held him there for fifteen minutes. Finally he came back to me."

Robert is still developing his own shamanic abilities. One night a woman in his ayahuasca group was possessed by malevolent forces. He found himself making gestures that suddenly came to him—"I felt I was throwing her spirit back in her body." The etheric energy surrounding her seemed to jump away from her and leap into his belly. From his belly, he spat it out in gobs of phlegm. This conversion of evil-spirit energy into yucky physical stuff is something described in many books about shamanism (I have since seen tribal shamans do it), but I had never heard an account from a Western insider before.

"I suspect that I am an agent for whatever spiritual powers I represent," he said. "Sometimes I feel more like an agent than a person. I communicate with my clients psychically—they tell me what they want me to do in my dreams and I do it." He stubbed out his cigarette. "This is going to sound crazy to you. I have these long dreams where I am given personal tours through the White House and the current president invites me to dinner. I had some good meetings with Clinton, even with Reagan. But I could never reach Bush, and I doubt I will get through to his son."

"What do you think these dreams mean?"

"Through the dreams I am like an ambassador for these other forces, trying to intercede for them."

I was listening, semidetached, to Robert's shamanic spew, when I suddenly realized what I had been doing since my trip to Gabon: I had been working to wake up my spirit. My intellectual drive for understanding was cover for my spiritual development. In fact, the Bwiti initiation had begun a semiautonomous process giving me increasing access to what I could only think of as "the spirit world." I was getting hints of this through my dreams, plus the deepening visions from ayahuasca and other psychedelics. Even the elves demonstrated that my channels were open to new frequencies—the elves, I thought, had manifested themselves only because I was ready for them.

At the time I returned from Gabon, the Bwiti trip had seemed like a joke, later a profoundly personal revelation; now I realized it was something else entirely. Through iboga I had seen my "self" as a kind of object, a projection from some deeper order. I had realized my connection to a transpersonal reality, some source that existed outside linear time. Over the span of several years, the effect was a deepening sense of certainty. To the extremely limited extent I had started to know it, the "spirit world" seemed to work on impersonal or unconscious principles. It was like a cosmic bureaucracy employing its own PR department, its own off-kilter dream-logic and sense of humor. The spirit forces were constantly playing with human limitations, dangling possibilities before our puny grasps at knowledge.

Of course Richard was a gardener by trade. Of course he was the Kennedys' gardener. My new archetype for understanding the world revealed a pattern that worked on every level. If it was madness, it was a deliriously logical madness. The plants, and the transformative knowledge within them, are at the center of the story—"the matrix of all possible stories," as Ginzburg described it.

. . .

"IT IS NECESSARY to cultivate your garden," Voltaire wrote. At the end of *Candide,* the aphorism is offered as melancholy consolation, but it now seemed the opposite. Living in the nonpsychedelic Age of Enlightenment, Voltaire could not have suspected the powers of psychic transformation hidden within green growing things.

Another lecturer at the Palenque conference was Kathleen Harrison, an ethnobotanist, once the wife of Terence McKenna. Beautiful, black-haired, in her late forties, she worked with the Mazatecs, living with a family of healers for a few months every year. The Mazatec language and culture has been protected because they inhabit inaccessible mountains. Harrison talked about life in the mountains, far from roads. "When you walk a stone path, you look, you monitor. Every day is a pilgrimage, a cycle." While inaccessibility protects native cultures, roads threaten them with acculturation and loss of tradition.

The mushrooms, central to Mazatec traditions, come in many varieties. Each variant has its own purpose. "The mushrooms are different beings," she said. One is used for divination, another for healing, another for good luck upon starting a new undertaking. This meticulous discrimination reminded me of the Indians in the Amazon who recognize many different types of ayahuasca vine, each one causing different visions. These differences are imperceptible, even to highly trained Western botanists. As Lévi-Strauss described in *The Savage Mind*, Indians are attuned to botanical subtleties at a level beyond our comprehension.

Harrison spoke of another visionary plant, *Salvia divinorum*. A plant from the mint family, it was only discovered by the West in the 1950s. Diffusion of information about *Salvia* has been slow, which is fitting, as the experience of this plant is subtle—according to the Mazatecs, her spirit is "shy like a deer." I had tried *Salvia* several times in New York and found it unpredictable, ranging from dissociative to empathic. It had a peculiarly orthogonal effect, as though giving a view into a universe linked, at an odd diagonal angle, with our own. On my first attempt, I felt as if I was trapped forever in a time-loop, although the entire experience lasted less than five frightening minutes.

When you study psychoactive plants, botanical details become significant. The personality of the plant, or its spirit, expresses itself in its way of growing, its habits of development, its history of human use. *Salvia* is a square-stemmed plant that grows straight up, its stalks and leaves reaching out in symmetrical pairs. It is a pure cultigen, which means it cannot be found in the wild. The plant was only discovered, by Gordon Wasson, in the gardens of a handful of Mazatec healers. Although it flowers in white blossoms (in a slide projected by Harrison, the *Salvia* flower looked spectacular, angelic), *Salvia* never, or almost never, produces seeds. To propagate itself, it grows until it reaches a certain height, then falls over, and where it falls, a new plant shoots up. The Mazatecs have no mythology, no folklore, to explain *Salvia*—they also call it Ska Pastora, the leaves of the shepherdess, and associate it with the Virgin Mary—and it is not known how long they have used it. The plant is surrounded by a delicate aura of secrecy.

The psychoactive component of *Salvia*, salvinorin A, is potent in doses measured in micrograms, similar in power to LSD. Generally only nitrogenous compounds affect the brain, but the salvinorin A molecule is not nitrogen-based. Technically, the chemical is something called a neoclerodane-diterpenoid, made up of carbon, hydrogen, and oxygen atoms. The neurochemical basis of its activity on human consciousness is completely unknown.

One year before her visit to the Mazatecs, Harrison had been diagnosed with arrhythmia, an alteration in the rhythm of the heartbeat. Her doctors wanted to treat her with medication or surgery. She put off treatment until after her trip. In Oaxaca, the shamans suggested a *Salvia* ceremony. They ate a thick cigar made from fresh leaves, which can grow to nine inches in length. "We performed the ritual in total darkness," she recalled. "They told me I had to pray out loud with them, to beseech the *Salvia* spirit, and not to laugh. They said laughter scares away the spirit."

Suddenly she was no longer in the dark, rough-walled temple. She saw that she was in a large garden. Across the garden was a "beautiful woman dressed in white and about ten feet tall," silently tending to the plants. "As I looked around, I saw I was standing next to the shaman and his wife in the last row of plants. They told me to keep praying. I realized that we were also plants in her garden." The tall woman—the *Salvia* spirit—slowly made her way to Harrison. In the vision, the spirit passed its hand right through her. "It was a wonderful feeling, a tingling warmth going through me," she said. "I wished that I would always feel that way." The garden vision began to fade. She begged the spirit for guidance, asked what she should do with her work as a botanist. She was told, softly, "Show them the edge of the garden." Back in the United States, she went to the hospital, and was told that her heart problem had vanished. In a reversal of roles, the plant had revealed itself as a gardener of human beings.

There are many accounts on the Internet of people taking *Salvia* without knowledge of the plant's ritual meaning or use. One account described instant transportation into the *Salvia* realm after smoking two hits of an extract:

> I felt a tall, female entity put her hand on my shoulder and . . . physically pull me backwards. I then became aware of the presence of a number of these strange entities, they seemed to be surrounding me in a circle or semicircle. I remember hearing phrases spoken sharply in some language unknown to me. These beings wanted me to be absolutely clear about

something: I think it was their name. . . . I know this sounds fucking crazy, but it sounded like "Divorum," and/or "Divinorum—Salvia divinorum." . . . I felt as if I were being interrogated by a panel of superior life forms. . . . I believe that part of the message the spirit was trying to make very clear was that Salvia is truly divine—"of the gods," and must be approached with care and respect.

Stories such as Kat's and Robert's are certainly suggestive, but what exactly do they suggest? Are they admissible evidence of some kind of other order manifesting itself through the lost domains of nature? Or are they no different from reports of faith healers or psychics, alien abductees or visionaries, indicating latent powers or quirks of the human mind that cannot be quantified? If we can accept that they are not mass-delusions or con jobs or synaptic fritzes, then all of these phenomena, taken together, reveal deep and complex levels of interaction between the human mind, physical reality, and the natural (and supernatural) world.

Perhaps these words from a Peruvian shaman help to explain the relationship between healer and herbs: "The *curandero,* upon invoking the power of the plants within his curative power, also influences them. He imposes his personal spiritual force over the plants, giving them that magic power which becomes, let us say, the power that plants contain as a result of having been rooted in the earth and partaken of its magnetic force. And since man is an element of the earth, with the power of his intelligence he emits this potentiality over the plants. The plants receive this influence and return it toward man, toward the individual in the moment when he invokes. In other words, all of the spirit of the plants is fortified by the influences—intellectual, spiritual, and human—of man. He is the one who forms the magic potentiality of the plants."

For the Mazatecs, according to Harrison, "the leaves of a plant hold and transfer energy." They believe "that plants actually participate in energy transmission. The inherent character and energy in plant material is behind a lot of their rituals." The energy of the plants is a true source of healing.

It was a great pleasure to hear Harrison talk about the Mazatecs, the native relation to plants, the spectacular powers of plant medicine. The brand-new gnosis of psychedelia in the Western world has been, throughout its brief and volatile one-hundred-year history, male-dominated territory, with words by Leary and Castaneda and Kesey, set to music by Pink Floyd and Jim Morrison. Harrison contextualized the subject from a perspective of female depth and compassion; like the striking of a bell, hers is a new tone in the discourse.

To hear her speak was to get a sense of what this area of plant-wisdom might become: not some fringe New Age element or middle-class nightmare, but a source of redemptive energy for a society in denial about its effect on the planet, and spiritual despair. She talked about the importance of ritual in psychedelic use, of creating some kind of context, intention, and "sacred space," rather than just spacing out. "I see so many people wallowing in confusion and physical self-destruction, coming from a culture where they have no training, at loose ends. I don't see how it is helping the individual or the collective the way it is being done now."

This was Robert's point also. The founders of the entheobotany conference, McKenna among them, had done valuable work, scouring the world for new magical plants, learning from the shamans, testing new combinations of herbal extracts and chemicals from different climates. But the next question is one of utility: What to do with what has been learned?

During his lecture, Jonathan Ott, the author of *Pharmocotheon,* an encyclopedic source book on shamanic inebriants, said that Westerners couldn't become shamans in the traditional sense. "I don't think it is possible for anyone in our world to be a shaman. They are the scientists of the preliterate world. The closest thing in our world is people like Sasha Shulgin, Terence, or me."

Robert convinced me that Ott was wrong. There were limits to Leary's and Alperts's hedonist/therapeutic model of psychedelic use—or even the quack-scientist-mystic model of McKenna and Ott. Perhaps the only way to go beyond those limits is to plunge into shamanism as a living spiritual practice, as Robert has done. McKenna seemed to recognize this himself: "The last best hope for dissolving the steep walls of cultural inflexibility that appear to be channeling us toward true ruin is a renewed shamanism," he wrote. "By reestablishing channels of direct communication with the Other, the mind behind nature, through the use of hallucinogenic plants, we will obtain a new set of lenses to see our way in the world." Although excised from Western culture, shamanism is a universal phenomenon, integral to the human relationship with the planet that gives us life. "It comes up from the earth," Robert said.

Chapter 32

THROWN-AWAY
KNOWLEDGE

I took an afternoon off from lectures to explore the Palenque ruins. Palenque was, until the ninth century, a major ceremonial center, a huge city and Mayan temple complex abandoned for unknown reasons at the pinnacle of its power. The city was lost in the jungle, overgrown and forgotten to everyone except the local, secretive Lacandon Indians until its rediscovery in the late eighteenth century. Most of its structures are yet to be unearthed or half-consumed by the jungle. Walking off the path, you find large piles of rocks that are the crumbled remnants of ancient temples. Atop the Temple of the Smoking God there is a fabulous frieze of a smirking shamanic master holding a long pipe with tendrils of smoke curling out—DMT anyone? Another famous carving, preserved at the Palenque museum, is the cover of the tomb of Pakal, Palenque's great king. The ornate tableau either depicts Pakal falling down through the jawlike gates of the Underworld or, according to UFO researcher Jacques Vallee, operating the controls of a jeweled spaceship. Another carving shows priests clustered around a small entity identified as one of the "gods." This creature, plug-shaped and otherworldly, resembled the squiggly extradimensional beings that I saw during the *yagé* ceremonies of the Secoya.

Palenque may have been abandoned, along with many Mayan centers, because of some prophecy, some divine order, or perhaps the calendar foretold catastrophe—nobody knows for certain. However, it is known that, in Central America, astronomy and astrology were highly developed enterprises. Centuries later, due to prophecies based on astronomical conjunctions, the Aztecs expected the appearance of a "White God" on the exact date that Cortés arrived—that is why they failed to put up an effective struggle despite their vast advantage in numbers.

Inspired by psychedelic visions, McKenna studied accelerating novelty and the I Ching and predicted an as-of-yet unimaginable summation in the year 2012. He later found that the Mayan calendar prophesies the end of the present historical era and the beginning of a new cycle in 2012, at the moment when our sun comes into momentary alignment with the galactic center.

McKenna theorized that the linear structure of time could be a temporary illusion, and that time might actually be a wave form, fractal, or spiral. He used the "King Wen" sequence of the I Ching to plot time as a wave form representing increasing complexity or the "ingression of novelty" into human consciousness. He speculated that in the last years leading up to the crest and collapse of this wave, we might see a speeded-up replay of all of human history as cartoon farce. By this logic, the destruction of the World Trade Center might be in "resonance" with the Tower of Babel, while the global military campaign of the United States might resonate with the rapid expansion and collapse of the Roman Empire or the Crusades. He proposed that the current simultaneous processes of technological advance and global destruction might be something like a chrysalis stage, in which humanity was incubating technology, awaiting a dimensional shift, or preparing the way for an evolution of consciousness.

Using mathematical calculations elaborated in a computer program, "Time Wave Zero," McKenna projected 2012—December 21, to be exact—as a major transformation point in human history. Perhaps the end of history as we now know it. He presented this as a potentially positive thing, the entry into hyperspace and galactic citizenship. The "concrescence point" could be "the culmination of a human process, a process of toolmaking," he wrote in his book *The Invisible*

Landscape. "'The appearance in normal space-time of a hyperdimensional body, obedient to a simultaneously transformed and resurrected human will . . . may be apocalypse enough."

McKenna's writings on 2012 contribute to a worrisome trend in psychedelic thought—I admit that I feel it within myself—toward predictions of apocalypse or imminent world transformation. This might be because psychedelics reveal so many new potentialities, convey so many different speeds and possible levels of conscious activity, that the human mind automatically attempts to construct an eschatological narrative from the chaos. In a sense, the simplest narrative proposes that our current technological evolution is speeding us dizzily toward an imminent conclusion or cataclysm.

Up until his death from a brain tumor in April 2000, McKenna was the leading prophet and proselytizer, the nonstop pontificator, for the contemporary psychedelic movement. He writes in *True Hallucinations* that after decades of psilocybin use, "I had apparently evolved into a sort of mouthpiece for the incarnate Logos. I could talk to small groups of people with what appeared to be electrifying effect." Indeed, McKenna's voice was a peculiarly memorable buzz saw. There are tapes of him talking at conferences, in high-speed nasal monotone, for twenty or more hours straight.

McKenna grew up in a small town in Colorado, then went to Berkeley in the 1960s, where he participated in the Movement, the political wing of the counterculture, and smoked DMT for the first time. From Berkeley, he went to live in the Far East. In Nepal, he sought out shamans of the Bon tradition, which predated Tibetan Buddhism, trying to learn more about the shamanic use of visionary plants. The pursuit of psychedelia was, for him, a political choice: "We had sorted through the ideological options, and we had decided to put all of our chips on the psychedelic experience as the shortest path to the millennium, which our politics had inflamed us to hope for." He, his brother Dennis, and a few friends decided to go to the Amazon in pursuit of a snuff made from DMT-containing plants, used by local Indians. In the end, they never bothered with the snuff. Instead, they became involved in a feverish investigation of *Stropharia cubensis,* "one of the largest, strongest, and certainly the most widely distributed of any of the known psilocybin-containing mushrooms," but, for reasons the McKennas never investigated, not popular with the locals.

Psilocybin became the catalyst for McKenna's eccentric career. Although Leary's Harvard project began with psilocybin, when LSD appeared in mass quantities, psilocybin was eclipsed and almost forgotten by the counterculture. Compared to LSD, psilocybin was a gourmet psychedelic in the 1960s, much less available and rarely synthesized. In fact, McKenna and his brother were the first to figure out a reliable method for cultivating psilocybin mushrooms at home. In 1976, they published a little pamphlet on their technique using the sobriquets O. T. Oss and O. N. Oeric. Still in print, the booklet has sold over 100,000 copies.

True Hallucinations, McKenna's account of his 1971 Amazonian escapade, is an end-of-the-sixties fable, a haunted tale of extraterrestrial contact and psychedelic delirium, including zany blips of telepathy and even omniscience. "Alchemy was the gnosis of material transformation. Clues seemed everywhere; everything was webbed together in a magical fabric of meaning and affirmation and mystery." The McKenna brothers believed their mushroom ally was communicating with them, giving them hints about the end of the world and the future of their species. Among the things the mushroom seemed to be telling them was that it was an ancient extraterrestrial intelligence, a kind of probe sent out to help humanity in its evolution, offering a symbolic partnership.

"We could feel the presence of some invisible hyperspatial entity, an ally, which seemed to be observing and sometimes exerting influence on the situation," McKenna later recalled about his youthful experiment.

> Because of the alien nature of the tryptamine trance, its seeming accentuation of themes alien, insectile, and futuristic, and because of previous experiences with tryptamine in which insectile hallucinatory transformations of human beings were observed, we were led to speculate that the role of the presence was somehow like that of an anthropologist, come to give humanity the keys to galactarian citizenship.

The inchoate, otherworldly visions that filled the air at La Chorerra, the Indian village in Colombia where they stayed, were too much to comprehend, and too elaborate to encapsulate here, but the shadow of those early revelations inspired the McKennas in all their further explorations.

Has humanity been contacted by alien beings? McKenna thought the typical model of extraterrestrial contact—wide-eyed aliens descending to earth in a shiny UFO—was too overtly a product of our own technological fantasies to be accurate. Other UFO theorists have also come to the same conclusion in the last decades. Some suggest that the UFOs and their crews are actually travelers from other dimensions, ancient spiritual beings clothing themselves in the garb of modern fantasy. The writer Michael Talbot has suggested that UFO encounters are neither objective nor subjective, but "omnijective" phenomena—a conjunction of observer and observed, in the same way a subatomic particle is neither wave nor particle, but what some physicists have dubbed a "wavicle." An easier way for a highly advanced species to disseminate itself, McKenna suspected, would be through spores, the hardest organic substance, deposited on asteroids and sent spinning through the galaxy until they crash-landed on some suitable planet. To support this wild theory, he noted the peculiar shape of the psilocybin molecule. "It is the only 4-substituted indole known to exist on earth. . . . Psilocybin has a unique chemical signature that says, 'I am artificial; I come from outside.' "

The cult of McKenna—among ravers, hackers, and Silicon Valley software engineers—remains an important phenomenon. For a long time he had a curious effect on me. When I didn't look at his work for a while, I recalled it as cartoonlike, trashy, excessively absurd. But when I turned my attention to his books, I was captivated, yet again, by his style, his sense of humor, and the freewheeling flow of his ideas. In that way his work parallels the entire subject of psychedelics, which, when you stop thinking about it, seems to vanish entirely, yet as soon as you take it seriously, expands until it threatens to transform your entire perspective on reality.

"The power of the Other is humbling and magnificent, but because it cannot be bent into power in this world, priestcraft turns away from it. It is the 'thrown away knowledge' of the Luis Senyo Indians of Baja, California. It is only seeing and knowing," he wrote in *The Archaic Revival*. Part of the pleasure of reading McKenna is the relief of communing with a thinker with no academic rubric, no ax to grind or foundation stipend to protect, willing to tee off on any of the transcendent and philosophical issues opened to his capacious mind by the massive, long-term ingesting of psychedelic compounds. As McKenna said during an interview, "The strange thing about psilocybin, my career, and this conversation is that it has to do with the empowerment of language. . . . The social consequence of the psychedelic experience is clear thinking—which trickles down as clear speech. Empowered speech."

McKenna happily accepted his marginalized status because his model of psychedelic exploration was closer to Huxley's than to Leary's or Ginsberg's. The attempt to transport LSD to the masses, using the media to spread the word, led to social confusion and political backlash. McKenna's idea was the opposite. He encouraged the deeper immersion of a small subset of alchemist/acolytes: "Instead of the horizontal broadening of the faith, I would be much more interested in a vertical strengthening of the faith by having the people who take these compounds take more of them, take different ones, and take larger doses. The real crucible of this research is the Self." He did not want to incite the government to further repression, and he pitched his ideas so far beyond the pale of mainstream concerns that they seemed completely unthreatening. McKenna cunningly crafted his public persona as crazy fool, the Irish raconteur with a mad gleam in his eyes.

I am now in a position to recognize, after visiting the psychedelic antipodes for myself, that underneath the teasing banter of McKenna's talks and his texts is dead-serious intent, a truly radical and real vision: "My assumption about psychedelics has always been that the reason they are not legal is not because it troubles anyone that you have visions, but that there is something about them that casts doubts on the validity of reality," he wrote. "They are inevitably deconditioning agents simply by demonstrating the existence of a nearby reality running on a different dynamic. I think they are inherently catalysts of intellectual dissent."

McKenna's *Food of the Gods* is an overview of sacred and profane drug use throughout history. Like Wasson, McKenna thought psychedelic plants might have catalyzed the development of human consciousness and the acquisition of language. He calls Adam and Eve's eviction from the Garden of Eden for tasting the fruit of the Tree of Knowledge of Good and Evil, "history's first drug bust." For him, the myth symbolically describes the collapse of humanity's symbiotic relation with a psilocybin-containing mushroom in an archaic "part-nership culture" where women controlled agriculture and plant knowledge. This collapse, for whatever reasons, led to the male-aggression-ruled "dominator culture" we know today: "Substance-induced changes in consciousness dramatically reveal that our mental life has physical foundations," he writes. "Psychoactive drugs thus challenge the Christian assumption of the inviolability and special ontological status of the soul. Similarly, they challenge the modern idea of the ego and its inviolability and control structures. In short, encounters with psychedelic plants throw into question the entire world view of the dominator culture."

To a great extent, history has been propelled by the quest for new tastes and new pleasures. The drive to satisfy the taste for new delicacies brought back by explorers created trade routes, colonialism, and, in the modern era, the revival of institutionalized slavery. "The early importation of African slave labor into the New World was for one purpose only, to support an agricultural economy based on sugar." Refined sugar, he notes, is an inessential additive and a highly addictive drug. The sugar addict tends toward a childish personality, given to tantrums, dominated by mood shifts. "The craze for sugar was so overwhelming that a thousand years of Christian ethical conditioning meant nothing. An outbreak of human cruelty and bestiality of incredible proportions was blandly accepted by the institutions of polite society." The entry of sugar and caffeine into Europe led to the coffee-house culture of eighteenth-century Paris. The "excessive raving" stimulated by strong cups of espresso incited the radical thoughts of the Enlightenment Philosophes and the radical deeds of the French Revolutionaries.

Alcohol, for McKenna, is the "dominator drug par excellence." "No other drug has had such a prolonged detrimental effect on human beings," he writes. "Alcohol and slavery often went hand in hand across the economic landscape. . . . A 'besotted underclass' was a permanent fixture of mercantile society whether in the home countries or the colonies." The opposite of hallucinogenic openness, alcohol leads to a narrowing of consciousness, a "condition of ego obsession and inability to resist the drive toward immediate gratification." Repression of women, frat rapes, and wife beatings are typical outcomes of the alcoholic lifestyle. In booze land, McKenna sighs, "Gone are the boundary-dissolving hallucinogenic orgies that diminished the ego of the individual and reasserted the values of the extended family and the tribe."

Throughout history, different civilizations developed a trans-species bond with a particular entheogenic plant. The early Vedic civilization had Soma; the ancient Greeks had some form of ergot or perhaps several psychoactive catalysts used in the durable Eleusian Mysteries, for two thousand years the essential initiation ritual of the ancient world. In every case, the connection was eventually broken—either changes in climate led to disappearance of the chemical catalyst, or a self-perpetuating ruling class or priesthood established its power by guarding, then concealing, and ultimately forgetting the Mystery. The compulsive modern quest for new tastes and artificial pleasures, ranging from sugar to oxycontin, has been an unconscious effort to re-capture the lost catalyst: "Each intoxicant, each effort to recapture the symbiotic balance of the human-mushroom relationship in the lost African Eden, is a paler, more distorted image of the original Mystery than the last."

One problem with McKenna's thesis in *Food of the Gods* is that the Mayas and Aztecs, highly advanced civilizations that incorporated use of psychedelics, at least among the priest class, were not exactly models of enlightened behavior. Human sacrifice was their favorite form of popular entertainment. Clearly, the use of psychedelic sacraments does not necessarily lead to the creation of a feminine-oriented partnership society with a penchant for boundary-dissolving orgies. Instead, it can lead to the attempt to match the volatile power and ambiguous spectacles of the hallucinatory realms with bloody and horrible acts of appeasement. The psychedelic impulse can become dangerous and decadent. McKenna makes a laudatory effort to put a happy face on material that may be ambiguous at its core, but psychedelic relativism, at the very least, reveals aspects of reality denied by mainstream materialism.

The postsixties psychedelics avatars, McKenna among them, believe that psychedelics are a fast-track method for revealing the dark matter of consciousness, a necessary antidote to the "dominator culture" of materialism: "Like a chemical habit, we are hooked on ego. And the psychedelic dissolves that chemical or psychological dependency and replaces it with the facts of the matter: how the individual fits into the life and organization of this planet, the vast amount of time all these things have been in existence and have worked themselves to their present status." Essentially, I agree, although the worlds revealed through psychedelics have their own valences, their own troubling ambiguities.

. . .

I TOOK A SWIM in the Mayan Queens' Baths, a waterfall splashing into a natural cove surrounded by limestone cliffs. The rocks around this pool look more like the faces of imprisoned gods, impassive elders, water cascading over their frowning features, than any rocks I have seen. As I swam, I thought about this: If the Indians, North and South, were right about so much—about the nature of spiritual reality, about all that we in the modern West have forfeited and forgotten—then perhaps the most heavy-duty Indian prophecies need to be taken seriously. The Hopi Indians in the Southwest, perhaps the original inhabitants of America, have inherited a series of ancient predictions. The Hopi seers described a "gourd of ashes" falling from the sky, destroying a city, a prophecy seemingly confirmed by Hiroshima. The probable gist of the near-future, according to the Hopis, is grim, to say the least: further environmental devastation; multiple assassinations of world leaders; nuclear war ("a spiritual conflict with material matters") started by India, China, or Pakistan; the United States destroyed before the next world cycle begins.

Out of the natural stone bowls of the Queens' Bath, I dried myself and walked the path between ancient ruined temples and twisting trees, the sunlight falling to the earth through the branches in gossamer strands. Howler monkeys chattered and whooped overhead. It was a beautiful afternoon in Palenque. That night, I decided, if possible, I would try DMT.

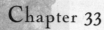

Chapter 33

I SMOKED DMT

Any place is the center of the world.

—BLACK ELK, *Black Elk Speaks*

And I did so.

It was past three A.M. at the Chan Kah hotel in Palenque. I was with John and Sara, two attendants at the conference. I held the long glass pipe to my lips, watched as the small beige clumps began to release themselves into the air. I inhaled—one, two, three breaths. The dry smoke was wickedly noxious and bizarre, with an extraterrestial plastic tang. As I had been warned, it was like smoking a shard of lawn furniture. With the next intake, the unfolding, the unveiling, began. Runes and geometric patterns filled the air, hovered around me, tattooed themselves over the walls, the furniture, the other people in the room. These images were copper- or golden-colored and I had only a few seconds to look at them. In those few seconds I saw an intricate interweave of sacred geometrical motifs—pentagrams, seals and symbols, golden triangles—drawn from every mystical and traditional source. As I was sucked into the golden funnel it seemed startlingly clear that all of those symbol systems were not just metaphorical codes but actual gateways to literal dimensions outside of our own. John, a video art student from San Francisco and DMT veteran, had described these patterns as the entry point—once you saw them, you were just one breath away. *I'm going to get there,* I thought to myself, surprised, even shocked. I took in one more deep plasticky breath and held it, and I started to go. John took the pipe from my hand. I fell back on the mattress as I shot out of myself like a rocket.

How to explain the rush, the terrifying and ecstatic trauma, of leaving your body, and your brain, and everything that is you, except some infinitesimal tendril that has no existence in space or duration in time, which is an astral probe spiraling out into the infinite, far beyond the shell you left behind?

I seemed to be projecting forward at an incredible speed. At the periphery of my vision I saw twisting white columns like high-tech swizzle sticks, as if I was following a ladder or lattice up, or in or out or all of the above, to hyperspace. I had the sense of floating through a fractal tapestry, a curving and infolding plane of synthetic, plastic, fantastic whiteness and gleaming colors in endless vibrant hues. This extradimensional realm I had pitched into was made, I felt certain, of data, of quantum equations, visible shamanic harmonics, and the self-weaving fabric of extradimensional superconsciousness. It was science fiction made fact. A dimension devoid of natural things, of plants and human need, of our weak and imprecise symbol systems. DMT land was an interweave of tantric mandalas, virtual reality fantasias, stained-glass aureolae; a ten-dimensional Walt Disney World projected into some far-fetched and far-flung future. There was, in that place, rushing toward me, an overwhelming force of knowledge and sentience. I knew it was impossible that my mind, on any level, had created what I was seeing. This was no mental projection. This was not a structure within the brain that the drug had somehow tapped into. It was a non-human reality existing at a deeper level than the physical world.

Suddenly I was rocketing through their cities. Multidimensional, jewel-faceted, hard and immaterial palaces where geometrical and tentacular constructions were being taken apart and reconstructed at such lightning speed that I cannot recall more than a tiny and trivial fraction. I was taken on a flyby at a tremendous velocity. There were beings in this place. They were humanoid, as far as I can remember, which is unfortunately not far enough. I recall a blue entity (a blue the color of certain celestial Buddhas in Tibetan *thangka* paintings), gesturing—in my memory I see him with one hand raised, waving at me. There were fountains and spinning mandalas like lit-up roulette wheels or flowering chakras that seemed organic as well as mechanical. At the center of the city there was a great fountain, like the fountain at the center of a Renaissance town square, where bits of data or perhaps mathematical potentialities or burbling new test tube universes were flowing in rainbow patterns of ultraviolet froth. This realm was in a state of continual transformation, yet solidified in synthetic matter. Everything I "saw" glittered with an artificial sparkle. There was something impersonal, detached, about my visit. It seemed as if the entities were tranquil, even unemotive, as they went about their work of cosmic supervision.

Everything seemed to be communicating to me a chattering greeting. Although I can't remember sound, I felt there was sound all around me. Weeks later I began to recollect it as high-frequency buzzing, clicks, and trills. As I recall, the beings in the DMT universe were saying to me, over and over again:

"This is it. Now you know. This is it. Now you know."

I began to remember that I had a body, although it was lost to me. I felt myself breathing. Every now and then I would swallow involuntarily. My breathing and my swallowing seemed like a program they were running. "I" seemed to be exactly like a program they were running in their fabulously impersonal cosmological system: As I breathed, they were breathing me.

"Now you know. This is it. Now go back. Now go back. Now you know. This is it. Now get out."

As soon as I recalled my human identity, I was flowing back into this world. I noticed there was something . . . a room containing me. I was lying stretched on a hotel bed. Then the engulfment quickly receded, returned to morphing geometric gold forms that spun down, quickly whirling out of existence as I returned to who I had been.

I was left with little doubt that I had visited what we, for lack of a more accurate word, traditionally call "spiritual reality." The trip supported the idea of a soul existing outside the body, woven into the extradimensional fabric of the cosmos. The cosmos, what McKenna called the "cosmic giggle," is something they were spinning, or we were spinning with them. I had been given more than I ever expected. I had been shown the hard kernel of everything that I wanted to know.

The DMT realm is "next door," behind every billowing curtain, hidden inside the dark matter of consciousness, now playing every night in disguised form in our dreams. It is so close to us, adjacent or perpendicular to this reality. It is a soft shadow, a candle flicker, away.

DMT is Direct Mystical Transmission. Drastic Magical Transport. It is, as McKenna put it, just too much. Once you have had the experience, you are permanently rewired. You can consign existentialism to the scrapheap as you wrap your old ontological constructs around this new pole. Of course, many questions are opened by the jolt, while only a few are answered. For me, the DMT vision suggests that we are incarnations in some way, sent from that place of boundlessness to this one of sticks and stones and hard knocks, perhaps over the course of lives Ping-Ponging back and forth between the dimensions with certain tasks to perform, or with knowledge to learn. Or perhaps what is happening is more ambiguous and multipurposed than we can language.

The experience called to mind Mircea Eliade's book *The Eternal Return*, in which he analyzes the consistent belief held by archaic cultures that all places in physical reality have a double in the spirit world. Every temple and city built by human beings actually relates to a "celestial archetype." Eliade writes: "Not only does a model precede terrestrial architecture, but the model is also situated in an ideal (celestial) region of eternity." The DMT city seemed to be something like a celestial metropolis, a fabulous ideal that our physical cities are a feeble attempt to imitate, utilizing blunt matter rather than bright magic.

For many people, ayahuasca—a slowed-down low-res interface of the DMT flash—seems to convey strong messages from the natural world, of nature as sentient energy and spirit matter, of the need to protect the planet we have been given. *Yagé* whispers that human beings are meant to be gardeners of this reality, journeyers, storytellers and singers, weavers of the sacred. DMT, on the other hand, conveys no overt human or humane message. It is a doorway you can step through to greet the beings who run the cosmic candy store. Spinning down from the immersive matrices of DMT, I suspected those beings were, in some way or other, superconscious entities who created and maintain our universe. They made us for some purpose, to play with us or to be us, to tantalize or teach us. But of course this raises only more questions: Who created them? Is that the only other dimension out there? If not, what other dimensions, what other forces, are acting upon us or seeking to communicate with us?

I was left with the notion that creativity is one purpose of existence; we are meant to evolve toward them, become like that, entities beyond the physical plane, and make universes, palaces of thought, gnostic hieroglyphs of our own, as they made this one. Building another universe—it would be the ultimate act of creativity we could imagine. But perhaps it is just one of their parlor tricks.

Beyond all of this, I mulled over the old litany of questions anybody would want to ask the spirits, if they could: Why so much suffering down here? Is this life a test in some way? Why are we, so often, so forsaken? And why is the DMT dimension so synthetic, as if it were built out of mathematics and machine logic, out of language evolved to some ecstatic equation? Are those beings like us, in some way, but perfected to a point where they dream-engineered themselves out of the time-space continuum? Are they, perhaps, ourselves, evolved to a point of disembodied immortality, having learned to bend and snap the time-space continuum like a twig? Are they ourselves so far in advance of where we are now that they can only communicate with us in orthogonal fashion, the way a three-dimensional being might try to express itself to a two-dimensional dweller of flatland in a language of incomprehensible dots and lines? Am I, are you, just a program running in some alien supercomputer? Is that what this universe is?

We have the DMT receptor. It is a trigger placed in our brain to launch us out there—try to get used to the idea. It is there so we can commune with *that* (or with it, or with them, whatever)—a trip that will eventually force us to revise our science texts and rewire our way of conceiving reality. Why has this experience been allowed to emerge into the modern consciousness at this precise time? To put it another way, why am I the first, after untold numbers of dreaming ancestors, to return to this startling source? As technology turns ever-more treacherous and our weather gets weirder, I suspect there is intentionality to it.

DMT flashes the question of free will: Is there any such thing? I still suspect there is—however much spiritual hierarchies are running this show, each of us can choose to create our role in it with the theater props lying around this quaint little planet. There may simultaneously be free will and a knowing of everything that happens and can happen; all kinds of paradoxes may coexist in those quantum interstices, those tiny curled-up dimensions of vibrating superstrings that physicists found, to their own surprise, hidden within this one. With DMT, once we know it is there, we are left with a choice that is itself a classic test of free will: All of us can choose to go there, push to activate the circuits that give us access to that impacted labyrinth. Or we can avoid it, cut ourselves off, deny its existence out of a completely sensible cowardice. Personally, I don't think the pure DMT flash is a journey we should take too many times; it feels intuitively threatening. But certainly we are meant to go see for ourselves, at least once or twice. The fact is that the portal exists. Not to explore it would mean denying our heritage of human curiosity.

. . .

I WENT OUTSIDE, a small smidgen of self stuffed into flesh, staring up at the spinning, chortling stars, feeling a mixture of astonishment and terror. *Well, that was amazing,* I thought. *Incredible. I am so grateful, so grateful. Thank God I never have to do it again.*

When I returned, Sara was already down and she was weeping. "I was fighting it at first," she said. But the DMT beings had come to her, in the treacly tradition of Hollywood, with open arms of love. They told her there was no reason to struggle against them. "They showed me my palm and my astrological chart," she said. "They said I had been sent into the world for a purpose." I admit that I was jealous of the love that had been showered on Sara by the DMT beings, who seemed to regard me with a more ambiguous detachment.

Ten minutes later, John smoked the glass pipe, fell back, and went out. He came down screaming "We are! We are!" over and over again, until the lights in other hotel rooms flicked on. A being had shown him its whirring praying mantis legs, he said. He saw a female entity sitting at something that looked like a computer. He told us how he had set free a praying mantis when he was five. The praying mantis had turned to look back at him before it hopped away, and at that moment he knew, with complete and utter certainty.

He knew that the mantis knew him.

Chapter 34

DIRECT MYSTICAL
TRANSMISSION

DMT was not a popular or well-known drug in the 1950s and 1960s. Although it was available in certain circles, its overwhelming speeding car crash effect was not to most people's taste. As I was writing this, I met an artist who was a teenager in the early 1960s. She tried DMT at that time and found it terrifying. She refused to describe her experience to me and blanched at the distant memory; however, she noted that it was the last psychedelic she ever took. Just as the revelations of mescaline were too traumatic and strange for the bourgeois intellectuals of the late nineteenth century, most of the psychedelic explorers of the 1950s and 1960s could not handle DMT. It is only in the last two decades that it has attained cult status, and its gyroscopic effects are impacting certain types of music, video games, and movies. At Burning Man, I was surprised when a raver, a kid in his early twenties wearing wide furry pants, told me, "When I first smoked DMT, it was like coming home." Are kids today being primed for the DMT flash by their overexposure to the sensorial culture of shock that surrounds them—the violent totality of DMT transport something like the toy surprise inside the mass media's hallucinatory Crackerjack box? As Walter Benjamin once noted, "Man's need to expose himself to shock effects is his adjustment to the dangers threatening him."

DMT is mind expansion as shock therapy, and McKenna has been responsible for its revival: "The dimethyltryptamine molecule has the unique property of releasing the structured ego into the Overself. Each person who has that experience undergoes a mini-apocalypse, a mini-entry and mapping into hyperspace," he wrote. "For society to focus in this direction, nothing is necessary except for this experience to become an object of general concern."

One of the organizers of the Palenque conference said he thought the best use for DMT was to "convince the doubters," and indeed, the unadulterated DMT trip seems to reveal that the cosmos is a far more populous place than we imagine. To quote McKenna again: "And what is the dimension beyond life as illuminated by DMT? If we can trust our own perceptions, then it is a place in which thrives an ecology of souls whose stuff of being is more syntactical than material. It seems to be a nearby realm inhabited by eternal elfin entelochies made entirely of information and joyous self-expression. The afterlife is more Celtic fairyland than existential nonentity; at least that is the evidence of the DMT experience."

As the monolithic corporate culture threatens to close over our head like a coffin lid, DMT can provide, for Western searchers, what peyote did for the Indians: instant proof, beyond any doubt, of the existence of a nonmaterialist Mystery worth exploring.

In 1990 the Drug Enforcement Agency approved a clinical study of DMT's effect on human subjects. Conducted by Dr. Rick Strassman at the University of New Mexico, the study was the first research on human response to a psychedelic drug approved for nearly two decades. Over five years, Strassman, a psychiatrist, gave repeated intravenous injections of DMT, in increasing dosages, to sixty subjects, studying their physiological and psychological responses to the drug, until he discontinued the project in 1995. Although interested in DMT's potential use in therapy, he also had a secret agenda.

"I firmly believed that there was a spirit molecule somewhere in the brain, initiating or supporting mystical and other naturally occurring altered states of consciousness," writes Strassman in *DMT: The Spirit Molecule*, his book on the study. Before DMT, he investigated melatonin. Discovered in 1958, melatonin is a hormone that controls our reaction to light and darkness, and has a function in sleep.

Produced in the pineal gland, it is very similar in structure to DMT and serotonin. After early explorations of melatonin proved disappointing—even at high doses it had no psychically transformative effect—he turned to DMT as a prime candidate.

DMT was first synthesized, but untested and shelved, in a Canadian laboratory in 1931. In the late 1940s, it was found to be a naturally occurring alkaloid in various plants and Amazonian snuffs. In the 1950s, DMT's effects were studied on hundreds of human subjects in Hungary by Dr. Stephen Szara. During the postwar years the psychology profession considered DMT, like LSD, primarily interesting as a "psychotomimetic," a compound imitating the effects of psychosis. Another discovery was made about DMT: "In 1972, Nobel prize–winning scientist Julius Axelrod of the U.S. National Institutes of Health reported finding it in human brain tissue. Additional research showed that DMT could also be found in human urine and the cerebrospinal fluid bathing the brain." In other words, DMT was an endogenous compound, produced by the brain for unknown reasons. After psychedelics were legally "restricted" in 1970, all studies of DMT stopped. (A question worth asking: Should any government be allowed to make a compound produced in our bodies illegal?) As Strassman notes, "Considering the intense pace of human research with psychedelics just thirty years ago, it is amazing how little today's medical and psychiatric training programs teach about them. Psychedelics were *the* growth area in psychiatry for over twenty years. Now young physicians and psychiatrists know nearly nothing about them."

Strassman recalled his own experience in medical school in the mid-1970s, when there were only two lectures on the subject. Psychedelics "began as 'wonder drugs,' turned into 'horror drugs,' then became 'nothing.' " He believes that the medical and psychiatric professions were traumatized by the way the era of psychedelic research abruptly ended. Many of the leaders in psychiatric research began their careers studying psychedelics: "The most powerful members of the profession discovered that science, data, and reason were incapable of defending their research against the enactment of repressive laws fueled by opinion, emotion, and the media." But as these researchers were scientists, not LSD priests, they turned their careers toward more supportable areas of study.

The unproven aspect of Strassman's thesis is that DMT, like mela-tonin, is produced by the pineal gland. Strassman suspects that the pineal gland, a singular organ buried deep in the brain, actually is, as Descartes and others have speculated, the seat of the soul. "The pineal gland of evolutionarily older animals, such as lizards and amphibians, is also called the 'third' eye. Just like the two seeing eyes, the third eye possesses a lens, cornea, and retina. It is light-sensitive and helps regu-late body temperature and skin coloration—two basic survival func-tions related to environmental light." He discovered that the human pineal gland "becomes visible in the developing fetus at seven weeks, or forty-nine days, after conception"—almost precisely the same time that the sex of the fetus is determined. He also learned that Buddhists believe the soul reincarnates forty-nine days after death. Astonished by this synchronicity, he evolved a hypothesis that the pineal gland is like a receiver that picks up the spirit—an extradimensional vibration that ex-ists outside the body—and DMT is the conductive element. "When our individual life force enters our fetal body, the moment at which we become truly human, it passes through the pineal and triggers the first primordial flood of DMT. . . . As we die, the life-force leaves the body through the pineal gland, releasing another flood of this psychedelic spirit molecule."

For Strassman, this theory would explain the pineal gland's unique structure and placement inside the brain. Formed from "specialized cells originating in the fetal mouth," the pineal "nearly touches visual and auditory sensory relay stations. The emotional centers of the lim-bic system surround it, and its position allows for instant delivery of its products directly into the cerebrospinal fluid." DMT is quickly de-stroyed in the blood by MAO enzymes, but if it was located in the pineal gland it could diffuse directly into the visual, auditory, and emo-tional centers of the brain. "This reasoning further develops the idea that decomposing pineal tissue affects residual awareness after death," he writes. DMT, released by the pineal after death, could diffuse through the "sensory and emotional centers" even without a function-ing circulatory system, allowing the departing soul the time to make the life review and enter the bardo domains detailed in the *Tibetan Book of the Dead*. A minimal flow of DMT might also catalyze the dream state during sleep.

If this theory were true, Strassman expected his DMT subjects would report variations on the classic "Near Death Experience" model—the tunnel of light, the life review, the transcendent ascension into fractal realities. Instead, his subjects were submerged in a disturbingly zany dimension. A few achieved full-blown mystical transcendence, but many entered zones that were one part Insane Clown Posse, one part leprechaun kitsch, spliced with the outtakes of *Plan Nine from Outerspace*.

Here is one typical report: "I saw what can only be described as a Las Vegas–casino type of scene, all flashing and whirling lights. I was rather disappointed. . . . I 'flew' on and saw some clowns performing. They were like toys, or animated clowns."

Here is another: "I felt like I was in an alien laboratory, in a hospital bed. . . . I was being carted around. . . . They weren't as surprised as I was. It was incredibly unpsychedelic. I was able to pay attention in detail. There was one main creature, and he seemed to be behind it all, overseeing everything. The others were orderlies, or disorderlies. They activated a sexual circuit, and I was flushed with an amazing orgasmic energy. A goofy chart popped up like an X-ray in a cartoon. . . . They were checking my instruments, testing things."

Here is a third: "There were four distinct beings looking down on me, like I was on an operating-room table. . . . They had done something and were observing the results. They are vastly advanced scientifically and technologically. They were looking just over the traction bar in front of me. I guess they were saying, 'Goodbye. Don't be a stranger.' " This subject noted, at the end of the trials, that DMT had shown him "there is infinite variation on reality. There is the real possibility of adjacent dimensions. It may not be as simple as that there's alien planets with their own societies. This is too proximal. It's not like some kind of drug. It's more like an experience of a new technology than a drug."

Common themes emerge in the reports of Strassman's subjects: In some cases, the aliens inserted a probe or cable into their eyes or forearms. Often the aliens seemed to be expecting the visit. At other times they were surprised but unruffled. Sometimes there seems to be one alien with a particular bond with the human visitor. The beings sometimes showed them colorful hieroglyphs of a highly complex visual language—this last a repeated motif in McKenna's DMT ravings.

Strassman's book is filled with sad exchanges between the doctor and his subjects. As they return to their bodies from alien realms that are more real than this reality, he makes feeble efforts to convince them that they have experienced some psychological projection or waking dream. The subjects react to his attempts with curt dismissal or annoyance. "When reviewing my bedside notes, I continually feel surprise in seeing how many of our volunteers 'made contact' with 'them,' or other beings. . . . The 'life-forms' looked like clowns, reptiles, mantises, bees, spiders, cacti, and stick figures." Poor Strassman: "It is still startling to see my written records of comments. . . . It's as if my mind refuses to accept what's there in black and white." He realized that many of the reports of his subjects duplicated classic accounts of UFO visits and alien contact. "The resemblance of . . . the alien abductions of 'experiencers' to the contacts described by our own volunteers is undeniable. How can anyone doubt, after reading our accounts . . . that DMT elicits 'typical' alien encounters?"

Although Strassman's research was not oriented toward psychotherapeutic goals, he writes that a major reason he stopped the DMT study was that he saw little beneficial impact on his subjects. "It was especially disappointing that no one began psychotherapy or a spiritual discipline to work further on the insights they felt on DMT," he writes. Why did Strassman imagine that dosing subjects with a drug causing extreme out-of-body and alien encounters in ten minutes flat would lead to New Age journeys of self-discovery? This idea appears both naive and patronizing, but it seems that the real reason he ended the study was fear—a nonspecific anxiety summed up by his "highly intuitive" massage therapist, who told him she saw "evil spirits hovering around you. They want to come through this plane, using you and the drugs." He was blackballed from his Buddhist community and told "Hallucinogens disorder and confuse the mind, impede religious training, and can be a cause of rebirth into realms of confusion and suffering"—despite the fact that most of the Western leaders of his center attributed their initial pull to mysticism to LSD trips.

As noted earlier, in the 1950s, researchers discovered that "set" and "setting" were the crucial determining factors for a positive trip. The mind-state and expectations—the "set"—of Dr. Strassman and his subjects might not have been up to the demanding paradoxes of inner-

dimensional travel—also lacking from his account is a shamanic element of sly, self-reflexive wit. The hospital ambience of Strassman's
DMT studies was also a problem, perhaps predetermining subjects to
envision themselves as patients or passive victims. These reports call to
mind Allen Ginsberg's initial response to LSD, given to him by doctors
in a windowless room of a Palo Alto clinic: "I thought I was trapped in
a giant web of forces beyond my control that were perhaps experimenting with me or were perhaps from another planet or were from
some super-government or cosmic military or science-fiction Big
Brother," he recalled. It may be the case that hospital settings are just
inappropriate for studies on the subjective effects of psychedelic substances.

Chapter 35

DO YOU TAKE RESPONSIBILITY?

One of the subjects in Strassman's study was Jim DeKorne, a New Mexico gardener and well-traveled psychonaut. On his high dose of DMT, he found himself flying toward a "space station": "I was aware of many other beings inside the space station—automatons: android-like creatures that 'looked' (all this transcends ordinary visual description) like a cross between crash dummies and the Empire troops from Star Wars. . . ." He opened his eyes to see the doctor and nurse as alien clowns with huge blubbery lips. DeKorne went on to write his own book, *Psychedelic Shamanism,* in which he explored his long-term relation to psychoactive plants and the entities encountered in what he terms *mind-space.* DeKorne's personal inquiry into shamanic realms yields a deeper level of insight than Strassman's Buddhist/psychiatric straight-man approach.

In the beginning of his book, DeKorne, with offhand humor, relates a number of episodes from his life that would be "considered by mainstream science as anomalous or paranormal at best, as delusions or fraud at worst." Some of the events involved psychoactive chemicals; others were spontaneously occuring states of trance or insight. He describes an LSD trip in which he felt compelled to grab an old Mexican machete he had hanging on the wall, then fell to his knees as a voice spoke in his head, asking him over and over: "Do you take responsibility? . . . DO YOU TAKE RESPONSIBILITY?!!!" He screamed *"Yes"*—"I felt certain that if I'd said 'no,' I would have dropped dead on the spot," he recalled. That night, after coming down, DeKorne had a dream: "My machete was in front of me, hanging suspended in a pure void of infinite darkness. Etched on the blade were Hebrew letters in living fire. . . . The machete disappeared and only the fiery letters remained suspended in the void. Then they began to move and re-form themselves in the Roman alphabet to spell 'SEPHIROTH' in fire." DeKorne was not Jewish. He had no idea what "Sephiroth" meant, and could not find the word in his dictionary. Two weeks later, browsing in a bookstore, he checked a glossary of occult terms and read: "Sephiroth: The ten emanations of God in the Jewish Kabbalah." He was stunned; he had only vaguely heard of the Kabbalah before.

He learned that his encounter corresponded to the "seventeenth path on the Tree of Life," although he never untangled all of the implications. The image of a sword, the notion of a crossroads, and the drug ergot—the source of LSD—were connected to it. He later read Stanislav Grof on LSD therapy and found this remark: "Individuals unfamiliar with the Kabbalah have had experiences described in the Zohar and Sepher Yetzirah [two classical kabbalistic texts] and have demonstrated a surprising familiarity with kabbalistic symbols." DeKorne, like Robert in Palenque, discovered an innate pull, as if his unconscious had its own traction or he was connecting with some residue from a previous life, toward shamanic and mystical exploration.

His experiences led him to adopt a Jungian view of the collective unconscious, and of an inner self that transcends the ego's constraints. His own life taught him that "The human psyche transcends corporeal existence, therefore we must be multidimensional entities. . . . The ego is not the center of the psyche, but only the space/time portion of a greater reality which unfolds and reveals itself from what the ego perceives as its own unconscious mind."

Like McKenna, DeKorne accepts the shamanic map of the cosmos; by this model, the world of physical existence is a "middle world" between the upper and lower realms accessed via altered states, intuitions, and dreams. It is easy for us to comprehend how a zero-dimensional point becomes a one-dimensional line, how a line extends into a two-dimensional plane, and how a plane is extended to become a three-dimensional cube. Just as time is an extra dimension that extends from space, the "imaginal realms," or "mind-space," are real domains that extend from the dimension of consciousness. "The shaman, in effect, is an ego who has learned how to reconnect with his source in mind-space (Jung's collective unconscious)," he writes. The explorer of "mind-space" first discovers a landscape, including beings and artifacts that relate to his own history, but in that new land he also encounters "other" extradimensional entities. The Gnostics had a word for this inner kingdom of spiritual beings. They called it the Pleroma, a Greek term for fullness or plenitude, later used by Jung.

Once you encounter the shamanic dimensions, you realize these other realms must have their own ecology, their own hierarchies and operational logic. DeKorne examines the models provided by Amazonian shamans, Tibetan Buddhists, Renaissance alchemists, and the Western occult philosophy of Aleister Crowley in an effort to comprehend the laws that govern the psychocosmos. Every mystical tradition posits the existence of spirits or deities that seek to compel the attention and belief of human beings. In the Upanishads, the term for such entities is "Devas." The Hindu text states: "Now if a man worships another deity, thinking the deity is one and he another, he does not know. He is like a beast for the Devas." The Gnostic term for such entities is "Archons." The Gnostics believed that the Archons feed on the human soul, "the dew from above," and they try to keep human beings imprisoned in the fallen world of physical reality and ignorance. DeKorne suggests that these "ultraterrestrial entities" are nourished by human belief and human will: "As monads of the imaginal realm, each Archon seeks to maintain itself, and will conceivably say or do whatever is necessary to gain our attention and worship. . . . Without worship, a god starves and is absorbed (eaten) by some other entity."

"Who can say that belief is not a form of energy, is not food or fuel used in more abstract realms of existence by entities we have always perceived as gods?" he asks. When voices speak in the heads of schizophrenic patients, they tend to demand bizarre behavior and self-sacrifices. Similarly, in the New Age culture of channelers, the channeled entities often speak in patronizing and demanding tones. "This cruel and arrogant . . . attitude of the Archons is only natural . . . if we compare their behavior with the way we treat food in our own dimension." Nobody, not even the most softhearted vegetarian, asks the feelings of a potato before devouring it.

This viewpoint is similar to that of the mystic Gurdjieff, who believed that everything, including psychic processes and thoughts, is actually a form of material—and all material is, to some extent, sentient. "Everything in its own way is intelligent and conscious," he said. "The degree of consciousness corresponds to the degree of density or the speed of vibrations. The denser the matter, the less conscious it is." In his view, the cosmos employs a system of "reciprocal maintenance," with each level of being feeding on the beings beneath it. The sentient souls of human beings sustain the higher vibrational demiurges above them.

DeKorne's book "holds to the shamanic model of multiple dimensions, accessed via human consciousness, in which dissociated intelligences feed off of human belief systems the way that we eat hamburger," he writes. "It is to these entities' advantage to keep us ignorant of their agendas; they would forfeit independent existence if we chose to become gods ourselves by devouring *their* energy instead of vice-versa." Through shamanic exploration, humans can learn to become partners, perhaps equals, with such imaginal entities, rather than nutritional supplements. "It follows that the wisely intentional use of any psychedelic drug is as a self-integrating, self-empowering catalyst. In this way the gods (Devas, Archons, spirits, belief complexes, etc.) cannot coerce our worship—we coerce theirs in the form of enhanced personal power." The lesson of shamanism, of visits to different realities, is that we have to grow up, become adults, and claim our own agency in the imaginal realm as well as the "real world" of physical reality.

Part of what I love about DeKorne's book is that he seems to accurately define not only the shamanic dimensions but something crucial about how the "real world" functions. In our lives, it is obvious that beliefs have independent energy and vitality. Beliefs compel followings and take on a life of their own, leaping from host to host. The belief systems active in controlling our world—whether called "patriotism,"

"free market capitalism," or even "high culture"—behave like danger-
ously independent forces, self-propelling viruses, or like demiurges,
devas, or Archons. Both Gurdjieff's philosophy and the psychedelic experience suggest that spiritual growth requires increasing our level of
self-awareness and refusing to identify with any external agency. Perhaps our belief systems, and even our socially constructed personalities
or egos, function like layers of insulation that must be stripped away if
we want to discover what we can become.

Part Eight

INCONCEIVABLE NEW WORLDS

There are different kinds of Spirits, according to the things over which they preside; some of them govern the Empyrean Heaven, others the Primum Mobile, others the First and Second Crystalline, others the Starry Heaven; there are also Spirits of the Heaven of Saturn, which I call Saturnites; there are Jovial, Martial, Solar, Venerean, Mercurial, and Lunar Spirits; there are also (Spirits) in the Elements as well as in the Heavens, there are some in the Fiery Region, others in the Air, others in the Water, and others upon the Earth, which can all render service to that man who learns their nature, and knows how to attract them.

—*The Keys of Solomon*

Chapter 36

NOT FOR HUMAN CONSUMPTION

I met Dave in Palenque. He had started a company selling experimental research chemicals that were labeled "not for human consumption," although most of them could be found in the back pages of Sasha Shulgin's books. Sitting by the pool one day, I heard Dave tell how he had studied to be a priest but dropped out to become a professional masseur. By some circuitous route—a typical tangled American odyssey—he made his way from the Miami Beach yacht scene to psychedelics and the cutting edge of mind-expansion. In Palenque, Dave invited me to join his private research group, giving me free and low-priced introductions to some new chemicals, as well as his regular catalog of little-known and unscheduled compounds. (Fearing intensified government surveillance, he would close his company the day after the September 11 terrorist attacks, even though his business was not clearly illegal.)

Back in New York, I ordered a few things from his catalog. They came to my home in plain envelopes labeled with intimidating chemical names. For $125, I bought one gram of a yellowish powder called DPT, dipropyltryptamine, a chemical cousin of DMT, substituting propyl for methyl.

Propyl and methyl are simple carbon compounds, two of the

building blocks of organic matter. There is, for example, methyl alcohol, wood alcohol, and propyl alcohol, rubbing alcohol. In gas form, there is propane and methane. The tryptamine molecule is the building block of many neurotransmitters, and of many psychoactive compounds. Serotonin is a tryptamine. As far as I can ascertain, DPT, unlike DMT, does not occur in nature, which means it did not exist until it was synthesized in a laboratory a few decades ago. While DMT, an endogenous chemical inside the body, is recognized by MAO enzymes and immediately neutralized, DPT, a new concoction, is not. Therefore it crosses the blood-brain barrier through direct sniffing or swallowing. But the most astonishing aspect of the two chemicals is that, despite their similarity, they reveal completely different worlds. Why is this the case?

In Shulgin's book and on the Internet I found accounts of DPT trips. Some described the effects as terrifying: "The whole universe falls apart, all colors in electrik air whirlpool into a mandala, eaten up forever. That's it, the world's over." Others felt, after smoking the drug, they entered, for the first time, the "clear light" of God. Another report was more narrative: "I was being led by a wise old man who I know was God. . . . I was handed a Torah for me to carry as a sign that I had been accepted, and forgiven, and come home." Shulgin also mentioned a church in New York, Temple of the True Inner Light, which uses DPT as its sacrament. Clearly DPT was a serious mind-warper. I put the slim envelope of powder in the refrigerator, where it sat for months.

I am often caught between a desire for new and intense altered states and anxiety. When you pass through a doorway to what may actually be a different dimension, there is no guarantee that you will emerge as exactly the same person you were before. After your first serious LSD or mushroom or DMT trip, you really are never quite the same—you have been given an alternate perspective on your psyche, you have been relativized. You may spend the rest of your life suppressing the memory, but it is still there inside of you. After DPT, I understood what Don Juan told Castaneda: "We are men and our lot is to learn and to be hurled into inconceivable new worlds."

Psychedelics are catalysts for transformation, and when you take them, you have to be ready to transform. Our society seems to be changing rapidly, but the psychedelic realms move with a tremendous velocity. They make the achievements of our present-day technology seem tragically antique. While these chemicals should not be demonized or trivialized, they also cannot be reduced to therapeutic tools. They are more powerful than our categories. Someday, they may help us establish a science of the spirit. At the moment, all we can say is that they should be treated with tremendous respect. It is good to be scientifically precise about dosages and reaction times, to know, as best as you can, what the chemical will do to you, and why you are taking it. Because I didn't know exactly what DPT was, or what I wanted from it, I bought it and then sheepishly left it alone.

My cautious resistence to the DPT lure continued until one night, after a party. For the first time in months I was drunk. I was with two old friends, twin brothers, who were eager to try the DPT in my fridge. We each snorted a line, and for me it was an interesting disaster. I was both drunk and tripping. On the one hand, the world was a woozy mess; on the other hand, I was seeing it with a razor-edge precision and in the most vibrant colors. When I closed my eyes, I saw muticolored three-dimensional triangles rotating in deep space. I realized later that I had foolishly used alcohol to overcome my fear of DPT the way I used to drink for the courage to talk to girls at bars. I didn't like DPT. The DPT realm seemed icy, annihilating. I told my friends over and over again, "This is evil. This is not to be explored. This is the wrong doorway." In retrospect, I don't think I was exploring the DPT realm on that trip. I think, instead, the DPT realm was beginning its exploration of me.

Because this is a story not just about chemicals but about occult correspondences and psychic events, I will note that later that night we went out to a bar and started talking to the people next to us. For some reason I talked about the end times and 2012, the Hopi and Mayan prophecies. One of our neighbors described a vivid dream she had when she was a teenager that had stayed with her ever since: "I was in a spaceship full of people. We were lifting off from Earth. I looked back at the Earth and there was brown crust where the land had been. We shot into space and went a long way. Then an angel appeared to us. He said that God had decided to rejuvenate the Earth, even though we had ruined it. He was going to start again, do it all over from scratch. For the time being we were going to have to wait in limbo. And he pointed to a vast gray space where many people were already waiting. We had to leave the spaceship to go there."

It was another few months before I tried DPT again.

In the meantime, another new friend from Palenque accepted my invitation and came to New York. This was Charity the fire dancer. Twenty-four years old, skilled at Tarot and ceremonial magic, a professional stripper, she was the fearless and pixielike embodiment of the new culture I had found at Burning Man. In Mexico, I told her I could find her a free place to stay in New York, and she hitchhiked all the way from Palenque with her cat, Prometheus, catching rides from truckers at truck stops. Unlike me, Charity had no fear of new psychedelics. She kept a list of all the drugs she had tried, and the number was up to forty-three. I told her I had this DPT stuff around, and of course she wanted to try it.

Charity and I took DPT at my house one night—once again, I had to overcome an intense initial reluctance. Finally I put some of the yellowish powder into a pill and swallowed it, but got no effect. She sniffed a line, and almost instantly went into a trance. When her trip was over, she told me I had to try sniffing it. She had seen incredible things.

Sometimes, when you trip, it seems that all of the psychic matter, swirling around in the hours and days beforehand, gathers together, like particles galvanized by a magnet, and pushes the journey in a certain direction. These influences can seem like the karmic trace of some larger pattern or subconscious intention. Earlier that night Charity had told me about the "psychic vampires" who roamed the streets of San Francisco, some of them homeless hippies, who would pick up vibrations from strangers, talk to them, and suck their energy away. I laughed at this. We also talked about the books of Zecharia Sitchin, whose scholarly research convinced him that a race of extraterrestrial giants had created human beings, long ago, to serve them as slaves—a variation on the concept of the "Archons" from Gnosticism. According to Sitchin, the magnificent cruelty of the alien race that created us was beyond our imagining.

Charity cut two big lines of the DPT on the table, and I snorted one. The powder burned my nasal passages. Bitter residue dripped down the back of my throat. I stretched out on the couch. I closed my eyes and entered the DPT realm.

We were listening to moody techno music. With each change in beat, with each skitter of sampled noise, I saw a brand-new and extremely detailed demonic realm swirl before me in cobalt, scarlet, purple gossamer hues. At moments there seemed to be some incredibly elegant yet violently orgiastic party taking place with beautiful females in evening gowns and men in Edwardian topcoats in the spacious parlors of a huge and opulent mansion. At other times there seemed to be bat or butterfly-winged creatures—long and quivering antennaes, velvet coats and emerald eyes, stiletto talons—rising into otherworldly skies, wandering futuristic cities. I had an impression of tremendous vanity. "I" was being used as a mirror for the DPT beings to admire themselves. But their realm was far beyond what can be expressed in ordinary language in its speed of transmutation, its shivering quicksilver beauty.

The worlds revealed were like endless facets of a twirling diamond—I felt the real possibility of being trapped inside any of those facets, a kind of soul-prison, for eternity. That was the terror of it. As with smoking *Salvia,* I had the sense that some part of me had always been stuck in this Gothic DPT prison, trapped there eternally. I somehow understood that this was not my first visit, nor my last.

For a flicker of forever, I was imprisoned in a postmodern bar surrounded by gleaming mirrors with a hyperslick lounge lizard wearing a white mohawk and synthetic fabrics. He was sitting at the bar, drinking a highball. There were no doors or windows in this room, no escape possible. The graphics of this vision were high-res and hyperperfect. Other shards of the DPT realm shared this sci-fi quality. DPT was a postmodern demonic MTV psychedelic.

The sleek, rhythmical mesh of the music seemed woven into the lurid fabric of the darkness, the revelation of sinister forces coming to life behind my eyelids.

Like DMT, the level of visual organization of the DPT realm was far beyond anything that the synaptical wiring of my brain could create—it was, in its own peacock-feathery way, not just as real as this reality, but far more real, crackling with power. I felt from the entities exploring my mind a kind of contempt, a disdain for human beings trapped in our pitifully unsophisticated domain, our meat realm. They seemed somewhere between bemused and enraged that we had trespassed.

In shamanic cultures, the taking of entheogenic substances is always surrounded by ritual. A circle of protection is created, the four directions invoked, the spirits asked for their blessing through an offering of tobacco and prayer. Because we were sniffing a chemical powder in a modern New York apartment, a chemical without a long history of human use, it didn't even occur to us to take such precautions. I was jealous of Charity because she managed to get to the kitchen sink and throw up. She vomited four or five times in a row—later she said she saw a male entity in the sink with a kind of device or machine that he was using to soak up the energy she was expulsing, jeering at her as he did it. The demon told her his name but she couldn't recall it. I couldn't throw up. I suspected that I had finally, and completely, managed to destroy myself. I was convinced I would never recover from this onslaught. I staggered to the CD player and changed the music to Bach, which helped a little. With my eyes opened, transformational energy seemed to be crawling over everything, flickering and receding like waves of sentient power—vampiric electricity. My hands looked and felt like claws made out of wires. When I opened my eyes on ayahuasca, I also felt and saw energy passing like a wave form, but it was more human somehow. Here the speed of the waves was much faster and more brutal than the *yagé* flares. The experience was unmammalian, futuristic, inhuman.

Not only was it suddenly obvious that there was such a thing as a soul, it was also clear that I was in danger of losing mine permanently.

I somehow understood that the DPT realm had evolved over an incredibly long period—millions of years, if time has the same kind of meaning to its inhabitants as it does to us. I realized there are diabolical hierarchies, secret cabals, vast libraries of wickedness to be studied over millennia. It was obvious that we little human beings have absolutely no idea what is going on in the cosmos. The word *baroque* doesn't even begin to describe the jaded emptiness and sublime beauty of that evanescent empire. A little bit like soft candle-flimmer worlds one sees on hash and opium, but etched in perfect solid-state reality—more than photographic. The sleekness of the DPT dimension was beyond belief.

About half an hour into the trip, past three A.M., I called my friend Tony.

"This is total magic, total sorcery. I am watching endless Gothic demon universes mirroring each other," I babbled. "If someone could be at home here, learn to control things here, they could gain such power they could just walk right through the walls of the White House, do anything, but it wouldn't matter, because they would already be part of such an ancient conspiracy." I had begun to pace around the house, and as I paced, I found that I was moving my arms in the air, making "passes" like the shamanic gestures described in Castaneda's work. These gestures came to me intuitively. They helped control the overwhelming sense of assault.

"Daniel, don't be taken in by it. It's just samsara," Tony said. His voice was a soothing lifeline. He laughed at me. He tried to convince me that the trip would end soon, that I wasn't permanently fried. He told me I should have known what I was doing, since I had called DPT "evil" after my first attempt.

"What's that music you're playing in the background?" he asked.

"Bach," I told him. "It's the only thing that's keeping me together. Perhaps that's why they are here; the demons are attracted to the music. They are crowding in here to be close to it."

"Well, that's nice," he said.

"There's nothing nice about that!" I screeched at him. "They are totally defiant. They don't give a shit about us; we are their puppets."

But at this point the trip was starting to wind down. In a few minutes Charity and I were back in that miraculous illusion of stability we call "reality" once again. I felt incredibly relieved. "Wow, I can't believe it," I said to Tony. "Reality . . . this is definitely a good thing!"

In the next few days, however, I learned that I wasn't quite back in reality after all, or if I was, it was a new, hypercharged one.

I was supposed to leave to meet my girlfriend in Berlin the next day. In the morning my travel agent came up with an affordable last-minute ticket. On the plane, I sat next to a German woman dressed in black. I was reading *The Invisible Landscape* by Terence and Dennis McKenna, and I noticed she seemed startled after she read a few words from the back cover over my shoulder. She had read the word *shamanism*. Halfway through the flight, she told me she had been having a series of dreams over the past months in which two American Indians, a couple, came into her house and told her that she was meant to be a shaman, that she wasn't supposed to get married. She was meant to devote herself to shamanism totally. The dreams mystified her. She had never thought about shamanism and she had little idea what it was. "Do you know anything about it?" she asked.

I tried to explain the basics of shamanism and gave her the titles of some books to read. Also I told her what I believed, what I had learned from Robert: "The Indian cultures have been almost wiped out, but shamanism is an essential human phenomenon connected to the earth. Right now, the shamans of the past are looking for candidates who can carry on the traditions. They have zeroed in on you as a possible candidate. You can choose to follow this or ignore it, but I definitely recommend that you learn more before making a decision."

The woman had a tribal pendant around her neck—on it was a pattern of lightninglike zigzags around a central circle—and I asked her about it. "Somebody gave this to me on a beach in Mexico," she said. "They said it was a Navajo protection symbol."

I do not think the world is orchestrated as a paranoid conspiracy designed to fit my wildest fantasies. Yet I had an intuitive, uncanny sense that this symbol had been sent to me—to show me that I was being protected, somehow, that I was being taken through a process. Even though I was freaking out, I had to trust that the process was good. In shamanic cultures, synchronicities are recognized as signs that you are on the right path.

I was in Berlin because Laura's father had been stricken with cancer. The entire family was assembling for the weekend. Because Laura was pregnant and wouldn't be able to travel later, she was staying with her parents for several weeks.

Whenever I was left alone, I found myself walking around the house and making conducting gestures again. I was afraid I was turning into an obsessive-compulsive, but I could control the gestures when other people were around. At night, I barely slept.

With my eyes closed, I watched vivid imagery unfold in little film loops. I saw a huge column of fire shooting up from the center of Stonehenge. I envisioned myself walking into the flame column, being obliterated and shooting up into space. This felt so good that I did it again and again. Then I saw the surface of another planet, covered in coral and spongelike growths. A smirking alien was standing next to one of the sponges, and he kept flowing through the organic folds of the plant, then reassembling himself. He and the plant were fused in magical symbiosis.

Finally I fell asleep. I dreamt of a boy standing in the woods, yelling over and over again at the top of his lungs: "Long live ethnopharmacology!"

Another night I had two extremely vivid dreams in which I was pursued by a bearded man. In one dream I threw a party in an apartment where I once lived. Aggressive strangers showed up and stole my books from the shelves. A bearded man came up to me.

"I used to live here," he said.

"Do you want to come back?" I asked.

"Yes," he said.

Back in New York, I still felt very strange—fizzy and nonordinary, with a buzzing around the temples. It was my second night at home and I was jet-lagged. Ten minutes after I turned out the lights and got into bed, a large mirror in the other room fell off the wall and loudly crashed facedown on the floor. It didn't break.

All night I dreamt that the bearded man was hitting me in the head with a pillow over and over again, and laughing as he did it. I tried to hit him back but my swings were feeble misses.

When I awoke in the morning, feeling groggy, I went to get a yogurt from the refrigerator. I opened the tightly closed silverware drawer and reached for a spoon. Right under the spoons was a large and ominous bug. It did not look like a New York bug at all—it was winged, honey-brown, with a long curly tail, and it quickly wriggled out of sight.

I screamed and slammed the drawer shut.

Fuck, I thought. The DPT trip had unleashed an angry poltergeist in my house. How could this be? I have never had a belief or even the slightest interest in poltergeists or the occult, but the signs couldn't be more obvious. Suddenly I was in the midst of something for which I had no frame of reference, no preparation. What had I done? Once again, as often before, I cursed myself for my fascination with these chemicals.

I walked around in a panic. I went to the East Village and sat at a cafe. On the way I stopped in a Tibetan Buddhist store. I asked the clerk if he had any symbols of protection, and he sold me a small metal *dorje*, the Tibetan lightning bolt symbol used in meditation. I still felt fizzy. I had a tingling around my left temple and my left hand was buzzing strangely. Clutching the *dorje* in my fist, I called Charity and told her about the situation.

"Oh man," she said. "We've got to clean that thing out of there before your girlfriend comes back with the baby."

It turned out that Charity, from her days of San Francisco witchcraft (modern paganism was another phenomenon I had always dismissed), knew all about exorcisms and entities. She had carted with her, all the way from Mexico, an entire kit bag of magical implements, including a large and beautifully smooth black obsidian ball that someone in Palenque had given her and some quartz crystals. While I knew that quartz was used for shamanic healing, to realign energy patterns, I did not know that obsidian was considered to have the power to absorb negative spiritual energies. "This ball is so excellent, it just sucks all that stuff right up," Charity said. She also brought ceremonial candleholders (tacky little sculptures of a cat and an elephant, which became the Egyptian god Bast and Indian god Ganesh for the duration of the ceremony), and Aleister Crowley's elegant Tarot cards. I met her and we went back to the apartment.

"I can already feel it," she said when we were in the lobby. And it was true—the air in the building seemed electrically charged, more so in the elevator, and in the apartment, the charge was like a distinct physical presence. Charity put the obsidian ball down on the ground in the center of the living room. We both watched, astonished, as it took the ball an extremely long time to stop trembling, finally rotating in smaller and smaller circles until it came to rest. She organized a quick magical ritual, consulting the Tarot cards several times. I had also never given Tarot cards much thought, but now I was watching them as if my life depended on it—I felt, in some obscure and woozy way, perhaps it did.

She picked a card with lightning bolts all over it, "Swiftness." "So we'll be swift," she said. She picked "Fortune," suggesting a change for the better. She picked "Futility"—my heart sank—but opposite it, "The Queen of Cups," my court card. "Because your card is a water sign, we've got to do something with water," she said, quickly analyzing the situation like a technician faced with an engineering problem. She soaked the obsidian ball in salt-water, then held it in the toilet and flushed a few times.

"Take that bullshit out of here," she commanded.

At the end of the ritual, the atmosphere in the apartment seemed changed, cleared out. It was, we thought, safe again.

It was safe until later that night, when I returned from visiting Tony. Once again, I felt the apartment crackling with an electrical occult buzz. My temple and left hand started buzzing again. I had been jokingly complaining to Tony about the supernatural forces taking such obvious manifestations—a falling mirror, a big bug. It was all so silly, so comic book–like, even flirtatious. Once again, the joke seemed to be on me as I lay in bed and felt increasingly creeped-out and panicked.

I went into the living room and sat in front of the obsidian ball. I picked up the *dorje* and chanted a bit—nonsense words, Asiatic-sounding, insectile, similar to what I recalled of the Secoya language, came into my head and I called them out. "Ching! Ching! Gada-ching! Gada-gada-ching!" I rapped the hard surface of the black ball with the Tibetan *dorje,* then I held it in my palms and looked into the polished surface of the obsidian sphere.

My entire visual field turned gray.

All I could see were a few rectangles of refracted light in the center of the ball; thick grayness covered everything else.

I turned away from the ball and looked around the room.

After two seconds, my vision went back to normal. I looked back at the ball.

My entire visual field turned gray yet again.

I grabbed my jacket and ran out of the house. Once in the street, I called my friend Michael from my mobile phone. Michael is twenty years older than me; a poet and novelist with an impressive knowledge of alternative healing and indigenous cultures; it was he who first told me about ayahuasca. For an hour, as I paced around the streets, Michael tried to calm me down. He told me some Buddhist meditation techniques to "get you back in your body." He told me that even if there were some "other" out there, and he was not convinced there was, I had to recognize that aspects of my mind had manifested all of this stuff. "It takes two to tango," Michael said. Rather than fighting against it, I could accept it, integrate it within myself.

Michael told me to imagine a buddha hovering over me, shooting pure white light through my body, turning me into blinding white light, flushing everything negative or bad into my central channel where it would go into my intestines and ultimately come out of me as shit. At the end of the meditation, Michael told me to imagine this buddha coming down to me as I merged with the white light.

I followed his instructions, and it seemed to help. I felt selfless, emptied out, and even empathic toward my entity visitor. Soon I fell asleep. By the next morning, the world had returned to normal. There was no more buzzing, no more tricks.

This story may seem ridiculous, yet the psychic reality of the DPT encounter and its aftermath overwhelm most ordinary events. I offer it as a cautionary tale. There are aspects of the story that remain, for various reasons, impossible to tell. Suffice it to say that after DPT, I strongly suspect an ordinary death is not the worst thing that can happen to a human being. There may be far worse fates.

Chapter 37

NEW SENSATIONS

For over a year I had carefully studied my dreams, waking three or four times a night to write down images, conversations, disjointed narratives, and semiconscious visions. Sometimes, lying in bed on the threshold of sleep, I would see myself as a corpse devoured by birds, or I would be processed through some kind of cosmic sausage-grinder. In one dream I was crucified and my body paraded through an African town by laughing Bwiti tribesmen. In another, I was given directions to undertake the alchemical "Great Work" in an airport lobby. My dream life changed in other ways as well. I would fall asleep thinking about some esoteric concept, and throughout the night I would awaken repeatedly to find my unconscious mind was still holding the idea tightly, turning it around in different ways. I began to realize that sleep can become an extension of waking awareness, not just an extinguishing of it.

The change in my dream life suggested some kind of shamanic or esoteric initiation. It felt as though the ideas that fascinated me were slowly filtering from my thoughts into my bloodstream, permeating my cells. Despite these hints, despite my fascination with the subject, I assumed that shamanism would remain a phenomenon "out there" that I was studying, in the distanced and analytical way I had always pursued intellectual subjects.

According to Gurdjieff, intellectual knowledge—technical or academic mastery of any subject—is always shallow and one-dimensional. "Knowledge by itself does not give understanding. . . . Understanding depends upon the relation of knowledge to being." He thought that ancient cultures cared about one's quality of being, developed through self-discipline and spiritual training, while modern society only values what is quantifiable: "People of Western culture put great value on the level of a man's knowledge but they do not value the level of a man's being and they are not ashamed of the low level of their own being." If understanding is linked to being, then certain types of phenomena can only be comprehended when the observer has changed: "There are things for the understanding of which a different being is necessary." This transformative process takes place in stages, over time.

It is hard to calculate precisely, but in small-scale tribal societies probably one out of every twenty-five or thirty people receives a shamanic calling. Since shamanism seems to be a universal phenomenon, this statistic should be cross-cultural, which means there are at least ten million people in our culture who potentially fit the shamanic role. Some of those people are currently alternative healers of some sort, some are artists or psychologists, and I have no doubt that many of them are imprisoned in mental hospitals, or they are among the muttering homeless who refuse integration into society. Whether or not they realize it, they are people, like myself, for whom contact with the invisible world is as essential as ordinary knowledge or material gain or any reward that the "real world" can offer.

This is what I suspect happened when I made my alliance: A somewhat mischievous being from a higher-vibrational realm melded itself into my consciousness.

For a few weeks after the events, I felt this other "it" as a new perspective inside my mind. My perceptions seemed more acute, my thoughts zingier. There were certain aspects of reality that I seemed to be picking up without conscious intent. For instance, walking around the streets of New York I was conscious of the way symbols and logos in advertisements and on clothes stood for unconscious forces, how they shaped and manipulated social reality. All logos, all symbols, seemed to draw energy from the occult dimension, the DPT realm.

Even watching a basketball game on television became unbearable—
the manipulations were so obvious. The underlying messages—beer
for self-oblivion, jeep for planetary destruction and accelerated extinction—so mind-numbingly clear. Post-DPT, I had to overcome a new
sense of contempt for humanity, myself included, as well as an increased sympathy for the devil.

I studied the DPT reports on the Internet with more care. Several
of the DPT takers echoed my impressions: "I felt as if DPT were a sinister, sinister being that was laughing at me. Humans are so weak. DPT
destroys you," wrote one of them. Some worried that they had torn
apart the fabric of reality: "It's very obvious the human world was as
stable as a house of toothpicks, amazing it didn't fall apart sooner in
history, but the hideous human angel hasn't been crawling along the
planet that long at all, and now someone pulled the plug out accidentally." This writer also passed, at high speed, through Gothic realms
where beings appeared in parallel dimensions. Many takers of DPT experience the classic rising of kundalini energy—the Hindus call it
shakti—from the base of their spine to the top of their skull, sometimes leading to out-of-control body shudders. Unsurprisingly, DPT often seems to generate an extreme fear reaction.

As noted earlier, Rick Strassman theorizes that DMT, nn-
dimethyltryptamine, is the "spirit molecule" that releases the soul into
the spirit realm. If that is the case, I suspect it is possible that DPT
serves the same function in some other realm—the supernatural world
of magical entities sketched by Aubrey Beardsley and described by
Aleister Crowley. Perhaps DPT is the "demon molecule," recognizing
that demons are ambiguous entities in many traditions. In Tibetan
Buddhism, all deities have both their benevolent and wrathful aspects.
The wrathful deities in Tibetan Buddhism are depicted as frightening
monsters, drinking blood out of skulls, multiarmed, with fangs and
talons. As the flipside of the Buddhas, and ultimately aspects of the inner self, such deities call to mind an old proverb: "The devil is God as
He is misunderstood by the wicked."

In making this alliance, in this speculative interpretation, not only
did I have no control once the process was set in motion, but the entity
that integrated into me had little choice in the matter as well. "I" was
somehow part of his evolution, his inquiry, as much as he was part of

mine. Other forces were involved in guiding the merge, but don't ask me who or what they are. As Gurdjieff noted, "All the phenomena of the life of a given cosmos, examined from another cosmos, assume a completely different aspect and have a completely different meaning." He also said: "The manifestation of the laws of one cosmos in another cosmos constitute what we call a miracle."

There might be validity in the idea that the demons or djinns "are attracted to the music." The disembodied splendor of their higher-vibrational realm may bore them after a while. Through communion with a human being, a spirit from the supersensible realms gets to smell, taste, love, fuck, all our sense-realm experiences. On our side, perhaps we can utilize some tiny aspect of its higher vision and its powers—I don't know, at this point, exactly what for, but perhaps that remains to be revealed at some future point.

If the universe has a spiritual purpose, perhaps the soul develops new powers and possibilities as it passes through various incarnations that are stages in its development. In my dream, the DPT demiurge came into my house and said to me: "I used to live here." There was a strong feeling of familiarity to the episode. Perhaps, in some previous incarnation, centuries or eons or even worlds ago, we once made this same bargain. The incubus's memory just happens to be better, and longer, than mine.

I almost never buy clothes, but on the plane to Berlin, I began to see myself wearing a deep red or purple velvet Vivienne Westwood suit with an Edwardian cut to it. I thought how cool-looking and comfortable such a suit could be, and even sketched myself wearing it. It was nothing like my normal dressing style. On the plane back to New York I was reminded of the suit again. A week later, in SoHo, I happened to walk past the Vivienne Westwood boutique. Down in the basement they were having a sample sale. I found one copy of the exact suit I had been thinking of, in deep crimson. I put it on. It fit. At 70 percent off, I could even afford it.

Chapter 38

MAGICAL THINKING

Before taking DPT, I had started to reread Carlos Castaneda's books on the Yaqui sorceror Don Juan. I anticipated writing dismissively of Castaneda as a phony anthropologist who perpetuated a fraud. As Jay Courtney Fikes writes in *Carlos Castaneda, Academic Opportunism and the Psychedelic Sixties,* "Castaneda's claims that he was a sorcerer's apprentice, and that don Juan's teachings constituted a 'Yaqui way of knowledge' are unsupported by photographs, field notes, or tape recordings." Fikes believes Castaneda simply recognized a good marketing niche and cashed in.

After DPT, however, Castaneda's depictions of the sorcerer's world seemed plausibly insightful. Don Juan explores tricks-of-the-eye universes, realms of otherness revealed in mirror-scratches or the shadow-throwing flickers of candle flames. He contacts parallel dimensions of beings at once extremely threatening and powerful, yet evanescent and ephemeral. Don Juan's sorcery is a dangerous pursuit of knowledge that the sorceror considers ultimately meaningless. "Seeing," as Don Juan embodies it, requires detachment toward ordinary reality.

"A man who follows the paths of sorcery is confronted with imminent annihilation every turn of the way, and unavoidably he becomes keenly aware of his own death," Don Juan says. "The idea of imminent death, instead of becoming an obsession, becomes an indifference." Through DPT, I saw the road open up toward amoral knowledge and occult power. What was most frightening was its seductiveness, its nonhuman glamour.

I could no longer argue with the idea of ambivalent spirit-realms conjoined with this one. The rules of navigating in these realms may be, as Don Juan lays them out, extremely specific and seemingly arbitrary. Without a guide, the dangers for the integrity of the psyche may be as imposing as the knowledge to be gained.

Post-DPT, I turned to the occult tradition of the West. Impressed with Charity's deft handling of the Tarot, I found myself peering into the histrionic writings of Aleister Crowley. Like Castaneda, I considered Crowley to be mere adolescent entertainment. Alas for me, I could no longer dismiss him so easily. The DPT journey, and its aftermath, showed Crowley's work, and Castaneda's, as more than spooky fantasy.

Crowley's scholarly project was to find definite correspondences between mystical traditions, linking the I Ching and Egyptian mysticism and the Tarot. "The laws of magick are closely related to those of other physical sciences," he wrote. He laid out a model of the cosmos with many higher dimensions and endless beings inhabiting them, made of subtler stuff than us. "It is one magical hypothesis that all things are made up of ten different sorts of vibrations, each with a different vibration, and each corresponding to a 'planet.'" This theory—based on the Sephiroth, the ten emanations of God in the Kaballah—has a neat poetic resonance with modern "superstring theory" in physics, which postulates ten dimensions of space-time.

In the 1920s, Crowley wrote, "Magick deals principally with certain physical forces still unrecognized by the vulgar; but those forces are just as real, just as material—if indeed you can call them so, for all things are ultimately spiritual—as properties like radioactivity, weight and hardness." Crowley considered the Tarot, based on the Kaballah, to be an accurate model of the forces and spiritual hierarchies at play in the universe, a tool given to us by higher-dimensional forces.

Most people in the modern world reject the possibility that the self might have occult and transcendental dimensions that are intentionally obscured by ordinary life. The possibility that such knowledge exists, and that you can receive direct experience of it, through psychedelics or other means, is upsetting, even frightening. I now suspect that this is the reason that psychedelics have been strenuously suppressed by mainstream society and rejected by psychiatry. As T. S. Eliot wrote, "human kind cannot bear very much reality." We have chosen not to know.

All of Carl Jung's researches led him to conclude that the unconscious as it was revealed through psychoanalysis had occult and paranormal dimensions. Freud, despite his courage and brilliance, could not accept this possibility. He once confessed to Jung, as Jung described in *The Undiscovered Self,* that it was necessary to make a dogma of his sexual theory because this was the sole bulwark of reason against a possible "outburst of the black tide of occultism."

> In these words Freud was expressing his conviction that the unconscious still harbored many things that might lead themselves to "occult" interpretations, as is in fact the case. . . . It is this fear of the unconscious psyche which not only impedes self-knowledge but is the gravest obstacle to a wider understanding and knowledge of psychology.

Jung believed that the individual cannot achieve true awareness without exploring the occult domains of the psyche (which does not mean they have to literally conjure up demons). He looked at the metaphors for the quest for self-knowledge hidden in Gnosticism, and in alchemy, where the injunction "Visit the interior of the earth" referred to techniques of seeking transcendent knowledge and power by delving into higher states of consciousness and integrating them into the self.

The roots of European alchemy can be found in Gnosticism, a heretical offshoot of Christianity that flourished in the first centuries A.D. The Gnostic version of Christ is a Leary-like advocate for direct spiritual experience over faith. In the "Gospel of Thomas," one of a group of Gnostic texts discovered in a jar in the Nag Hammadi desert at the end of the Second World War, Christ said, "Open the door for yourself, so you will know what is." In that same text, which may predate the biblical scriptures and equal them in authenticity, Christ also announced, "If you bring forth what is within you, what you bring forth will save you. If you do not bring forth what is within you, what you do not bring forth will destroy you." Either of those phrases could stand as a psychedelic credo. With his visions, his ability to transform energies, and his mastery of healing, Christ could be seen as a prototypical shaman. In the Gospels, Christ says, "Seek and you shall find." The unstated corollary to this is, if you do not seek, you will not find.

. . .

THE HIERARCHIES of invisible beings I had seen on DPT—as if I was a reflecting surface, a mirror for them to preen themselves—now seemed to be present everywhere. Walking in a community garden on East Houston Street, featuring flowering paths and a small pond with turtles in it, I saw emanations of that higher-order occult dimension in the swooping flourishes of rare flowers, in the pseudopsychedelic patterns traced across a turtle's scaly skin. It was suddenly obvious to me that the Darwinian theory of evolution, the Western rational perspective on world biology, with all its flaws and gaps, could not be the whole story. It was true to a limited extent, but there were other truths as well. Life on earth has been sculpted into multitudinous forms by higher-dimensional beings for the enjoyment of their own skill and our delight. As I watched a turtle's eye rotate in its socket, I had to admit that they were master craftsmen.

As I was reading about the Kaballah and the Western occult tradition, feeling oppressed by Crowley's maniacal tone, I ran into an old friend who had moved to San Francisco and was just in town for a few weeks to curate a show at a downtown gallery. I had known Neil in New York for many years. We had shared an insatiable appetite for parties and art openings. Our mutual friends considered us rivals for the title role of New York bon vivant.

Neil seemed essentially unchanged after five years. Tall and narrow, he wore antique suits and patterned ties, looking a bit like an ascetic missionary from the 1940s on his first trip into the jungle. It turned out that Neil had become deeply involved in studying the work of Rudolf Steiner. Steiner was an Austrian-born philosopher and occultist from the turn of the century, who claimed to have developed a scientific approach to studying spiritual phenomena. Neil was even living in a church founded under Steiner's guidance. I knew nothing about Steiner except that he had created Waldorf schools and founded something called anthroposophy.

Neil had received an initial push toward mysticism through psychedelics. He described a DMT trip from the early 1990s during which he shut his eyes and beheld a sight which astonished him: an infinitely deep tunnel whose glowing walls were covered with constantly changing runic script and visual symbols. "Then I became aware that I was surrounded by several gigantic beings who were guiding my attention into this tubular apparatus, which they had been propping up in front of my face as if to distract me from their activities. When I discovered them hovering around me, they smirked and winked at me, probing into my head with their fingers as if inspecting the contents of my mind. The masculine ones looked a bit like King Neptune, with long curly beards, but hunched over and very earthy. The females were absurdly voluptuous and struggled for my attention with playful antics."

When the effect began to wear off, Neil lit the pipe a second time. "As I sat and inhaled, I stared into the burning chunk of DMT in the pipe. When I closed my eyes, I was immediately transported back to the vivid, liquid reality of these beings, except that the red glow in the pipe had become a molten sun within the magnificent bowl of a much larger pipe being smoked by one of the beings. They were all sitting with me in a circle, and the one with the magical pipe offered it to me ceremoniously. They communicated through these image-tunnels, and each had a unique persona conveyed through the quality of images within their tunnel. I had the distinct feeling that they were starved for human attention and were overjoyed that I had made the journey to them. Although I was amazed to meet them and eager to grasp their visual discourse, I knew that it was too much for my puny intellect."

When the trip seemed about over, he lay down on the bed and received a final intense flash. A feminine figure approached him from above. She held a luminous tablet from which emerged a stream of transforming symbols: "The motifs of all the world's civilizations flowed out of her in an animated tableau—Egyptian and Babylonian figures, Native American patterns, Eastern mandalas, Hebrew and

Greek script, a crucifixion scene, everything you could imagine. It was with this that I was welcomed back to a comparatively drab reality. Of course, I wanted to understand my experience. All my previous psychedelic trips had shown me the creative handiwork of the spiritual world, the swirling patterns and whatnot. Now I had met the beings responsible for it!"

At around the same time, a musician friend turned Neil onto anthroposophy. He recognized the beings he had met on DMT as the "elemental beings" described by Steiner in numerous works, particularly his book *Man as Symphony of the Creative Word*. These nonphysical or "supersensible" beings live within the processes of nature and help construct the physical universe. They are related to the gnomes, nyads, dryads, and sylphs seen by country folk throughout history and preserved in myths and legends. For Steiner, they were part of a vast order of supersensible entities he encountered through his own clairvoyant experiences.

"Steiner explains how opposing forces act on human beings all the time," Neil told me. "One of these forces he calls 'Luciferic,' which is the force that pulls us away from physical reality upward into dream and fantasy, visionary realms, and abstract theorizing. According to Steiner, Lucifer is not an evil being himself, but he causes evil to occur when people allow themselves to be lured by his offer of inflated self-esteem and escape from the responsibilities of life. There is an opposing force that pulls us down toward the earth, chaining us to the mineral realm of the material world and death. This force is identified by Steiner as Ahriman, named after the dark earth-spirit of Persian legend. In order to be truly human, we must strive to achieve balance between these different forces. It's only when we find the center that we can consciously appreciate the extremes. Psychedelics are heavily weighted toward the Luciferic realm, expansive but escapist. They give access to worlds that you may be eager to see but may not be prepared for." Neil compared it to crashing a party, rather than waiting to be invited.

"Don't you think that it depends on the individual?" I asked. "After all, you probably wouldn't have found your way to Steiner if it wasn't for psychedelics."

"Obviously the drugs are here for a reason, but that doesn't mean they are good for us. The beings we meet on psychedelics may or may not have our best interests at heart. I think they benefit from our attention in ways we don't fully understand. There may be a sort of 'organ trade' going on in these realms. 'Oh, here's a liver I can use!' All spiritual traditions that I know of teach that crossing the threshold without preparation is fraught with peril." He quoted a song by the British post-punk band Magazine: "My mind ain't so open that anything could crawl right in."

I immediately started reading Steiner's work. Steiner explains that different types of spiritual training were appropriate for different epochs of human evolution. He called the spiritual consciousness of the ancient world and the shaman a "dusk-like clairvoyance." In the present world, according to Steiner, that type of consciousness is no longer appropriate. He devised a method of spiritual training based on meditations and cognition, using the highly developed thinking power of the modern mind to rediscover the lost spiritual realms. Steiner believed we had developed our modern empiricism in order to rediscover spiritual cognition in freedom—without compulsion or atavism.

According to Steiner, in the higher realms, beings are not separate from each other as they are in the physical world: "To have knowledge of a sense-perceptible being means to stand outside of it and assess it according to external impressions. To have knowledge of a spiritual being through higher consciousness means having become completely at one with it, having united with its inner nature."

The higher spiritual realms consist of beings made entirely of thought: "The actual world of thought is what pervades everything in the land of spirits, like the warmth that pervades all earthly things and beings," Steiner wrote. "Here, however, we must imagine these thoughts as living, independent beings. What we grasp as a thought in the material world is like a shadow of a thought being that is active in the land of spirits."

Steiner describes a hierarchy of consciousness, from the lowest pebble to the highest spiritual being. On earth, a person who achieved truly rational consciousness (of course, for Steiner, rationality would include spiritual awareness) would have reached the highest level of thought that we can imagine, while minerals exist at the lowest level of mental activity (for mystics, it seems that nothing, not even a pebble, is completely devoid of consciousness). In the higher realms, you find beings whose lowest level of existence is rational thought. Within this multidimensional hierarchy, elemental beings range from subphysical demonic beings to exalted workers shaping the forces of external nature. Neil paraphrased Steiner: "The elementals are hard at work keeping the planet alive, but the ones that give us their attention tend to be less concerned with the healthy unfolding of humanity than they are with their own development, which may prove to be at the expense of our own, and that of the earth."

Neil had doubts about the psychedelic community. "People are entering the lower realms of the spiritual world unbidden and unprepared, exposing themselves to delusions and deceptions. In reality, they are placing their faith in the mischievous imps of the spiritual world. I have no desire to stop anyone from pursuing their destiny, but the soul-wrenching chaos of the psychedelic experience seems to lend itself to a sense of panic and dissipation. If one wants to have a positive effect on the world, inner calm and discrimination are absolutely necessary."

. . .

IN 1997, largely inspired by the jewel-like multicolored landscapes I beheld with eyes closed on several mushroom trips, I decided to go to Nepal. The prismatic fast-changing psilocybin scenes seemed direct evocations of "Buddha Realms," those sumptuous paradisical lands ruled by enlightened unearthly beings, described in many Buddhist texts. After a few visits, I found myself drawn toward the stylized artifacts of Tibetan art, the *thangka* paintings and mandalas used as aid to meditation.

With the money I made writing a never-published article about a humiliating visit to a "Free Love Summer Camp" in the Oregon woods, I booked a ticket to Kathmandu, a city of crumbling Hindu temples, ancient stone streets, and dire poverty. I thought, perhaps, that Tibetan Buddhism might be a path for me. I visited several temples and monasteries. The solemn rituals of chanting monks and the stylized slow-motion pageantry of the costumed dances to celebrate

Losar, the Tibetan New Year, were beautiful. But I didn't like the hier-
archical and nondetached feeling of the Westerners who clustered
close to the high-powered lamas.

From Nepal, I went to Dharmsala, the headquarters of the Dalai
Lama and Tibet's government-in-exile, in northern India. I appreciated
the smiling faces and earthy warmth of the Tibetans, monks and com-
moners, but I was once again put off by the graspiness radiated by the
Westerners. I had picked up a lung infection during a Shiva festival
in Kathmandu—to celebrate Shiva, the city with the third worst air
quality in the world burned fires of garbage all night long—and spent a
week coughing, waiting for either the Indian antibiotics or Tibetan
homeopathic remedies to take effect.

By accident, I was in India at the time of the Hindu festival Kumbh
Mehla, which is in the *Guinness Book of World Records* as the largest
gathering of people in the world. Every three years, around twenty
million people travel across the country to bathe in the River Ganges
on one of three auspicious dates. At first I thought the combination of
Hindu mobs and bad sanitation would make Kumbh Mehla a tourist
nightmare. Finally, sick of the Tibetan Buddhist circus, I decided to
check it out.

The festival turned out to be well-managed and orderly, despite its
immensity. It was a joyful, almost biblical, spectacle. I stayed in
Rishikesh, a holy city of pastel-colored ashrams, the place where the
Beatles went in the sixties to study Transcendental Meditation with the
Maharishi. Rishikesh was idyllic and vegetarian. Clans of Hindus
dressed in bright colors and flowing robes paraded cheerfully through
the narrow, carless streets. Kumbh Mehla also attracts sadhus from all
over India; these yellow-robed, trident-carrying followers of Shiva
range from sincere holy men to smirking shysters eager to extract do-
nations, pick up chicks, or sell *ganga* to tourists. I stayed at a laidback
ashram for Westerners, run by a bald guru in his nineties. The ashram
cost a dollar a night, including breakfast, and for another dollar you
could attend yoga and meditation classes spaced throughout the day.
Hinduism seemed sloppier, more anarchic than Tibetan Buddhism.
Hanging out on the banks of the Ganges—clean to swim in because of
its proximity to its source in the Himalayas—old holy men in long gray
beards would come up to converse with me in broken English about

the nearness of God. Wild monkeys chattered in the trees. A pilgrim in the streets stopped to tell me, sincerely, that he was sure we had known each other in an earlier life.

Kumbh Mehla marks a mythological event. Long ago, the gods were fighting over a vial containing the nectar of immortality. Four drops of this nectar fell into the Ganges at the four spots where Kumbh Mehla is celebrated. If you bathe in the Ganges during the right moment of the festival, you wipe away the bad karma, like a psychic crust, accumulated over all of your past lives.

The actual festival was held, that year, in the nearby and equally festive town of Haridwar. On the auspicious mornings, hordes of devotees clustered for miles up and down the riverbanks. On the first festival day, I did not enter the water myself, but I witnessed a riot of the Naga Babas. The Naga Babas are the most extreme and ascetic clan of sadhus. Most of them live in caves high in the Himalayas, coming down for the festival once every three years. They parade—naked, carrying weapons, covered in gray ash—through the town before bathing in the water. They are followed by gurus from across India, on chariots, surrounded by their disciples. Among the Nagas, self-mortification is de rigueur. As they paraded, I saw that some of them had cut the tendons in their penises to prevent erections. Others kept one arm raised in the air—they had stayed like that for years, until the appendage was thin and shriveled. By tradition, the Nagas entered the water first, to be followed by the Hindu hordes. I never understood why they were rioting—it had something to do with the exact order in which they would enter the water—but I watched as those emaciated mystics picked up large rocks from the street and hurled them into the crowds. They charged around, menacing the police with their weapons. I cowered in a restaurant, watching the melee through the metal grate the proprietors had quickly pulled down.

Fascinated by Kumbh Mehla, I delayed my return flight. I spent several weeks in Rishikesh, trying to learn yoga. On the next auspicious morning, I found myself luckily wedged into the center of Haridwar right across from the Nagas. This time, at the right instant, I joined the joyful multitudes bobbing up and down in the clear blue Ganges water.

Of course, at that point, I did not believe in karma.

. . .

ALTHOUGH HE WAS an esoteric Christian, Steiner believed, along with Hindus and Buddhists, that human beings pass through many incarnations. Health problems and personal crises and good fortune that manifest along the way are the residues of one's former actions, the karma accrued in previous lives. He also thought that, through spiritual training, it is possible to remember your past incarnations, as the Buddha did when he achieved enlightenment, recollecting all of his lives up to that instant.

"It is often asked why we do not know anything of our experiences before birth and after death," Steiner wrote. "This is the wrong question. Rather, we should ask how we can attain such knowledge." At the moment my provisional belief, stitched together from Buddhism, Western mysticism, quantum physics, and psychedelic shamanism, is that what we experience as the "self" is actually a kind of vibration or frequency emanating from an invisible whole that exists in a higher dimension. Buddhists see this reality as illusionary samsara; it is a product of our consciousness, our karma. If the Buddhists are right, then the only way to change the world is to transform our consciousness. Psychedelics are only catalysts for that deeper process of inner development.

Accepting Steiner's ideas for a moment, my actions over the last years, however much they seemed self-willed and haphazard, began to reveal an esoteric logic. After Kumbh Mehla, I went, due to the "lucky draw" of a magazine assignment, through the Bwiti initiation in Africa. Then I drank ayahuasca with Don Caesario and the Secoya. After DPT, I was forced to revise my thoughts yet again. I confronted the ambiguity, reality, and power of the occult orders. The DPT trip and its aftermath was bizarre, yet eerily familiar. I felt, I still feel, as though I had activated some circuit of Nietzschean "eternal recurrence," recovering something I had known before.

According to Steiner, along with the self that we perceive in daily life, the intractable "I," there is another self, a hidden spiritual being, which is the individual's guide and guardian. This higher self is the double, which "does not make itself known through thoughts or inner words. It acts through deeds, processes, and events. It is this 'other self' that leads the soul through the details of its life destiny and evokes its capacities, tendencies, and talents." The direction of our life is set out by that other self, a permanent being that continues from life to life. "This inspiration works in such a way that the destiny of one earthly life is the consequence of the previous lives." The pull of these far-flung archaic rites in India, Gabon, and the Amazon had exerted something like a magnetic attraction, and seeking out these contacts, I intuited that I was prodded along by that hidden, higher aspect of my being.

Epilogue

THE ANGEL OF HISTORY

Nothing bores an ordinary man more than the cosmos.

—WALTER BENJAMIN

Is history a purposeless mass of incident and coincidence, or is there some driving force, some meaning behind it—what Walter Benjamin called "the angel of history" watching over our steps?

This book charts my own groping-in-the-dark progress, based on a quest for self-knowledge using psychedelics as tools, from a neo-Freudian materialist and mechanistic perspective on reality to one that is Jungian, Gnostic/Buddhist, outrageously mystical. My view of history has changed accordingly. It now seems to me that the human race is being propelled like a Ping-Pong ball through an evolutionary wind tunnel by forces not entirely but largely outside of our control. These forces have been called spirits, gods, demons, demiurges, disincarnate entities, and a host of other names. Displaying themselves in various forms—as elves, angels, burning bushes, dream messengers, or the inscrutable alien abductors on UFOs—they may be emissaries from a vast ecology of supersensible beings. At the higher levels, they know where we are going and how we might get there. They see at least a few of the branching paths ahead of us, the traps and hidden snares. Some of them have our best interests at heart. Many want to drag us down or smash us against the rocks. Others just enjoy a good joke.

W. B. Yeats wrote: "Many poets, and all mystic and occult writers, in all ages and countries, have declared that behind the visible are chains on chains of conscious beings, who are not of heaven but of the earth, who have no inherent form, but change according to their whim, or the mind that sees them. You cannot lift your hand without influencing and being influenced by hordes. The visible world is merely their skin. In dreams we go amongst them, and play with them, and combat with them. They are, perhaps, human souls in the crucible—these creatures of whim."

Yes it is ridiculous, but here it is: I have had the classic spiritual awakening, catalyzed by use of psychedelics, those blighted chemicals that symbolize the crushed hopes of a failed era. I have become a "crazy fool," one of "them," the ones who have been discarded by this world, whose visions are greeted with mockery, dismissal, or fear. And I am much happier for it.

One result of my research is that I now feel strangely impersonal—an age-old result of the influx of information that is part of the awakening of the spirit. I suspect that I, this improbable pinchbeckian imposter, this rag doll of flesh and flapdoodle, arrived here to continue the ancient spiritual work of my unknown ancestors—kabbalists on one side, druids on the other—and, if such things exist, previous incarnations. The inheritor of untold generations of mystical yearnings, of chantings in dark caves and around stone circles, of exiles and long pilgrimages across starry deserts, I am no longer just myself—I am something other and older, the archetypal outsider, the archaic wayfarer of myths and legends. Of course I lack any hard evidence for this; yet I intuit it as unfathomable truth, as pieces of my private puzzle. Every time I drink ayahuasca—to me the most profound and healing of all the mind-expanders found in potions and herbs and pills—I am in touch with that ancient and questing part of myself, that strand of childlike wonder twisted around my soul like a jungle vine.

I am writing this truthfully, yet part of me recants, doesn't accept, sincerely hopes to reject the whole tangled argument and return, tail between legs, to the consensual, daily-newspaper view that is, I know, hopeless and deranged in its one-dimensional portrait of a doomed world, yet oddly comforting in its flat certitudes. I am sick of finding myself fluttering, like some unwieldy albatross, farther and farther away from the margins of the mainstream.

The nature of reality is spiritual, not physical. Everything we see around us is animated by sentient essences, dainty sub-Planck-length flimmers of cosmic wit: plant spirits, sylphs and dryads, thunder beings, twisted genies of nationalist fervor, predatory demons of corporations unleashing new chemicals (terrifying to envision the malformed and enraged asuras of aspartame, olestra, malathion), astonishing devil empires revealed by brand-new tryptamines. The earth itself is a spiritual being that formed us out of mud and DNA to achieve its own destiny.

Since the Indians are right about the shamanic cosmos, I am wary of the gloomy Indian prophecies, consistent in their vision of imminent historical breakdown and unleashed horrors ahead—natural catastrophes, nuclear wipeouts, biochemical assault, melted ice caps, polar shifts—now approaching us at high speed. The destruction of the World Trade Center may turn out to be a prelude or birth pang, first in a series of convulsions, before modern civilization is expunged from the planet and forgotten forever, unless there is a quick and unlikely reversal of current trends.

The consciousness of modern humanity and the planetary crisis mirror each other. Humanity is staring through the keyhole, the ozone hole, onto an increasingly degraded planet and its own shortsightedness. Addicted to oil as if it were crack, we are chopping down the world's tropical forests at an astounding rate—as much as 1 or 2 percent a year. When modern civilization finishes draining the world's resources, when this house of cards collapses, we will see ourselves stripped down to our essence and whimper for forgiveness like third-grade bullies caught by our teachers, unable to comprehend what went wrong. Against the floods, genetic pollution, bacterial onslaughts, radioactive infernos unleashed by human stupidity or aggrieved nature, our technologies will pop like toy guns. Watch the fun as the stock markets continue to seek profit, down to the last seconds of recorded history, betting on the margin-calls of disaster relief and reinsurance agencies.

What is "profit" anyway? What is the greed that is motivating a frenzied humanity to destroy the planet and degrade itself? If a media mogul pockets so many hundreds of millions of dollars a year while leaving his children and grandchildren a world without clean air, Amazonian jungles, the purple splendor of coral reefs, or animals, where is his profit? If a chemical corporation profits by spreading toxins across the globe that will rematerialize as cancer in the flesh of their own anxious stockholders, where is the profit? To what Martian retreat or Lunar Club Med do these madmen—ourselves!—see themselves retreating when they have finished fucking this planet like an old whore?

Modern scientific thought is a very recent development. The underlying logic of capitalism is tied to materialist empirical convictions about the nature of reality that have, in fact, already been outmoded. Physics has been forced to recognize an inextricable relationship between subject and object, observed and observer, consciousness and cosmos. As Dr. Stanislav Grof writes in *Beyond the Brain*:

> Scientific thinking in contemporary medicine, psychiatry, psychology, and anthropology represents a direct extension of the seventeenth-century Newtonian-Cartesian model of the universe. Since all the basic assumptions of this way of viewing reality have been transcended by twentieth-century physics, it seems only natural to expect profound changes sooner or later in all the disciplines that are its direct derivatives.

Despite its narrow-minded belief in its own mastery, Western materialist science cannot comprehend the nature of consciousness. Consciousness may be much more an intrinsic property of matter and living cells than we have dared to let ourselves imagine.

Astonishing experiments have been done with plants and polygraph machines. Lie detectors wired to plants have shown, through an increase in electrical impulses, that plants were aware of who stood in the room with them, and what the intentions of those people were toward them. Even before an experimenter could cut off a plant's limb, when the severing was just an idea held in their mind, the targeted plant would begin to register frantic displeasure.

What if plants are, at some level, conscious?

Every time I take mushrooms or LSD, I feel a cheerfully nutty but intuitive certainty that trees are watchers, plants are sentient beings, patiently aware of their place in the ultimate scheme of things—of course, this could be a delightful form of drug-induced paranoia. For the Indians, of course, plants are spiritual beings just as much as we ourselves; they are our fellow travelers and partners. Psychoactive plants are particular emissaries from the "Green Nation" who have developed the ability to share their wisdom with human beings.

What else might share consciousness with us?

What if everything does?

I have heard from various people of one experience they had while smoking the fortified leaves of *Salvia divinorum*, a profound and eerie alteration of self that lasts all of five minutes, in which they dissociated, then realized they were experiencing the world as an inanimate object—a window, wood floorboard, vinyl cushion, couch, or television set. "Suddenly I was the window in my living room," one friend told me. "I was looking out into the street and then back into my room at myself sitting there. That was all I could do."

How could a few smoked leaves of a plant cause such an effect? Could it be, as biologists strive to see all mentation, simply a physical action of the brain? What if, instead, everything that we create takes on, in some perpendicular dimension, a psychic reality and sentient awareness of its own?

Other reports of smoked *Salvia* trips are equally jarring but utterly different. Daniel Seibert, the researcher who isolated salvinorin A, the active component of *Salvia,* accidentally took a massive overdose of this substance (he did not imagine that, like LSD, salvinorin A could be active in micrograms) and found himself a ghost visitor to his early childhood homes, passing through them one after another. "The houses were completely detailed and real," he recalled. "I could walk around, open closets or drawers and see all the stuff exactly as it had been." Seibert and others also report entering strange *Salvia* realms where everything around them has not changed except that the world is suddenly made entirely out of stacks of coins or pebbles—some element of the material world replicating itself like three-dimensional wallpaper or tiling, a kind of holographic nightmare.

Such an idea—that everything we create acquires some kind of consciousness—is not that far away from certain concepts in social theory, such as Marx's notion of the fetish character of commodities, which act within markets as if they had wills of their own. As Walter Benjamin once noted, "In the end, things are merely mannequins, and even the great moments of world history are only costumes beneath which they exchange glances of complicity with nothingness, with the petty and the banal."

When you take psychedelics, after the initial fear and past the stage of psychological processing, you sometimes reach a calm place where metaphysical concepts arise, seemingly of their own accord. These self-organizing structures of possibility float to the surface of consciousness where they open like floral bouquets. On ayahuasca, I have had the thought that the jungle is Nature's free space for creativity, where new life forms are bred and released as poetic experiments— which is why it feels so sacred. Children intuit its sacredness without even going there—from a few pictures in books or some television images. The next thought to open was that we, human beings, were also loved, by all the unknown swarms and manifold phalanxes of sentient entities beyond the realm of the sensible, for our own creative efforts, no matter how mass-produced, ill-conceived, or half-formed they may be. We are loved for our creativity, which is a kind of infinite potential.

It is a peculiar fact noted by theorists of extradimensional physics: Only in three dimensions can there be such a thing as a knot. Knots are impossible in two dimensions, and equally impossible in any of the higher realms, the tesseract- and Calibi-Yau–shaped Rubik puzzles, of hyperspace. Perhaps we, temporarily embodied, trapped, in this reality, are like the knots of physical forces, holding the cosmos in place.

"As I see it," Jung wrote in his memoirs, "the three-dimensional world in time and space is like a system of coordinates; what is here separated into ordinates and abscissae may appear 'there,' in space-timelessness, as a primordial image with many aspects, perhaps as a diffuse cloud of cognition surrounding an archetype." This would have seemed nonsense to me a few years ago, but I have seen, in rainbow shimmers of ayahuasca visions, and through the more traumatic transportation device of DMT, that it may be true.

The shamanic antipodes of the known and familiar and seemingly rational have their own vaudevillian logic. What is almost most disconcerting about the other dimensions is this: After you have risked your sanity, the disapproval of friends and family, to get there, you find, amid the shards of prophecy and myth, the revelations of terror and utopian bliss, a love of bizarre low-brow comedy, two-bit puns, tinplate stereotypes, and cartoon shtick. The joke is one mask that the Unknown, the Other, wears to conceal itself, to keep itself beyond the grasp of human understanding. That is why one of the shaman's most efficient tools is laughter, which, wielded with the efficiency of a surgeon's scalpel, brushes the mind shadows away.

Over the course of several months, I found, in my dreams, I was getting the message, again and again, to take more—and more—psychedelic drugs. At parties, groovy guys in sunglasses would come over to offer me DMT. In a strange city, I was led to an underground drug counter where I could buy mind-altering compounds from overly solicitious clerks. An old friend offered me ketamine during a Central Park softball game. I found little white doughy pastries full of ecstasy for sale at the local deli, then commercial packages of "magic mushrooms" in a Mexico City supermarket. DPT made a disguised appearance also. At a fancy midtown restaurant, the waiter offered me the daily special: 300 tiny diabolical creatures in a sauce. Sensibly, I declined. There was a kind of lurid vaudevillian urgency to the way the dream-figures kept pushing me to further, and faster, exploration.

I didn't get it. Did some frisky aspect of my unconscious want me to expand my psyche in more directions? Was this a healthy impulse? Finally, as I began to suspect there might be a spirit world spinning around and suffusing our physical realm, I wondered if these offerings were being made by ambiguous or ominous forces who did not have my best interests at heart. Perhaps they were luring me on toward overuse and self-disintegration. Perhaps, as Dr. Strassman was told during his DMT trials, they wanted to use me to get into this world.

Clearly, psychedelics are ambiguous tools. But all tools are ambiguous. The tools of science can be used to weaponize anthrax or smallpox, to ring the world with nuclear warheads, to turn an open society into a paranoid distopia of telesurveillance. Psychedelics provide an accelerated method for exploring what Huxley called the "far antipodes" of the mind. Meditation, lucid dreaming, or Gurdjieff's system of "self-remembering" are slower but less dangerous pathways.

In one of his books, Steiner wrote that the core of the earth is made out of the stuff of black magic. Whether he meant this metaphorically or literally, it seems to be the fate of contemporary humanity to draw all forms of black magic up to the surface. Perhaps this is why our dreams, as well as our politics, tend to be suffused with dark matter, with fear and anger and unconscious rage.

If I wasn't studying my dreams, I would not have learned I was getting these constant inducements from other beings or other parts of my psyche. Perhaps I would have simply felt the desire to increase my intake of drugs and followed the impulse. Currently, I suspect our entire society suffers from a similar syndrome. Because we deny our intuition, because we don't believe in spirits or listen to our dreams, because we have banished our potential shamans to mental institutions and homeless shelters, because we have imprisoned ourselves within virtual shells of technology, it may be pathetically easy for ambiguous, supersensible entities—demons or devas, Archons or rakshasas—to continually operate on our minds, filling the vacuum we have created with sludge, anesthetizing us to deeper levels of wisdom.

If that is the case, then we, the privileged inheritors of an increasingly insecure and globally destructive empire, can be seen as suffering from demonic possession on a vast scale. The parasites manipulating us hide within our egocentric materialism and spiritual nihilism. They laugh at us in our dreams. Their will is enacted by multinational corporations that can be seen, shamanically, as ambiguous sentient entities that prefer to act outside of human control, in occult ecologies of information and high-speed financial markets. Like all Archons, these corporations, often branded by mythological symbols, increase their own power by compelling human belief and sacrifice to their greatness. Their aim seems to be the transformation of the earth into a non-human wasteland.

Where will we find shamans powerful enough to suck the spiritual poison from our social body and vomit it out for us? Wizards who can tame these demons? Visionaries who can point the way forward? There is only one place. Unlikely as it seems, we have to become our own shamans, wizards, and seers. As spiritual warriors, we must take responsibility for the plight of our species. To break the spell of our culture's death-trap deceptions and hypnotic distractions, we need the courage to confront what lies behind the open doors of our own minds.

вiblioςraρhy

Anderson, Edward F. *Peyote: The Divine Cactus*. University of Arizona, 1996.

Alverga, Alex Polari de. *Forest of Visions: Ayahuasca, Amazonian Spirituality, and the Santo Daime Tradition*. Park Street Press, 1999.

Argüelles, José. *The Mayan Factor: Path Beyond Technology*. Bear, 1987.

Artaud, Antonin. *Artaud Anthology*. City Lights, 1965.

———. *The Peyote Dance*. Farrar Straus, 1976.

———. *Selected Writings*. University of California, 1976.

Baum, Dan. *Smoke and Mirrors: The War on Drugs and the Politics of Failure*. Little Brown, 1996.

Benjamin, Walter. *The Arcades Project*. Harvard, 1999.

———. *Illuminations*. Harcourt Brace, 1968.

———. *Reflections*. Harcourt Brace, 1986.

———. *Selected Writings, Volume 1: 1913–1926*. Harvard, 1996.

———. *Selected Writings, Volume 2: 1927–1934*. Harvard, 1996.

Bennett, J. G. *Gurdjieff: Making a New World*. Harper & Row, 1973.

Bohm, David. *Wholeness and the Implicate Order*. Routledge, 1995.

Burroughs, William, and Allen Ginsberg. *The Yage Letters*. City Lights, 1963.

Castaneda, Carlos. *A Separate Reality*, Simon & Schuster, 1971.

———. *The Teachings of Don Juan: A Yaqui Way of Knowledge*. University of California Press, 1968.

Chatwin, Bruce. *The Songlines*. Penguin, 1987.

Clastres, Pierre. *Chronicle of the Guayaki Indians*. Zone, 1998.

Clifford, James. *The Predicament of Culture: Twentieth-Century Ethnography, Literature, and Art*. Harvard, 1988.

Cocteau, Jean. *Opium: The Diary of a Cure*. Grove, 1958.

Crowley, Aleister. *The Book of Thoth (Egyptian Tarot)*. Weiser, 2000.

———. *Moonchild*. Weiser, 1970.

Davis, Erik. *Techgnosis: Myth, Magic, and Mysticism in the Age of Information*. Random House, 1998.

Davis, Wade. *One River: Explorations and Discoveries in the Amazon Rain Forest*. Simon & Schuster, 1996.

DeKorne, Jim. *Psychedelic Shamanism: The Cultivation, Preparation, and Shamanic Use of Psychotropic Plants*. Breakout Productions, 1994.

Devereux, Paul. *The Long Trip: A Prehistory of Psychedelia*. Penguin, 1997.

Dickstein, Morris. *Gates of Eden: American Culture in the Sixties*. Harvard, 1997.

Didion, Joan. *The White Album*. Simon & Schuster, 1979.

Dobkin de Rios, Marlene. *Hallucinogens: Cross-Cultural Perspectives*. Avery, 1990.

Edelman, Gerald M., and Giulio Tononi. *A Universe of Consciousness: How Matter Becomes Imagination*. Basic, 2000.

Eliade, Mircea. *The Myth of the Eternal Return*. Princeton, 1971.

———. *Shamanism: Archaic Techniques of Ecstasy*. Princeton, 1964.

Eliot, T. S. *Four Quartets*. Harcourt Brace, 1943.

Epps, Garrett. *To an Unknown God: Religious Freedom on Trial*. St. Martin's, 2001.

Evans-Wentz, W. Y. *The Fairy Faith in Celtic Countries*. Carol, 1994.

Evola, Julius. *The Hermetic Tradition: Symbols and Teachings of the Royal Art*. Inner Traditions, 1995.

Fernandez, James. *Bwiti: An Ethnography of the Religious Imagination in Africa*. Princeton, 1982.

Fikes, Jay Courtney. *Carlos Castaneda, Academic Opportunism, and the Psychedelic Sixties*. Millenia, 1993.

Flaherty, Gloria. *Shamanism and the Eighteenth Century*. Princeton, 1992.

Fortune, Dion. *Psychic Self-Defense: A Study in Occult Pathology and Criminality*. Aquarian, 1985.

Frye, Northrop. *A Natural Perspective: The Development of Shakespearean Comedy and Romance*. Columbia, 1965.

Furst, Peter T., ed. *Flesh of the Gods: The Ritual Use of Hallucinogens.* Waveland Press, 1990.

Ginsberg, Allen. *Journals Early Fifties–Early Sixties.* Grove, 1977.

Ginzburg, Carlo. *Ecstasies: Deciphering the Witches' Sabbath.* Random House, 1991.

Gitlin, Todd. *The Sixties: Years of Hope, Days of Rage.* Bantam, 1987.

Govinda, Lama Anagarika. *Foundations of Tibetan Mysticism.* Weiser, 1969.

Greene, Brian. *The Elegant Universe: Superstrings, Hidden Dimensions, and the Quest for the Ultimate Theory.* Vintage, 1999.

Grof, Stanislav. *Beyond the Brain: Birth, Death and Transcendence in Psychotherapy.* SUNY, 1986.

Hardt, Michael, and Antonio Negri. *Empire.* Harvard, 2000.

Harner, Michael, ed. *Hallucinogens and Shamanism.* Oxford, 1973.

Hayes, Charles. *Tripping: An Anthology of True-Life Psychedelic Adventures.* Penguin, 2000.

Hayter, Alethea. *Opium and the Romantic Imagination.* University of California, 1968.

Hobson, J. Allan. *The Dream Drugstore: Chemically Altered States of Consciousness.* MIT, 2001.

Hoffman, Abbie. *Revolution for the Hell of It.* Dell, 1968.

Holland, Julie, ed. *Ecstasy: The Complete Guide.* Park Street Press, 2001.

Huxley, Aldous. *Brave New World.* HarperCollins, 1998.

———. *The Doors of Perception.* Harper & Row, 1954.

———. *Island.* Harper & Row, 1963.

Jameson, Frederic. *The Ideologies of Theory: Essays 1971–1986.* University of Minnesota, 1988.

———. *Postmodernism, or, the Cultural Logic of Late Capitalism.* Duke, 1991.

Jansen, Karl. *Ketamine: Dreams and Realities.* MAPS, 2001.

Jay, Mike, ed. *Artificial Paradises.* Penguin, 1999.

Jung, Carl. *The Archetypes and the Collective Unconscious.* Princeton, 1980.

———. *Memories, Dreams, Reflections.* Vintage, 1965.

———. *Psychology and Alchemy.* Princeton, 1980.

———. *The Undiscovered Self.* Little, Brown, 1957.

Kennedy, John G. *Tarahumara of the Sierra Madre.* AHM, 1996.

Kerenyi, Carl. *Eleusis: Archetypal Image of Mother and Daughter.* Princeton, 1967.

Kramer, Jane. *Allen Ginsberg in America.* Fromm, 1997.

Kramer, Peter. *Listening to Prozac.* Penguin, 1993.

Larsen, Stephen. *The Shaman's Doorway: Opening Imagination to Power and Myth.* Station Hill Press, 1988.

Leary, Timothy. *Flashbacks: An Autobiography.* Houghton Mifflin, 1983.

————. *The Politics of Ecstasy.* Ronin, 1998.

————, Ralph Metzner, and Richard Alpert. *The Psychedelic Experience: A Manual Based on the Tibetan Book of the Dead.* University Books, 1964.

Lee, Martin A., and Bruce Shlain. *Acid Dreams: The Complete Social History of LSD: The CIA, the Sixties, and Beyond.* Grove, 1992.

Lévi-Strauss, Claude. *Myth and Meaning,* Schocken, 1978.

————. *The Savage Mind.* University of Chicago, 1966.

————. *Tristes tropiques.* Simon & Schuster, 1973.

Lewin, Louis. *Phantastica.* Park Street, 1998.

Lilly, John. *The Center of the Cyclone: An Autobiography of Inner Space.* Bantam, 1973.

————. *The Scientist: A Metaphysical Autobiography.* Ronin, 1997.

Luna, Eduardo Luis and Steven F. White, ed. *Ayahuasca Reader: Encounters with the Amazon's Sacred Vine.* Synergetic, 2000.

Lyotard, Jean-François. *The Inhuman.* Stanford, 1988.

Lyttle, Thomas, ed. *Psychedelics Reimagined.* Autonomedia, 1999.

Mailer, Norman. *The Armies of the Night: History as a Novel, The Novel as History.* Penguin, 1968.

Mathers, S. Liddell MacGregor, trans. *The Key of Solomon the King (Clavicula Salomonis).* Weiser, 2000.

Matthiessen, Peter. *At Play in the Fields of the Lord.* Random House, 1991.

————. *Indian Country.* Penguin, 1992.

McGinn, Colin. *Conscious Minds in a Material World.* Basic, 1999.

McKenna, Terence. *The Archaic Revival: Speculations on Psychedelic Mushrooms, the Amazon, Virtual Reality, UFOs, Evolution, Shamanism, the Rebirth of the Goddess, and the End of History.* HarperCollins, 1991.

————. *Food of the Gods: The Search for the Original Tree of Knowledge.* Bantam, 1992.

————. *The Invisible Landscape: Mind, Hallucinogens, and the I Ching.* HarperCollins, 1993.

————. *True Hallucinations: Being an Account of the Author's Extraordinary Adventures in the Devil's Paradise.* HarperCollins, 1994.

Merker, Dan. *The Ecstatic Imagination: Psychedelic Experiences and the Psychoanalysis of Self-Actualization.* SUNY, 1998.

Metzner, Ralph. *Ayahuasca. Human Consciousness, and the Spirit of Nature.* Thunder's Mouth, 2000.

Meyerhoff, Barbara G. *Peyote Hunt: The Sacred Journey of the Huichol Indians.* Cornell, 1974.

Michaux, Henri. *Darkness Moves.* University of California, 1994.

————. *Miserable Miracle*. City Lights, 1967.

Narby, Jeremy. *The Cosmic Serpent: DNA and the Origins of Knowledge*. Tarcher/Putnam, 1999.

————, ed. *Shamans through Time: 500 Years on the Path to Knowledge*. Tarcher/Putnam, 2001.

Neihardt, John G. *Black Elk Speaks: Being the Life Story of a Holy Man of the Oglala Sioux*. University of Nebraska, 1961.

Newberg, Andrew, and Eugene D'Aquili. *Why God Won't Go Away: Brain Science and the Biology of Belief*. Ballantine, 2001.

Newland, Constance A. *Myself and I*. New American Library, 1962.

O'Flaherty, Wendy Doniger, trans. *The Rig Veda*. Penguin, 1981.

Oss, O. T., and O. N. Oeric. *Psilocybin: The Magic Mushroom Grower's Guide*. Quick American, 1991.

Ott, Jonathan. *Ayahuasca Analogues*. Natural Products, 1994.

————. *Pharmacotheon: Entheogenic Drugs, Their Plant Sources and History*. Natural Products, 1996.

Ouspensky, P. D. *The Fourth Way*. Vintage, 1971.

————. *In Search of the Miraculous*. Harcourt Brace, 1949.

Pellerin, Cheryl. *Trips: How Hallucinogens Work in Your Brain*. Seven Stories, 1998.

Pendell, Dale. *Pharmako/poeia: Plants, Powers, Poisons, and Herbcraft*. Mercury House, 1995.

Perkins, John. *The World Is as You Dream It: Shamanic Teachings from the Amazon and Andes*. Destiny, 1994.

Plant, Sadie. *Writing on Drugs*. Farrar, Straus, and Giroux, 1999.

Proust, Marcel. *Remembrance of Things Past*. Vintage, 1982.

Puharich, Andrija. *The Sacred Mushroom: Key to the Door of Eternity*. Doubleday, 1959.

Pynchon, Thomas. *The Crying of Lot 49*. Bantam, 1967.

Rätschl, Christian, and John R. Baker, ed. *Yearbook for Ethnomedicine and the Study of Consciousness*. Verlag für Wissenschaft und Bildung, Berlin, 1994, 1997/1998.

Redgrove, Peter. *The Black Goddess and the Unseen Real: Our Unconscious Senses and Their Uncommon Sense*. Grove, 1987.

Rienzo, Paul de, and Dana Beal. *The Ibogaine Story: Report on the Staten Island Project*. Autonomedia, 1997.

Reynolds, Simon. *Generation Ecstasy: Into The World of Techno and Rave Culture*. Routledge, 1999.

Robinson, James M., ed. *The Nag Hammadi Library*. HarperCollins, 1990.

Roszak, Theodore. *The Making of a Counter Culture*. Anchor, 1969.

Saunders, Nicholas, Anna Saunders, and Michelle Pauli. *In Search of the Ultimate High: Spiritual Experiences through Psychoactives.* Random House, 2000.

Schultes, Richard Evans, and Albert Hofmann. *Plants of the Gods: Their Sacred, Healing and Hallucinogenic Properties.* Healing Arts Press, 1992.

Shiva, Vandana. *Monocultures of the Mind: Perspectives on Biodiversity and Biotechnology.* Zed, 1993.

Shulgin, Ann and Alexander. *PIHKAL: A Chemical Love Story.* Transform, 1991.

———. *TIHKAL: The Continuation.* Transform, 1997.

Siever, Larry J., and William Frucht. *The New View of Self: How Genes and Neurotransmitters Shape Your Mind, Your Personality, and Your Mental Health.* Macmillan, 1997.

Smith, Huston. *Cleansing the Doors of Perception.* Putnam, 2000.

Solomon, David, ed. *LSD: The Consciousness-Expanding Drug.* Putnam, 1964.

Staal, Frits. *Exploring Mysticism.* University of California, 1975.

Steiner, Rudolf. *How to Know Higher Worlds: A Modern Path of Initiation.* Anthroposophic, 1996.

———. *An Outline of Esoteric Science.* Anthroposophic, 1996.

———. *Self-Transformation.* Rudolf Steiner, 1995.

Stevens, Jay. *Storming Heaven: LSD and the American Dream.* Harper & Row, 1987.

Stolaroff, Myron J. *The Secret Chief: Conversations with a Pioneer of the Underground Psychedelic Therapy Movement.* MAPS, 1997.

Strassman, Rick. *DMT: The Spirit Molecule: A Doctor's Revolutionary Research into the Biology of Near-Death and Mystical Experience.* Park Street, 2001.

Talbot, Michael. *The Holographic Universe.* HarperCollins, 1991.

Taussig, Mick. *Shamanism, Colonialism, and the Wild Man.* University of Chicago. 1987.

———. *Mimesis and Alterity: A Particular History of the Senses.* Routledge, 1993.

Thompson, Hunter S. *Fear and Loathing in Las Vegas: A Savage Journey to the Heart of the American Dream.* Random House, 1971.

Tompkins, Peter, and Christopher Bird. *The Secret Life of Plants: A Fascinating Account of the Physical, Emotional, and Spiritual Relations Between Plants and Man.* Harper & Row, 1989.

Torgovnick, Marianna. *Primitive Passions: Men, Women, and the Quest for Ecstasy.* University of Chicago, 1998.

Vallee, Jacques. *Passport to Mangonia: On UFOs, Folklore, and Parallel Worlds.* Contemporary Books, 1993.

Wasson, R. Gordon, Stella Kramrisch, Jonathan Ott, and Carl A.P. Ruck. *Persephone's Quest: Entheogens and the Origins of Religion.* Yale, 1986.

Waters, Frank. *Book of the Hopi*. Ballantine, 1969.

Watts, Alan W. *The Joyous Cosmology: Adventures in the Chemistry of Consciousness*. Random House, 1962.

————. *This Is It*. Vintage, 1973.

Weil, Andrew. *The Natural Mind: An Investigation of Drugs and the Higher Consciousness*. Houghton Mifflin, 1986.

Wiener, Jon. *Come Together: John Lennon in His Time*. Random House, 1984.

Wolfe, Tom. *The Electric Kool-Aid Acid Test*. Farrar Straus, 1968.

Zaehner, R.C. *Mysticism: Sacred and Profane*. Oxford, 1961.

acknowledgments

Thanks to Richard Boulter, Michael Brownstein, Jay Crosby, Charity Egli, Adam Fisher, Kathleen Harrison, Gerry Howard, Neil Martinson, the National Arts Journalism Program, Mick Taussig, and Anthony and Jonathan Torn.

index

about the author

DANIEL PINCHBECK is a founding editor of *Open City*, and he has written for such publications as *Rolling Stone, Men's Journal,* and the *Village Voice,* where sections of this book have previously appeared. A native of New York City, he can be reached at www.breakingopenthehead.com.